WITHDRAWN

TIP & TRADE

TIP AND

HOW TWO LAWYERS MAD

TRADE

LLIONS FROM INSIDER TRADING

Mark Coakley

ECW

Published by ECW Press
2120 Queen Street East, Suite 200, Toronto, Ontario, Canada M4E 1E2
416-694-3348 / info@ecwpress.com

LIBRARY AND ARCHIVES CANADA CATALOGUING IN PUBLICATION

Coakley, Mark
Tip and trade : how two lawyers made millions from
insider trading / Mark Coakley.

ISBN 978-1-55022-986-8
ALSO ISSUED AS:
978-1-55490-964-3 (EPUB); 978-1-55490-986-5 (PDF)

1. Cornblum, Gil, 1970–2009. 2. Grmovsek, Stan.
3. Insider trading in securities—Canada. 4. Securities fraud—Canada.
5. Lawyers—Canada—Biography. 6. Stockbrokers—Canada—Biography. I. Title.

HV6805.C62 2011   364.16'80922   C2010-906740-1

Design, cover illustration, and typesetting: Ingrid Paulson
Printing: Transcontinental   1   2   3   4   5

Mixed Sources
Product group from well-managed
forests and other controlled sources
www.fsc.org Cert no. SW-COC-000952
© 1996 Forest Stewardship Council

The publication of *Tip and Trade* has been generously supported by the
Canada Council for the Arts, which last year invested $20.1 million in writing and publishing throughout Canada, by the Ontario Arts Council, by the OMDC Book Fund, an initiative of the Ontario Media Development Corporation, and by the Government of Canada through the Canada Book Fund.

 Canada Council   Conseil des Arts
for the Arts   du Canada
 Canadä   ONTARIO ARTS COUNCIL
CONSEIL DES ARTS DE L'ONTARIO

PRINTED AND BOUND IN CANADA

ECW PRESS
ecwpress.com

To the law students of tomorrow

CONTENTS

Gil Cornblum

Stan Grmovsek

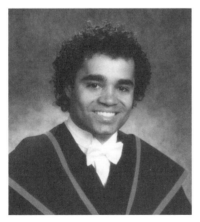

Mark Coakley

PART ONE

....

Fall and Winter 2007

The double-minded man is unstable in all his ways.

James 1:8

1 | AT THE PEAK

Gil I. Cornblum was a young corporate lawyer, and in the afternoon of October 23, 2007, he was at the peak of professional success.

Gil had spent almost two decades climbing the legal ladder — earning a combined law-MBA degree from Osgoode Hall Law School in 1994, then passing the bar exams, then moving to Manhattan to serve at the giant Wall Street firm of Sullivan & Cromwell, then coming home to run the Toronto office of another huge U.S.-based law firm, Dorsey & Whitney.

Gil was now 37. Around five foot five in height. Of Romanian descent, he had been born in the Israeli town of Ashkelon. His family had brought him to Canada as a young boy. Gil had thick, brown hair, which he wore parted on the right side. He had a naturally round face and was at this time slightly pudgy. His eyeglasses had large, round lenses that gave him a slightly owl-like appearance. He had thick eyebrows; big, sensitive-looking brown eyes; ears that stuck out. Gil smiled often but rarely openly enough to show his teeth.

A friend from his days at Sullivan & Cromwell would later describe Gil as a "sweet soul," adding that he had been the only lawyer at that high-pressure megafirm who "didn't seem to have an axe to grind. He was nice to me — and that meant a lot. It was unusual."

Married since 2000, Gil now had a young son. His attractive wife had recently recovered from a rare, aggressive form of breast cancer.

Gil's legal specialty was helping non-U.S. corporations sell their shares on U.S. stock exchanges — a complicated job in which a lawyer's mistake could cost a client millions of dollars. You needed the concentration of a high-wire walker to take a deal to completion — and nobody did this work better than Gil. He was also a well-experienced expert in other kinds of cross-border corporate transactions, such as helping a Canadian corporation take over a U.S. one.

October 23, 2007, was the second of a two-day educational conference held in downtown Toronto, at the Four Seasons Yorkville hotel. It was called the Intensive Course in Securities Law and Practice.

Forty-five corporate lawyers from across North America gathered in a comfortable conference room to, as advertised, "learn from leading securities lawyers at this intensive, hands-on and practical course."

- Comply with the hierarchy of securities regulation
- Best ways of managing contacts with securities regulators
- Strategies for co-operating with Canadian, cross-border and international regulators: who to deal with and when
- Learn how to minimize risk of secondary market liability
- Effective tips on preparing an initial public offering and learn about special considerations for cross-border public offerings ... and more!

This course was the peak of Gil's professional life; Gil was there not just to learn but also to teach. This was an honour, clear and public proof that he had been recognized by his peers as a leader of the profession and a role model for younger lawyers. He was one of the bright stars of the North American legal profession.

Gil had attended many events like this over the years, but this was only the third conference where he had been scheduled to stand up in front and lecture to other lawyers. The first time had been in 2005, at the International Finance Forum in Toronto, held by the International Association of Young Lawyers. Gil had lectured an audience of other young lawyers from around the world about "Business Trusts in the United States." (Trusts are legal creatures similar to corporations.) The second time had been in 2006, in Toronto again, at an Osgoode Hall Law School Professional Development Program called U.S. Securities Law: What Canadian Practitioners Need to Know. Gil had lectured about "Continuous Reporting for Foreign Private Issuers." (This had been about how non-U.S. corporations issuing shares in U.S. stock markets had to provide information to the U.S. government.)

The course leaders of the October 2007 conference were two lawyers, Mark Bennett and John Vettese, both of the Bay Street law firm Cassels Brock & Blackwell. Mark and Gil were good friends, and their respective law firms had a special relationship that profited them both.

Bay Street in Toronto, like Wall Street in New York, was a symbol of a nation's elite financial system. Most law firms known as "Bay Street firms" were physically located on downtown Bay Street, but not all of them were; the label was based less on geography than on size, power, and prestige. Bay Street firms handled all the biggest corporate deals, paid eye-popping salaries, and often had well-connected ex-politicians working for them as "rainmakers," helping to bring in those big deals.

The men and women preceding Gil at the podium were all Bay Street or Wall Street lawyers at the peak of the profession: Heather Zordel (of Cassels Brock & Blackwell), Charlie MacCready (of Heenan Blaikie), Steven Molo (of Wall Street's Shearman & Sterling), Geoff Shaw (of Cassels Brock & Blackwell), Tom Swigerts (of Gil's firm, Dorsey & Whitney), Brian Koscak (of Cassels Brock & Blackwell), Greg Hogan (of Cassels Brock & Blackwell), Philippe Tardif (of Borden Ladner Gervais), Lisa Damiani (of Davies Ward Phillips & Vineberg—we will encounter this firm again later), and Mark Gelowitz (of Osler, Hoskin & Harcourt). Gil was scheduled to be the second-last speaker, followed by Sean Farrell (of McMillan Binch Mendelsohn).

In light of later events, it is tempting to speculate about Gil's thoughts as he sat through the lectures and PowerPoint presentations that preceded his own.

What did Gil think when Heather Zordel explained that the purpose of insider-trading restrictions was to "ensure that everyone has equal access to material information on which to base trades or hold decisions and an equal opportunity to act?"

Did Gil react when Charlie MacCready, lecturing on "Canadian Securities Regulators," talked about how the government used "market surveillance activities" such as "trading analysis to identify breaches of the trading rules, including illegal insider trading and patterns of trading manipulation"?

Was Gil paying any attention when Steven Molo took the podium to talk about the "U.S. White Collar Enforcement Environment," describing the "growing intensity of the enforcement environment— more investigations, greater number of individuals prosecuted, larger fines, additional penalties"? Did Gil hear Molo's warning that in the United States corporate lawyers would now face a "triple threat" from the Department of Justice, the Securities and Enforcement Commission, and each state's attorney general?

When Tim Swigert, another Dorsey & Whitney lawyer, spoke about "Best Practices for Managing Investigations and Enforcement," did Gil hear his colleague describe the "sophisticated surveillance systems to monitor all trading activity in real time"? Swigert explained how an investigation could lead to a finding of guilt (in civil court) for stock market frauds such as insider trading or tipping. That finding could lead to penalties of up to $1 million per offence, plus repayment of illegal profits, plus payment of the costs of the investigation and trial, plus a criminal conviction and prison.

Was Gil listening at all?

o o o

When it was his turn to walk to the front of the Four Seasons conference room to take the podium to speak, Gil stood in front of a screen showing his PowerPoint presentation. The first screen showed the title of his lecture: "Overview of U.S. Securities Regulations Cross-Border Transactions."

Gil spoke knowledgeably about all of the various U.S. federal securities laws that regulated the U.S. stock markets, the most important being the Securities Exchange Act of 1934. It had been passed by

President Franklin D. Roosevelt during the Great Depression in response to the Wall Street crash of 1929. The 1934 act made insider trading illegal in the United States for the first time. (Before Roosevelt's presidency, insider trading in the United States was common and only mildly controversial; the Massachusetts Supreme Court would describe insider trading as a "perk" in the case of *Goodwin v. Agassiz*). The 1934 act also created the Securities and Enforcement Commission. Gil described the functions of the SEC, including its widely feared Division of Enforcement—responsible for market-fraud investigations, civil actions, and referrals to the FBI.

Gil also spoke to the crowd of 45 top corporate lawyers about other U.S. laws, such as the Insider Trading Sanctions Act of 1984 and the Insider Trading and Securities Fraud Enforcement Act of 1988. Like the prior lectures, his subject matter was too technical and complicated for most non-lawyers to understand. Lawyers trained in fields other than corporate law (like me, an ex-litigator) would also have found most of Gil's lecture baffling.

So let's get to the point.

The crime of *tipping* is when someone who works for a corporation steals information about it and gives the stolen information to an outsider, so that the outsider can make a profit or avoid a loss on a stock market.

The crime of *insider trading* is when someone who works for a corporation steals information about it and uses the secret information to make a profit or avoid a loss on a stock market.

By 2007, tipping and insider trading had been illegal in both the United States and Canada for decades, and the penalties had grown harsher and harsher over time. An inside trader who got caught could be punished in civil court (seizure of property) and/or criminal court (prison). As Martha Stewart showed, certain inside traders could also end up being judged by a third kind of court, the court of scandalized public opinion, with possibly the harshest punishments of all.

So we have met a young, successful lawyer named Gil Cornblum, who was at a conference in Toronto where other lawyers lectured to him about market fraud in general and insider trading in particular. We have watched Gil step up to the podium to speak to the assembled Bay Street and Wall Street lawyers on various topics, including U.S. insider-trading laws.

A detail is missing. The reader should know that Gil had more than a professional interest in stock market fraud. He had a big secret, shared with only one person. Nobody at the Intensive Course in Securities Law and Practice knew it. Nobody at Dorsey & Whitney, or at any other law firm, knew it. Nobody at his temple knew it. Gil's parents, brother, and wife did not know it. Only Stan Grmovsek knew it.

Only Stanko Jose Grmovsek (pronounced "*gur-MOV-seck*") understood the pressure and stress that attacked Gil every day. Stan was the only person in the universe who knew that Gil did not just lecture about insider trading—no, no, the truth was that Gil did it himself, on a massive scale. He had made between 100 and 150 illegal insider transactions over 14 years, both in the United States and in Canada, on both Wall Street and Bay Street. Again and again and again, he broke the lawyer's oath of loyalty and integrity.

From his secret crimes, Gil had gained many millions of dollars. He kept most of his share of the loot in a bank in the Cayman Islands. It was not under his real name, of course; the account was registered to INM. Stan had picked the name for Gil's secret bank account. The letters stood for "I Need Money."

But that was not true—Gil did not really need these proceeds of crime. He earned about a million legitimate dollars a year as a partner at Dorsey & Whitney. He had a big house in one of Toronto's best neighbourhoods and almost no mortgage. He had lots of savings, investments, many beautiful and valuable pieces of art.

And Gil knew that, if he lost all of his material wealth, his family would still love him; his family was the most important part of his life, the source of his greatest joys and anxieties.

Most of Gil's illegal profits sat untouched, year after year, dwindling away in poorly picked, poorly managed investments. Gil spent little of his secret treasure. So why did he steal it?

o o o

Sometimes Gil's inside information was stolen from his own clients. Sometimes it was stolen from clients of other lawyers at his law firm. Gil was a snoop and a spy.

One technique—which he and Stan called "spelunking"—involved Gil wandering the halls of a firm, usually very early in the morning before anyone else arrived, looking for documents with clues about upcoming deals. Gil would find them on lawyers' desks or secretaries' desks or in the fax room or in the photocopy room or elsewhere. When he found an interesting document, he would often return on following nights to find newer documents showing how the deal was progressing.

A simple technique involved Gil engaging lawyers in conversations about their files, hoping that something would slip out. Gil would also eavesdrop on conversations between other lawyers. He overheard rival lawyers blabbing secrets in skyscraper elevators, during a fancy lunch near Wall Street, at a busy Starbucks near Bay Street, and elsewhere. "Conflict checks"—in which lawyers are asked if they have ever represented a certain client—could also reveal upcoming deals.

Another technique involved Gil logging on to a law firm's computerized document management system. When he snooped in a computer system, he would sometimes leave behind electronic tracks.

Sometimes a law firm and its clients would use code names for pending transactions to keep news of the deal from the stock market. When Gil found information about a coded deal, he or Stan would investigate and research (often on the Internet) until they figured out who was in the deal and what it was all about.

After Gil tipped Stan on an upcoming deal, Stan would use the information for trades on the stock market in one of two ways. He would either buy shares in the company being taken over, knowing that its shares would rise after the deal's announcement, or he would "short" the company doing the takeover—that is, bet that its share price would go down—knowing that this would likely be the reaction of the stock market after the announcement.

○ ○ ○

Gil would later say about the start of his insider-trading career—when he was working for the giant Wall Street law firm Sullivan & Cromwell in the 1990s—that

> generally, I learned about transactions from other lawyers in the M&A group or banking group who were working on trans-actions. . . . Generally, I had lunch and dinner with people at the firm, met people in the hall. I mean, when lawyers meet the first thing they talk about is what they're working on, who they're working for, whether that person is a good person to work with, what they're working on, interesting, not interest-ing, exciting, not exciting, what type of work they're doing, why someone is doing something exciting and someone isn't. . . . I was interested in the transactions, but I wasn't grilling them. . . . Well, you know, law firms are full of paper. People would leave, you know, documents on shelves outside their desks. I spent a lot of time in the fax room sending things through, receiving things. So I saw things there. I would see things in the room where people package documents to go at night. . . . I saw something there in the document preparation room, photocopy room. You see paper everywhere. I was natu-rally curious what it was.

At least once at Sullivan & Cromwell, Gil learned of a deal from other lawyers chit-chatting in an elevator.

Many of the deals at Sullivan & Cromwell had code names, but, as Gil would later say, "Sometimes it was so obvious that, you know, research wasn't needed." Gil and Stan shared the work of research whenever it was needed.

Gil was known for his odd habit of showing up at the Sullivan & Cromwell office early in the morning, earlier than 5:00 a.m. When he was asked about this, he would chortle and say that he liked to get in early so he did not have to stay late. The real reason why Gil often arrived so early at 125 Broad Street was so that he could roam the offices of Sullivan & Cromwell when they were deserted, spelunking and stealing information from clients.

Stan would later say, "We had discussed that you could never work late enough in New York, there's always someone working very late, but you can come very early because people like to sleep in. So I would call him in the morning at, say, 3:30 . . . to wake him up, and he would go to work, he would be at work by 4:15."

Gil did not like waking up so early, so Stan in Canada (who had erratic sleeping habits) had the task of phoning Gil in Manhattan for his wake-up calls. "Rise and shine, Gil!" Gil could have used his alarm clock, but he petulantly demanded wake-up calls so that he would not suffer alone. Since the profits were divided evenly, he argued, the waking-up early part should be shared evenly as well.

When spelunking from office to office at Sullivan & Cromwell, often on the 30th floor (general reception) or the 28th floor (mergers and acquisitions), Gil would usually carry a book in one hand and a stapler in the other.

Stan asked, "Why?"

Gil explained that, if he was ever discovered in a lawyer's office or some other inappropriate location, he would show the book and explain his presence by saying, "I was looking for this book."

And the stapler?

If the story about looking for the book did not convince the lawyer of Gil's innocence, Gil told his best friend, "Then I'd use the stapler to hit the guy and kill him!"

Stan believed it.

Every day Gil hid his actions and feelings from everybody he knew — except for far-away Stan. Every day Gil lived in fear of getting caught.

He would later say, "It was a very rough period for me, very down, very depressed. Notwithstanding the $80,000 salary, it was a very, very tough emotional time for me. . . . Moving to a new city, no friends, practising U.S. law instead of Canadian law. . . . I felt, you know, like a foreigner, like someone who was, you know, ill prepared and didn't really understand, you know, anything, worthless and a fraud."

2 | THE TROLL UNDER THE BRIDGE

"Kingcityguru" was a name that Stanko Jose Grmovsek used online. He liked to write opinions on Internet chat-sites such as Televisionwith outpity.com and Fivestarvideopoker.com and Sherdog.com and to leave brief comments after articles on the liberal-leaning news-site Huffingtonpost.com. Stan was a "troll," meaning that he liked to visit chat-sites to insult strangers and offer obnoxious opinions.

On October 6, 2007 (two weeks before his friend Gil's Intensive Course), Stan commented on a Huffingtonpost news article titled "Boy Band Guru, Alleged Pedophile, Is a GOP Donor." Stan's response to this story about the ex-manager of N'Sync and the Backstreet Boys was "I believe a Democratic President was a rapist or, at the least, a sexual harasser. Cuts a bit closer to the Democratic party than this story does to the Republican, but why challenge your convictions?" This comment was irrelevant to the subject but managed to insult ex-President Bill Clinton, provoke his supporters, smear all Democrats as hypocrites and, mainly, confuse the issue.

When Stan woke up the next morning, he turned on his computer and pointed-and-clicked his way back to Huffingtonpost, where he read an article titled "The Greenest Countries and Cities on Earth." He commented,

If you claim to be green, but are against nuclear production of electricity you are a fraud! . . . We should assist [the poor] by providing nuclear electricity to the world and should start by at least achieving the same level of use in the U.S. as they do in France (80%). — [N]ote: please don't come back with your ill informed comments about waste as nuclear fuel is the most energy efficient in the world as it retains 95% of its energy generating potential which means that it is the ultimate recyclable fuel (Israel has just developed such a method).

Stan seemed to have an obsession with nuclear electricity — of the over 900 comments he left on Huffingtonpost between 2007 and 2010, about half of them dealt with the subject, repeating the same misleading arguments. (He did not know or care how much of France's energy came from nuclear; he made the statistic up.) Stan's monotonous comments were often left at the ends of articles that had nothing to do with nuclear power. Stan clearly delighted in annoying environmentalists (whom he mocked as "globalwarmingmongers" — a quip copied from Fox TV host Glenn Beck). There was another, hidden reason for his one-man pro-nuke PR campaign: Stan owned a portfolio of shares in uranium-mining companies, and he pumped out propaganda for nuclear energy to boost the value of these shares and make himself richer. (He was already very rich.) Stan also invested heavily in gold and gold-mining companies, which explained why he often (like Beck) urged readers to buy gold.

On non-political sites, Stan would sometimes reveal a more gentle side of his character. On the chat-site Televisionwithoutpity, for example, he liked to discuss some of his favourite TV shows: *Dexter*, *Californication*, and *House*. Stan watched a lot of TV (he had an expensive, big-screen model) and had strong passions about TV. Sometimes he would interrupt a rant about a TV show to discuss his personal life.

In the morning of October 7, 2007, Stan wrote on the *Dexter* page of Televisionwithoutpity,

If I may offer an aside, my son is 5 and has started a collection of comic book action figures. The question he asks most often is "Is this guy good or bad?" In almost every case I am forced to answer "He is sometimes good and sometimes bad—it depends on the situation and the time in his life." These comic book characters like Batman, Wolverine et al. have a near timeless appeal because they are not one dimensional but comprise an extreme of the best and worst in all of us. I think the writers for *House* and *Dexter* seem to have taken that same view with their protagonists. These characters (like T. Soprano before them) are the most interesting on television because they are both so complex and so extreme: a really mean and nasty Doctor that saves the lives of those that others cannot [House]; a horrible and demented killer that protects us by killing those that would kill the innocent [Dexter]. I thought of that again yesterday when I was watching an interview with an author of a book on Idi Amin (former Ugandan mass murderer and dictator) who went out of her way to note that "he was a very good father (despite all that killing and torture stuff)."

Stan left comments on these sites almost every day, sometimes many times a day, whenever he felt like it. He was unemployed and did not often leave his townhouse in the suburbs north of Toronto. Other than caring for his young son and daughter four days a week, with the help of a live-in nanny, Stan was free to devote his life to hobbies: TV, best-selling books, travel, gambling, spectator sports, and online trolling.

On October 19, 2007 (a week before Gil's conference), at lunchtime, he wrote on Huffingtonpost that "[Hillary] Clinton is the real Manchurian candidate. She is in the pocket of the Chinese government and America will suffer for it."

On the morning of Halloween, a week after Gil's conference, Stan wrote this on the *Dexter* page of Televisionwithoutpity: "As for serial killers, the most recent American example that comes to mind is the BTK killer—no one apparently suspected anything about him (he even did special work-outs to get extremely strong hands that might be akin to Dex's fighting skills) and he was only caught, I believe, because he had the ability to write backwards or something like that. So, yes, I believe that a serial killer can act normal without anyone giving him a second look."

Late in the night of Halloween, in response to a Huffingtonpost article titled "Henry Kravis' Transparent Greed," Stan wrote, "Don't be a playah hater. Hate the play, not the playah."

In the night of December 12, Stan was on the *Dexter* page of Televisionwithoutpity. Somebody else had commented, "I wonder how many people who work or have worked in criminal justice are posting here." Stan's sly response? "I suspect there are more than a few criminals lurking on this Board."

Later that day on Huffingtonpost, Stan trolled, "Anyone that says they will reduce CO_2 by 80% by 2050 is a liar or a nut. . . . What will happen to all the plants and trees without the CO_2 they need to grow?"

A few days later on the *Dexter* page of Televisionwithoutpity, Stan wrote,

> Dexter was flying his sociopath flag with pride this episode. From the Cleckley list [named after the author of *The Mask of Sanity*, this list was used to identify sociopaths] . . .
> 1. Superficial charm and good "intelligence"
> 2. Absence of delusions and other signs of irrational thinking
> 3. Absence of nervousness or neurotic manifestations
> 4. Unreliability
> 5. Untruthfulness and insincerity
> 6. Lack of remorse or shame
> 7. Antisocial behaviour without apparent compunction
> 8. Poor judgment and failure to learn from experience
> 9. Pathological egocentricity and incapacity to love
> 10. General poverty in major affective reactions
> 11. Specific loss of insight
> 12. Unresponsiveness in general interpersonal relations

13. Fantastic and uninviting behaviour with drink, and sometimes without
14. Suicide threats rarely carried out
15. Sex life impersonal, trivial and poorly integrated
16. Failure to follow any life plan
Thank you for that list. I guess I am OK since not all 16 apply to
me. What? 14 is not a lot. . . .

Three days later, just after midnight, Stan went back to the *Dexter*
page of Televisionwithoutpity and wrote, "Life lesson from the show:
AVOID CRAZY PEOPLE!"

o o o

Stanko Jose Grmovsek was 39. He usually gave his middle name as
Joseph. Six feet tall, 200 pounds. Stan was born in Canada, and his
parents were from Slovenia, part of the former Yugoslavia, near Venice.
Stan and his family were Roman Catholics.

Stan had small, narrow eyes that often seemed to squint; sometimes
his eyes made him look Asian. He looked people directly in the eyes. He
kept his hair in a short, almost military style that did not seem to need
combing. He had solid-looking shoulders and chest and a small pot-
belly. He was pale from rarely going outside. His voice was loud. Full of
confidence, he grinned a lot.

Like Gil, though, Stan had a big secret.

Stan actually had many secrets — such as what had happened to
him in the fall of 2004. Three police cars arrived at his house after a
loud, senseless argument between Stan and his then wife on their driveway, in front of their two kids. His wife told the officers that there was
a handgun inside. The police went into the house and found the cheap,
loaded pistol in a drawer in Stan and his wife's bedroom. Stan was
charged under the Criminal Code of Canada with four crimes, including the careless storage of a loaded firearm.

(His 9mm Bryco Jennings semi-automatic had a bad reputation
among gun experts because it was known for jamming after only one

or two shots. But Stan was not a gun expert, and, besides, one or two shots would be enough.)

Stan pleaded guilty in provincial court. Nobody at the court asked him why he owned the handgun. He was sentenced to a year of probation and told to report to a probation officer; he now had a criminal record.

Stan and his wife divorced and sold their matrimonial home.

Years later, single and living in a rented house in Woodbridge, Stan found himself thinking about an ex-fiancée. In November 2007, around the time of Gil's big lecture, Stan created a Facebook account just to look at the Facebook page of his ex-fiancée, Jennifer* (names with an asterix at the first appearance have been changed). He often made comments about her while trolling. He claimed that she liked "to steal things and call it art" and that, during sex, she had enjoyed punching him in the belly and being so punched herself. He claimed that they had been constantly drunk when together.

A long time ago Stan had promised himself never to try to contact his ex-fiancée. He had thought that if he ever did something bad would happen. More than 10 years after their breakup, Stan left an anonymous message on Jennifer's Facebook page: "Old crimes have long shadows," a phrase borrowed from Agatha Christie. Then he deleted his Facebook account.

Soon after leaving that odd and sinister message, Stan's shares in a northern Canadian mining company (Nova Gold) collapsed in price. Almost overnight Stan lost $600,000. That was not "dirty" money from one of his secret offshore accounts. That was over half a million dollars of "clean" money that he had laundered and smuggled into Canada with great hassle and expense. He had to borrow money from his ex-wife to cover the margin call. Even though Stan never repaid this money borrowed from his ex-wife, it was still a big and painful loss. Superstitiously, Stan blamed the loss on the Facebook message he had impulsively left for Jennifer.

He decided to earn the money back as quickly as possible. Even if he had to take some risks.

3 | PROJECT STORM

In the fall of 2007 (around the time Gil Cornblum was preparing for his Intensive Course lecture), Gil's law firm was hired by a company called A.S.V. to negotiate a merger with a company called Terex. Both were U.S.-based companies. The lawyer assigned to represent A.S.V. in this deal, Jonathan Van Horn, was based in Minneapolis. He was a partner in Dorsey & Whitney, a slender blond man with a hobby of preparing smoked meats. Although there was no Canadian aspect to this deal, Van Horn, like Gil, was an expert on cross-border transactions. Van Horn had worked in Dorsey & Whitney's Toronto office from 2002 to 2004. This deal was to be handled completely from the Minneapolis office, and there was no need for Gil to be involved.

A.S.V. was a company based in Grand Rapids, Michigan, that manufactured "compact track loaders"—tank-like rubber-track machines used for high-impact work such as earthmoving, landscaping, excavation, and tree cutting. It earned about $250 million in profit a year.

Terex was based in Westport, Connecticut, and was much bigger than A.S.V., taking in $9.1 billion in net sales in 2007. Terex manufactured a broad range of equipment used in industries such as surface mining, quarrying, construction, infrastructure, utilities, and refining. Terex also offered a complete line of financial products.

When lawyers handled sensitive, ultra-confidential corporate deals like this, they often assigned the file a code name for extra security. The A.S.V. and Terex deal was labelled Project Storm.

Even though they both worked at Dorsey & Whitney, and had worked together on deals in the past, Van Horn did not talk to Gil about Project Storm. Lawyers are generally not supposed to chit-chat about their clients, even to trusted colleagues; there should be a legitimate reason for sharing client information, such as the need to ask for advice or help. Gil was not supposed to know about Project Storm. But he did.

Gil learned about it by accident. He had found himself swamped with work in the late summer and had contacted Van Horn to ask for help. Van Horn had refused, saying that he was too busy with work of his own. Curious about what Van Horn was busy with, and suspecting that he had lied to avoid helping him, in Toronto Gil accessed Dorsey & Whitney's document-sharing computer program called NetDocuments (which Gil normally did not like using) to spy on his Minneapolis-based colleague. After seeing that Van Horn was working on documents linked to Project Storm, Gil investigated more deeply into the legal database — soon coming across some electronic documents showing the proposed takeover of A.S.V. by Terex. Gil knew that the stock price of A.S.V. would move sharply up if news of this takeover became public.

A perfect opportunity for insider trading.

Gil did not immediately rush out to buy shares in A.S.V.; he was too wise and experienced for that. Many planned corporate deals never actually happen, for one reason or another. Or a deal could happen but under conditions that would not cause the target company's stock price to rise.

Gil would monitor the progress of the A.S.V. and Terex deal over the coming months, waiting for the right moment to secretly start buying shares. He must often have schemed or brooded about it. When Gil was supposed to be listening to the other lecturing lawyers at the 2007 Intensive Course in Securities Law and Practice, was he actually daydreaming about Project Storm? When he lectured the other lawyers about law, was Project Storm at the back of his mind?

Although Gil was not supposed to know about Project Storm, computer records would later show that he accessed documents related to the deal at least 36 times between the fall of 2007 and the winter of 2008.

On December 22, 2007, at 11:00 a.m., Gil logged on to Dorsey & Whitney's NetDocuments system and looked at four documents in Jonathan Van Horn's file related to Project Storm. These documents convinced Gil that the negotiations between A.S.V. and Terex were going well and nearing completion.

A few hours later, at 6:12 p.m., Stan (under his alias kingcityguru) logged on to Huffingtonpost and read a news story titled "The Shock Doctrine in Action in New Orleans." Stan commented, "Anyone who has spent any time in N.O. will tell you that it was a City plagued by incompetence and corruption—both of which were encouraged by race-based voting and pandering. If you want to rebuild N.O. cut the subsidies and hand-outs and make it a tax-free zone for business and then step back as it revitalizes."

Later, at 10:30 p.m., Gil used his home computer to access Dorsey & Whitney's NetDocuments to view two more documents related to Project Storm.

Just before midnight, Stan used his home computer to respond to a Huffingtonpost comment:

Hard to take you and the prophets of "man made" global warming seriously when you are also not in favor of nuclear energy. Really, if we have "10 years" you can cut CO_2 emissions in the U.S. by half or more in that period by building 400 nuclear reactors on shuttered military bases and in doing so close all CO_2-emitting electrical generation (France gets 80% of its electricity from nuclear energy). . . . Maybe you don't want a solution?

On December 24, at 9:27 a.m., Gil again accessed NetDocuments from his home computer. (His wife had her own computer downstairs, networked to Gil's.) He found a document titled "Project Storm Timetable (Ver2)." This document convinced him that the time was finally right to take action. The A.S.V. and Terex deal was going to happen, no doubt about it. Gil could not miss this opportunity.

That day — Christmas Eve, also the birthday of Stan's ex-wife — Gil contacted Stan. That was not unusual; they were best friends who spoke on the phone almost every day and met for lunch almost every week. Their families had socialized and vacationed together. But this was not just another personal call: Gil tipped his best friend about Project Storm. Gil was the tipper; Stan would be the tippee and trader.

Although they planned to split evenly all of their proceeds of crime, Gil would later describe this Christmas Eve tip as a "gift" to Stan.

Soon after this conversation ended, Stan logged on to the E*Trade website from his home office and started buying A.S.V. securities on the NASDAQ stock market. He bought under different accounts — some under his own name, others under the names of his friends and family as well as the name of his ex-wife. Stan normally bought shares over a number of weeks, buying relatively small amounts of securities at a time to avoid attention. But this time he was eager to make up for the losses he had suffered recently on the northern Canadian mining stock, Nova Gold, so he bought lots of A.S.V. shares — in big, reckless blocks. On one day, he was the only person in the world buying A.S.V. shares.

By early January, Stan had accumulated 226,013 shares of A.S.V. common stock. He had also bought lots of A.S.V. options: a riskier but more profitable type of security. When you buy an option in a company, you do not actually buy any part of the company. Buying an option is a simple kind of "derivative"; an option gives you the right to buy shares in a corporation until a certain date, at a certain price. Let's say that it is now September, and you spend $1 to buy an option in company A that is for, say, $10 and lasts until November 1. Until November 1 comes, your option gives you the right to buy a share of company A for $10. If the market price of such a share goes over $10 before November 1, then you can use your option to buy the share for $10, then sell it to someone for a higher price, making a profit. If the market price of a share of company A does not go over $10 before November 1, then the option "expires" on November 1, and your investment disappears.

Gil's part of the conspiracy was complete when he tipped Stan. But—partly out of curiosity, partly for another reason—Gil continued to check on the progress of Project Storm over the following weeks. By mid-January 2008, he had logged on to this part of Dorsey & Whitney's NetDocuments 14 more times. Gil wrongly believed that there was no technical way for the Dorsey & Whitney partners, based in the United States, to monitor what he was doing in Canada on NetDocuments.

In the morning of January 14, 2008, a press statement disseminated by A.S.V. Corporate Affairs proudly announced, "Terex to Acquire A.S.V., Inc., Maker of Compact Track Loaders . . . through a tender offer followed by a merger." The press release also raved about "the global reach of Terex" and the "tremendous opportunity for expanding A.S.V. product sales," not to mention the "excellent strategic and cultural fit."

The press release quoted the Terex chairman as saying, "We expect that A.S.V. will add approximately $220–250 million in sales on a 2008 full-year basis," and the chairman of A.S.V. gloated, "We gain access to the resources and know-how of a much larger company with a very impressive global footprint." At the news, A.S.V. shares immediately jumped in price—just as Gil had predicted.

Soon after the announcement, Stan logged on to one of his E*Trade websites and started selling A.S.V. on NASDAQ. When all 226,013 of the A.S.V. common shares had been sold, plus the call options, they had scammed a profit of approximately $934,000 U.S.—more than making up for his $600,000 loss on NovaGold, which Stan imagined had been caused by his odd message on Jennifer's Facebook page. Project Storm had led Gil and Stan to another profitable, undetectable score—it seemed.

They had tipped and traded like this between 100 and 150 times since the early 1990s (they had lost track of the exact number of separate crimes), bringing in many millions of dollars. But this time was different. This time a U.S. government computer noticed a suspicious pattern in Stan's trades.

PART TWO

....

1990-94

I have watched the great minds of my generation flock to law school like migratory birds blown from their true course by prevailing winds. . . .

from *Double Billing*, by Cameron Stracher

4 | THE PLACE, THE TIME

Gil Cornblum met Stan Grmovsek for the first time in the fall of 1990, in the first week of Gil's first-year at Osgoode Hall Law School. Although Stan was also in the first-year class, it was actually his second year there—like Conrad Black, Stan had flunked out his first year at Osgoode. (Just one of many similarities between Stan and that ex-Canadian, hard-right newspaper publisher and convicted fraud artist.) Unlike Black, though, Stan returned to Osgoode the next year to try again.

There were two places in Ontario called Osgoode Hall. The original Osgoode Hall was a beautiful neo-Gothic building in the heart of downtown Toronto, just west of Bay Street, housing the Ontario Court of Appeal and the Law Society of Upper Canada (the Ontario Bar, which regulates Ontario lawyers). Osgoode Hall Law School had once been based in the building called Osgoode Hall, but in the 1970s the law school was moved to York University in North York. Later amalgamated into Toronto, in 1990 North York was an independent city just north of Toronto. The York University campus was often compared to Siberia due to its sprawling size, fields covered by drifting snow for much of the school year, and wind blasts that would wail between the widely spaced buildings. The heart of the campus was a little shopping mall called York Lanes, with fast-food outlets and fashion shops.

Osgoode Hall Law School was in a squat, red-brick building at the southern edge of the campus.

Many people studying or working at Osgoode at this time had an inferiority complex about the University of Toronto Law School. U of T had a nice campus downtown, and U of T Law School was considered Canada's best. (I would later apply to both and be accepted only by Osgoode.) At this time, Osgoode Hall Law School was sometimes mocked as "Was-Good Hall." It sometimes placed poorly in national rankings of law schools. Despite that, it had a long history of training many if not most of the great lawyers and judges in Canada's history, and its reputation among the general public was strong. Non-law folk would usually be impressed to learn that someone was a student at Osgoode, though they might not know anything about the institution or even that there were any other law schools in Canada.

In 1990, the world was changing fast. The Cold War had just finished, and Western capitalism seemed to have triumphed over Slavic communism. Gil's parents' homeland of Romania and Stan's parents' homeland of Slovenia were engulfed in economic chaos and civil war. New countries seemed to pop onto the map every month from the ruins of the USSR. Mikhail Gorbachev would win the 1990 Nobel Peace Prize. A different side of Western capitalism was shown in 1990 when Mike Milken, the "Junk Bond King" who symbolized Wall Street in the 1980s, was found guilty of insider trading and sentenced to 10 years in prison.

Also in 1990, the U.S. Securities and Enforcement Commission filed an action against Steven Glauberman, a senior lawyer at the Manhattan megafirm Skadden Arps. The Skadden lawyer would plead guilty to making at least $1.1 million in profit by using inside information on at least 29 corporate transactions.

Also in 1990, a partner at the giant law firm of Dorsey & Whitney, James O'Hagan, was charged with (among other crimes) insider trading — profiting $4.3 million in a single deal. The lawyer would plead guilty and be sentenced to 41 months in prison.

5 | ACROSS A CROWDED ROOM

There were 250 or so students in the 1990 first-year class at Osgoode. They were divided into sections based on the first letters of their last names. Cornblum and Grmovsek were both assigned to Section B.

A photograph of Section B, taken in Orientation Week, shows both of the young men. Gil (being shorter than average) is standing at the front and centre of the crowd of 50 students. He looks thinner than he ever would again. His face and eyes are directed to the camera, but his body is turned right while leaning to the left. Gil wears a white dress shirt with a crisply pressed collar. His lips are open and puckered together, as if he is saying "Oooooo."

Stan is at the back of the crowd (being taller than average), at the far right of the photo. He has on a white T-shirt; he is the only person in the picture with short sleeves. Stan has on a white baseball cap; he is the only person in the picture wearing any kind of hat. He wears a white-faced Swatch on his left wrist. His body is turned to the right, and he is leaning to the right. His mouth is open. From the curl of his upper lip, Stan looks to be saying "Hey!" or "Yeah!"

After this picture was taken, Gil stood in the crowd talking to another first-year student, of Slovenian background. This student knew Stan, having met him when Stan ran for the student government and was elected the "First-Year Rep" for Section B; this made Stan part of the Student Caucus. The Slovenian first-year student, while talking with Gil, saw Stan across the crowded room and called out, "Hey, Stan! Come here!"

Stan made his way through the crowd to the fellow Slovenian, who introduced him to Gil. Stan and Gil hit it off immediately. They started to hang out after class, talking "about nothing" for long periods of time.

There is another photo of Gil and Stan in the 1990 Osgoode yearbook. It was taken later in the year, for the membership of the Osgoode Hall Conservative Club. It shows them, both in white dress shirts and dark ties, standing with 11 other young Conservatives. Standing in the middle of the photo (almost directly beside Stan) is Michael Wilson, the Conservative federal minister of finance.

Stan and Gil would later meet Conservative Prime Minister Brian Mulroney, and both would shake his hand. While Stan was shaking Brian's hand, he said, "I was here [at the York campus] when they threw macaroni at you." Stan was referring to a student protest a year or two earlier against high tuition fees; tossed macaroni was used as a symbol of student poverty since it was supposedly all that Ontario students could afford to eat. When Stan mentioned the macaroni-throwing incident, the prime minister smoothly said, "That was quite a day," and moved on to shake the eager hand of another Conservative Club student.

Politics was everywhere at Osgoode Hall Law School in 1990, some of it provoked by the surprising victory of the NDP in the provincial election of September 6. The day after that election, in the first week of classes, the Property 1 professor for Section B walked into class and reminded the law students about the election results and Ontario's first social-democratic government. Stan would later write that this professor "strolled into class with a clenched fist pumped high saying, and I quote, 'After twenty years of working for it, we won. We won. The revolution has begun. . . .'"

All first-year students at Osgoode had to take Property 1, Property 2, Civil Procedure, Research and Writing, Torts, Contracts, and Criminal.

In addition to joining the Conservative Club with Gil, Stan volunteered for Mock Trial, a yearly song and dance and comedy extravaganza put on by Osgoode students.

Osgoode had two student governments. The Student Caucus dealt with academic issues, and the Legal and Literary Society dealt with non-academic issues and had a higher profile.

The Legal and Literary Society shared offices with the student newspaper, *Obiter Dicta*. Stan and Gil soon started volunteering for *Obiter Dicta*. (The name was Latin for "unimportant words.") Stan spent enough time hanging around the newspaper office to attract a comment in an October 1 editorial titled "People Are Wondering." The unsigned page 3 piece asked a series of goofy and obscure questions, ending with "10. Why Stanko Gorbachev changed his family name to Grmovsek?"

Stan had an unusual, difficult-to-pronounce last name, and this would not be the last time somebody made the Grmovsek and Gorbachev joke. A few lines down from the above editorial, in fact, the editors put Stan Gorbachev at number four on "The Hit List," apparently a list of people who had recently pissed off the editors. The editors would frequently misspell his last name, such as *Gromosvesok* or *Gropokvex*.

Obiter Dicta featured much less news than opinion. Often there would be no actual news at all—just front cover to back cover filled with law students ranting their opinions and attacking others.

In the October 1 issue, Stan started publishing a regular opinion column, under the pen name "Stan Goldwater Grmovsek." It was titled "Conservative Commentary" at first, but the spelling would soon change to "Konservative Kommentary." Stan replaced the Cs with Ks as a provocation, to associate his column with the Ku Klux Klan. The Goldwater nickname associated the author with Barry Goldwater, the harshly conservative U.S. politician who supported Joseph McCarthy's "Red Scare" tactics in the 1950s and opposed the Civil Rights Act of 1964.

Stan's first column began with this: "Well oh well, the left-leaning lunatic legion has finally found the foothold that will provide them with pre-eminent provincial power. I speak of none other than the NDP. Those reactionary red reaping radicals with their recrudescent reelings on redistribution and reorganization are gathering at the gates of government with their genuinely garish goal of giving greater social justice to Ontario." Stan criticized the NDP for wanting to raise taxes on rich people and to lower them on poor people. He argued for the reverse:

I ask you, why punish the proportion of the populace who have performed perfectly by exacting an excessive excise. . . . Society should show its displeasure with the perpetual and persistent purveyors of poverty, the poor, by tagging them with a terrible tax toll. The goal of my inverse taxation scheme is that we will be able to sufficiently reward the rich and punish the poor so that, God willing, we can take the glamour out of poverty and perhaps not make it such an attractive option for so many of our province's people.

Gil's first contribution to *Obiter Dicta* was a letter to the editor the following week, written in response to Stan's just-quoted column. The letter was titled "Deception":

Dear Editors,

I am writing in response to the Conservative Commentary column that you ran in last week's *Obiter*. It is clear to any reader with the least bit of perception that Stan "Goldwater" Grmovsek is not in fact the ardent Conservative that he purports to be but is in fact a Socialist in Fascist clothing. His column is so extreme as to be self-mocking. He is either attempting to give legitimate Conservatives a bad name or, and this is more psychological in deviation, he is attacking socialism in an attempt to repress his truly held beliefs. With the election of the NDP, the socialists of this province are no doubt squirming in consternation at the thought of the decreased number of issues to complain about. Is Stan "Goldwater" Grmovsek the one of their number who has been chosen to create an issue controversial enough to again inspire the socialist forces to action? Surely such a clever ploy is not below our Marxist masses? It is quite clear that the true Conservatives of this country are having enough trouble expressing their beliefs without having some alliteration prone asshole writing on their behalf. I'm not asking you to censor his column, but instead, I am asking that all readers not forget the old axiom of "never judge a book by its cover."

In light of later events, the "Deception" letter is remarkable. Gil was pretending to accuse Stan of pretending to be a conservative. But Stan was not pretending—he really was a conservative—and Gil, his friend, knew that very well. This letter gives us insight into their devious, cynical way of seeing the world.

The letter praised as "a clever ploy" the idea of living a lie to achieve a hidden goal. It seemed to predict the future, when Gil and Stan would live lies for money and personify deception.

Much later, Stan would admit to helping Gil write the "Deception" letter.

o o o

Later, Gil would say that he liked Stan because he was "interesting and amusing and loud and brash." Although Gil's personality was also "interesting and amusing," these were qualities that Gil usually kept hidden, for the benefit of only those closest to him, and nobody would ever use the words "loud and brash" to describe Gil. In his version, he and Stan became friends because they were so different, as in the cliché "opposites attract."

In Stan's version, also told much later, the appropriate cliché was "birds of a feather flock together." Stan said that they got along well because they were both "very quiet" and shared a dry sense of humour.

Both were basically telling the truth but each with a different emphasis—they were attracted to each other for both their similarities and their differences.

Both were unusually passionate about arts and literature and liked the same TV shows (for example *Star Trek* and *Seinfeld*). They loved science fiction, especially *Star Trek*. Gil identified with the double-sided Mr. Spock (half human, half Vulcan), while Stan was more the Captain Kirk type. They enjoyed comic books very much and agreed that Wolverine was the best superhero. Gil had a collection of rare comic books.

Both enjoyed being rude in their writings but not face to face with people. In social situations, especially involving those richer or more powerful than themselves, they were very pleasant company. Later, Stan would describe his own character as "very obsequious" and Gil's as "smarmy."

Both loved sweet foods — Gil's favourite snack was a chocolate cupcake with vanilla icing, while Stan was unusually passionate about fresh raspberries. Both also loved Taco Bell.

Both described themselves as belonging to the respective religion of their parents, and both claimed to believe in God, but neither paid much attention to the rules of their religion. Gil, a Jew, ate pork. Stan, a Catholic, enjoyed sex outside marriage and did not help the poor. They took the benefits of their religion with few if any of the restrictions.

Neither was born to wealth. Neither grew up in an expensive neighbourhood. Gil's family was slightly richer; his father was an engineer at Ontario Hydro, and his mother was a homemaker. Stan's father worked at a sheet-metal factory, and his mother was also a homemaker. Stan himself would work for many years at the sheet-metal factory during summer breaks from school, putting kitchen equipment together, once cutting his wrist badly on a piece of sheet metal, leaving a permanent scar. Because of his socio-economic background, Gil saw himself as an underdog in society; he would often make comments about himself such as "Not bad for a kid from the wrong side of the tracks."

Both were children of immigrants from Eastern Europe — Gil's family was originally Romanian (by way of Israel), and Stan's family was originally Slovenian. Like many second-generation Canadians, Gil and Stan knew at an early age that their parents had grown up in a culture very different from the one that they, the children, were growing up in. Often children of immigrants are cultural chameleons — able to "act Canadian" most of the time but also effortlessly slipping into the customs (if not also the language) of the old country at family events or community gatherings.

Both were first-born sons, with only one younger sibling: a little brother in Gil's case, while Stan had a little sister.

Both Gil and Stan were active supporters of Canada's Conservative Party and true-blue believers in modern conservatism — the political philosophy that mainly served the interests of the rich. They planned and expected to become rich; they had not come to law school to selflessly serve society and would have mocked anyone making such an idealistic claim. Modern conservatism, also known as neo-conservatism, justified the growing gap between the rich and the poor in moral terms. The rich were, as put in Stan's first article, "the proportion of the populace who have performed perfectly"—and were thus entitled to their property.

Gil and Stan strongly admired Ayn Rand, the amphetamine-gobbling author of *The Fountainhead* and *Atlas Shrugged*, who promoted the benefits of greed, hate, "rational selfishness," and the rejection of social responsibility. (Like Nietzsche, minus Nietzsche's honesty, intelligence, and literacy.) In *We the Living*, Rand howled, "What are your masses but mud to be ground underfoot, fuel to be burned for those who deserve it!" The "hero" of *The Fountainhead* is an arrogant architect of skyscrapers who refuses on principle to help others or accept help from them. He also rapes a rich woman, causing her to fall in love with him. Rand was a hero to U.S. Supreme Court judge Clarence Thomas and to Alan Greenspan, head of the U.S. Federal Reserve during the junk bond crash and the dot-com crash and just before the mortgages-and-derivatives crash.

Stan openly pushed his extreme right-wing views, verbally and in print, but Gil was more subtle and discreet. Other than the "Deception" letter, few of his published writings deal with politics. But the articles that do exist, along with his membership in the Osgoode Hall Conservative Club and my memories of Gil, suggest that his political views were as hard right as Stan's.

Modern conservatism itself is a kind of fraud. Its secret goal is to defend the interests of the rich. But in a democracy, the votes of the rich are not enough to get anybody elected. So how do conservatives win elections? By keeping their real goal secret and tricking middle-class and poor folk into voting for them. Successful conservative politicians wrap themselves in the flag and religious symbols, curry favour with police officers and soldiers, promise crackdowns on crime when crime rates are falling, use "wedge" issues, and exploit xenophobia and racism — with the necessary backing of massive corporate donations and constant propaganda from corporate-owned media. Gil and Stan's shared conservatism partially explains why they became both friends and fraudsters.

As was the case with Raj Rajaratnam of Wall Street and the Wyly brothers of Texas and Conrad Black of Britain—all outspoken conservatives who allegedly profited from massive corporate frauds in the 1990s—insider trading was a logical extension of Stan and Gil's political values.

How were Gil and Stan different?

Stan had a streak of toxic bitterness but was also an optimist and often happy-go-lucky. He derived deep joy from mental jousting and provoking his perceived inferiors. Stan was a survivor, a lemons-to-lemonade type who tried to make the best of every situation. Gil, on the other hand, was grim and gloomy, and his view of life was bleak. He suffered from pessimism and severe depression. They would never leave him. He enjoyed his time in the world less than most of us. Life was often a heavy burden that he dreamed of dropping.

Stan was taller than Gil and two years older. Gil literally looked up to Stan. In a physical fight between them, Gil would not have stood a chance. In 1990, Stan was 22 and Gil only 20. Stan's size and the age gap—combined with his personality and the fact that Stan was in first year for the second time—helped him to dominate Gil from the start. Until much later, Gil deferred to Stan.

In intelligence and education, however, Gil dominated. Everybody at Osgoode Hall Law School was smarter than average, but Gil stood out even there. People who were conceited about their intelligence would sometimes feel mentally outclassed in a conversation with him. Stan did not inspire such feelings.

Stan, having played football and basketball in high school, liked team sports and gambling; he had a talent for counting cards at games such as blackjack; Gil did not like team sports or gambling.

Gil liked long walks and occasional jogging; Stan did not.

Unlike Stan's parents, who spoke very little English, Gil's parents had immersed Gil in high-brow arts from an early age—giving him their opinions on Mozart's operas, for example. They encouraged him to read classics of children's literature—such as *The Secret Garden*, a lovely book about tragedy and rebirth that affected Gil strongly and that he would never forget—and he would read classic literature for the rest of his life. Stan preferred popular bestsellers, hard-right political screeds, and true crime books. Gil savoured classical, opera, and jazz music; Stan was into Leonard Cohen and George Thorogood. Both were outspoken haters of rap.

Gil had attended a prestigious and expensive private high school (University of Toronto Schools) and then studied economics at the University of Western Ontario, an institution famous for snobbery and elitism. He had studied French in Quebec during the summers of 1988 and 1989. His grades from Western were high enough to get him accepted at Osgoode even before he had completed his undergraduate degree. Gil would take the final courses of his undergraduate degree in the summer after his first year of law school—a very heavy academic load.

Stan would later say that Gil had the best memory of anyone he had ever met.

Although Stan also achieved very high grades in school, his all-round education was not nearly as good as Gil's. Stan had gone to a publicly funded Catholic elementary school and Catholic high school (where his nickname was Stinko) and then studied for two years at York before being accepted to its law school. Stan had not chosen a major and had picked only "bird" or easy courses, with the intention of getting grades high enough for law school. (He took every advantage or "edge" he could find to get high grades as an undergraduate. In one class, which had one professor and several teaching assistants, Stan was assigned to one TA but discovered that a different TA was giving students obvious hints about what would be on exams. So Stan stopped going to his own TA and started sneaking into this loose-lipped TA's class. That inside information helped him to get an A+ in the course.) Unlike Gil, Stan did not bother to complete his undergraduate degree after being accepted to Osgoode.

Gil was much more cultured and classy than Stan, who often played the buffoon. Gil was a quiet, mild-mannered person, and Stan's loudness and brashness were attractive to him. Gil usually repressed his own thoughts and urges. He instinctively avoided causing offence, afraid of attracting criticism or even attention. This might have been a safe way for a small, sensitive, Jewish boy to get through life—but was it satisfying? Did acting so civilized make Gil discontent?

I think that Gil dreamed of living like a wolf, but caution kept him in sheep's clothing. He was afraid to be himself in public situations, afraid to make waves or be vulnerable. Stan, however, rarely hesitated. Gil was delighted to find a new friend who revelled in conflict, chaos, and controversy. Stan shared Gil's feelings about many things, but, unlike Gil, he had the balls and the guts to put his feelings into provocative words and deeds. Gil lived vicariously through Stan—cheering and egging on his naughtiness.

○ ○ ○

Stan committed his first recorded act of fraud while a student at Osgoode Hall Law School. He put false information on an application form and successfully scammed the Ontario Student Assistance Program into lending him thousands of dollars that he did not really need. (Stan's writings often denounced social assistance such as OSAP. One of his favourite topics for outraged ranting was welfare fraud by the poor.)

Stan used this interest-free loot to invest in the stock market. Despite not having any inside information, he picked his stocks well—Nortel, Johnson & Johnson, and Greenstone. He held on to these shares and kept reinvesting the profits back into the stock market over the next few years. By the time Stan graduated from Osgoode, his investments had earned almost $310,000 in profit. (Greenstone was by far the best-performing stock; Stan's $25,000 investment in it grew to $300,000.) Stan eventually repaid his loan from the taxpayers of Ontario, but he kept the $310,000. No, the taxpayers of Ontario did not see a dime of that.

Later, in 1994, that $310,000 would be the seed money for Gil and Stan's first venture into crime.

○ ○ ○

In mid-October, Stan published another "Konservative Kommentary" article in *Obiter Dicta* under the headline "The Environment: What's It Really Worth?"

My plan involves a massive and unrestricted exploitation of all resources, from trees to fossil fuels. All trees should be cut down, every piece of coal dug and every barrel of oil drilled so that a glut of capital can be accumulated. I suggest that money, in its entirety, be funneled into the industrial research sector in order to foster the production of devices that can be used to solve the environmental problems that currently challenge us. I fondly envisage huge oxygen producing factories, giant orbiting solar shields, and various other man-made technologies permanently alleviating nature's shortcomings. . . .

Stan was not only writing for *Obiter Dicta* but also volunteering almost every Thursday night at the newspaper office to help get the next week's edition ready for the printer. This work involved printing articles and photos and cartoons from a laser printer and then using a wax-melting machine to put melted wax onto the backs of the sheets so they could be stuck onto large pieces of thick cardboard. It also involved free beer and pizza.

There were usually 10 to 20 volunteers each week, usually more men than women. Tipsy flirting between volunteers happened a lot. Gil did not volunteer at first for the layout nights.

On November 12, Miguna Miguna appeared in *Obiter Dicta* for the first time. He was a first-year student and recent immigrant from East Africa who attended classes in flowing traditional robes, sometimes carrying a tropical-wood walking stick. His opinion article was titled "Disgraceful Osgoode" and was a rambling but ferocious attack on Osgoode Hall Law School that seemed to come out of nowhere; his radical manifesto did not seem to be a response to anything that had been published earlier in the paper. Miguna wrote that

there are some people (both in and outside Osgoode) who hate the school. To this group, Osgoode represents elitism, arrogance and humiliation. To them, Osgoode is rotten and disgraceful. . . . Few (if any) Osgoode lovers question the curriculum. . . . Osgoode haters know that the so-called justice system is horribly corrupt and unjust. . . . Poverty has been criminalized and the poor driven into petty crimes and the grave while exploitation has been officially licenced. Hence, petty thieves receive heavy penalties while white-collar looters get away with everything — even murder! . . .

This article provoked much debate and controversy among Osgoode students.

Stan responded thus:

Dear Editors,

This letter is in response to the article entitled "Disgraceful Osgoode." In it, Mr. Miguna writes that "Osgoode lovers sing . . . as they prepare to jump into their capitalist boat on the road to exploitation and injustice." What an inept use of metaphor! Trying to connect the images of a capitalist "boat" to a "road to exploitation" is akin to the proverbial apples and oranges. . . . [T] o make such an egregious mistake, as Mr. Miguna does, leads me to question not only the reasoning but also the intellect behind the entire article in question. . . .

In the first *Obiter Dicta* of 1991, Stan brought back his Goldwater persona to argue for the creation of a TV station devoted to showing executions "of some of the vilest, most reprehensible and I hasten to add unemployed members of our society. . . . The highlight of Sundays will, of course, be the 'Budweiser Barabbas Hour.' Yes, during that hour, viewers can dial a 976 number to vote for which of two criminals will be executed and which will go freely back to society."

Stan got his first taste of negative publicity as a result of a letter to the editor he wrote for the February 11, 1991, issue of *Obiter Dicta*. Stan was friends with a fellow student, Barry Simpson*; they had worked together to design and typeset a book called *Constitutional Reform*, written by Osgoode professors Patrick Monahan and Lynda Covello. Under the headline "Green Card," Stan's ill-fated letter began thus:

Dear Editors,

B.K. Simpson, Osgoode Hall Law Journal Editor and all-round cool guy, died last weekend. Alright he didn't die, he got married. We don't know much about the bride, except that her immigration hearing had been scheduled for this week. Way to go Barry, but I hope you got the prenuptial agreement signed.

Sincerely,

Stan "Goldwater" Grmovsek

Konservative Kommentator and Sensitive Guy

Stan's "Green Card" letter triggered two outraged letters to the editor. One, signed by three female Osgoode Hall Law School students, was titled "Void."

Dear Editors, (but really Dear Stan Gvmovsek [sic])

This letter is in response to your offensive and unkind comment on the recent marriage of Barry Simpson and Elza Chekhov.*

To equate marriage with death reveals an unfortunate state of mind and maturity in the author. In the case of equal partners who love each other, such as Barry and Elza, relating their marriage to a death sentence for Barry was an offensive insult coming from a supposed friend. Even more offensive, however, was Stan's allusion to the movie *Green Card* in which a Frenchman contracts with an American woman to enter a phony marriage in order to secure a green card and, eventually, U.S. citizenship.

Barry and Elza love each other — as all of their friends know. And a true friend, out of respect for something as good as the relationship Barry and Elza share, would find it in great distaste for someone to trivialize and mar their special day. Stan has overstepped the bounds of friendship and basic human decency in his comments and, although it no longer surprises me that people like Stan have made it into law school, it does surprise me that the *Obiter* would consciously opt to print such libelous garbage. I want to apologize to Elza, a newcomer to Canada, for the unthinking idiocy of one individual.

The second letter on the subject, written by the recently wed Barry himself, was titled "Insult."

Dear Editors,
    S. Grmovsek's letter about our wedding highlights the void this year on the *Obiter*, a lack of responsibility and a lack of humour.
    It is a poor excuse for Mr. Grmovsek to tell me "sorry about the letter, it was late and I had had a lot to drink at the *Obiter* office when I wrote it." I expect no apology from Mr. Grmovsek, for he neither knows his own limits nor those of others, but I do expect a retraction from the editors.

On February 18, the *Obiter Dicta* editors apologized to Barry and Elza Simpson for printing "Green Card."
    The next week Stan Grmovsek was number three on the editorial "Hit List." His name did not appear in the paper for almost another month.
    After the "Green Card" letter, fewer women were willing to volunteer on Thursday nights at the *Obiter Dicta*. Stan had managed to change the atmosphere at the school newspaper office, making it a less attractive place for female students to hang out.
    Around this time, Stan nominated himself as a candidate for the following year's student government, running for the post of external affairs officer for the Legal and Literary Society. Gil also nominated himself, putting his name forward to be the second year-rep for the society.
    On April 1, the results of the Legal and Literary Society elections were announced. Stan came dead last in the voting for external affairs officer—collecting only 48 votes, compared with 115, 152, and 190 for the other candidates. Gil also came in dead last in the election—collecting only 27 votes, compared with 34, 59, and 59 for the other candidates.
    April 12, 1991, was Gil's 21st birthday. Gil was about to finish his final Western courses and earn his B.A. in economics. That would qualify

him to apply to transfer from Osgoode's three-year LLB program to the more demanding four-year joint LLB/MBA program. He was accepted into the joint program. That meant that, after having studied a year in the Faculty of Law, he would spend the next year studying business at York University's Faculty of Business. His third and fourth years would require him to take courses from both faculties at the same time.

Stan would later write that, during the summer of 1991,

> I was investigating whether to apply for the joint LLB/MBA program at Osgoode and spoke to Gil about it. We looked at the requirements and noted that an additional math credit was needed and that it could be obtained over the summer. I remember him saying than an MBA wasn't really necessary and that taking a math course over the summer would be a waste of time et cetera, et cetera. I agreed and spent that summer working construction for some extra money and goofing around. The school year starts in September, and I find that Gil is now in the LLB/MBA program after having completed the math credit over the summer. Clearly, he did not want another application competing with his.

Although Gil did not attend classes at Osgoode in 1991–92, he did start regularly volunteering on Thursday nights for *Obiter Dicta* layout. Every week he and the other volunteers would assign themselves a silly nickname (based on a common theme) to be listed on the masthead as if they were middle names. Some of Gil's self-assigned nicknames were Rockford, Capillaries, Product 19, The Ghoul, Stop Associating with Intellectual Inferiors, Go-Go, Law Firms Don't Hire Jews, The Pharaoh, Shrooms, and I'm Henry the VIII, I Am. Gil, like Stan, rarely missed a week.

In the first *Obiter Dicta* issue of 1991–92, Miguna Miguna wrote a lengthy sequel to the previous year's "Disgraceful Osgoode," in which he claimed that

> Osgoode racists are bitter. As a result, one Pan-Afrikan Law Society member was persecuted before a kangaroo tribunal, and summarily convicted even without a hearing. And that is JUSTICE

OSGOODE STYLE! Two or more Pan-Afrikan Law Society members were given failing grades. . . . We have resolved to fight and die for what we believe is just. . . . We promise to fight for nothing short of total justice even at the risk of facing academic penalties of D's and F's. . . . WELCOME TO THE BEAST, FIRST YEARS.

Stan and two other Osgoode students rose to Miguna's rhetorical bait. Stan wrote to the editors under the headline "Pathetic": "This letter is in response to Mr. Miguna Miguna's article entitled, 'Disgraceful Osgoode Part II: Because Osgoode has proven to be Rotten and Disgraceful.' . . ." Stan criticized Miguna's "hyperbole," "tendentious reasoning," and "anachronistic diction" and compared the African-born student to "the person that we all knew growing up who, on being required to repeat grade five, rationalized his failure by concluding that he was being held back 'because teacher didn't like me.'" Stan described himself as belonging to "the Racist, Capitalist Leeches of Osgoode Society" and questioned whether Miguna's article "was a clever piece of right-wing satire, a la last year's Konservative Kommentaries." Stan suggested that Miguna had written his article while high on drugs, then concluded with "Perhaps the only occurrence sadder than the death of an honest revolutionary is the dismissal of them, by their target audience, as little more than an insignificant, confused, and rambling source of pathetic amusement."

Confusingly for readers (most of whom, after all, were too busy with their expensive education to pay much attention), Stan's letter appeared in the same issue as Miguna's "Disgraceful Osgoode: Part 3," in which Miguna responded to Stan's criticism from the previous year. After referring to persons, corporations, and groups that "lay the golden egg," Miguna wrote that "Osgoode racists will claim that I've failed to use a proper metaphor—aha!" It seemed that Miguna had spent the summer brooding about Stan's "Metaphors" letter. The rest of Miguna's long article was in his usual style of radical rhetoric.

"Disgraceful Osgoode: Part IV" would soon follow.

Gibberish! That's what I call Messrs. Grmovsek's, McMullen's, and Ragonetti's reactions to my article "Disgraceful Osgoode:

Part II." . . . They attempted, without success, to assassinate my character rather than deal with the issues at hand. . . . Jamiliny Grmovsek, McMullen and Ragonetti are not qualified to talk about exploitation and oppression because they have failed to recognize their own racism! . . . I declare you irrelevant! I, however, appreciate the open demonstration of racism of Messrs. Grmovsek. . . . Jamiliny Grmovsek, however, does not tell us how his hypothetical grade five classmate (was he Black?) cannot be said to actually failed (or held back) on perceived real or imaginary grounds. . . . [Miguna describes how anonymous grading had been introduced at Osgoode to prevent discrimination against women.] Could it be that Jamiliny Grmovsek, McMullen, and Ragonetti forgot this fact (remember, they are very bright intellectual cream!) or are they just RACIST CHAUVINIST PIGS?

I have no idea what "Jamiliny" means, but it does not seem to be a compliment.

Despite his law school work and investments and school activities, Stan always managed to find time to watch lots of TV. In the fall of 1991, he noticed many Bell commercials advertising the then new feature of caller ID. Stan, often an early adopter of technology, already had it on his phone.

On December 16, as he was flipping channels between two celebrity-worship TV shows, *A Current Affair* and *Entertainment Tonight*, his phone started ringing. He picked it up and said, "Hello?"

An unfamiliar female voice said, "Your number's on my phone."

Stan, confused, said, "Excuse me?"

The stranger repeated, "Your number's on my phone."

Stan said, "What?"

The woman's voice grew both louder and slower. "Your . . . number's . . . on . . . my . . . phone!"

Stan (according to him) then said, "Miss, Ms., Mrs., or Madam, I think that fact has been established, if only in your mind. But let me assure you that no one from this house intentionally or, I suspect, unintentionally called you. If such a call was made, it was done so in error, and I apologize."

The woman said, "I have a son named Sean."

"It's been nice talking with you," Stan said.

After the woman again said, "But your number's on my phone," Stan hung up.

Then he looked at the caller ID on his phone and saw the woman's number. He dialled it.

She said, "Hello?"

Imitating the woman's voice, Stan said, "Your number's on my phone!"

"What?"

"Your number's on my phone!" Stan repeated.

"What?"

Stan added, "I have a cousin named John!"

"What?"

"Your number's on my phone!"

She hung up.

Stan went back to watching *A Current Affair*, which was showing a documentary video about "a nymphomaniac housewife-prostitute" and her "voyeuristic sheriff-husband." Just before the show was about to present a re-enactment of one of the prostitute's sexual trysts, Stan's phone rang. Stan answered with a "Yello?"

Sean's mother was back on the phone. Hearing Stan's voice, she said, "Oh oh," and hung up.

Stan guessed that she had been going through her caller ID's memory and must have mistakenly redialled his number. So Stan called her back.

She picked up her phone and said, in a timid voice, "Hello?"

Stan, hoping to start the cycle again, said, "Your number's on my phone!"

The woman shouted, "Fuck you, asshole!"

Just before Stan heard the click of her hanging up again, he cried out, "Merry Christmas!"

6 | KIRK A.J. RINTOUL, CLASS OF '88

On February 10, 1992, *Obiter Dicta* published an anonymous letter from a bitter Osgoode graduate. The letter was titled "Bigot?"

Dear Editors,

    I am ashamed to be a graduate of Osgoode. . . . Osgoode has become a national joke in recent years. I apologize to new people I meet for having attended Oz.

    Let me explain. I recently arrived back at Osgoode after three years and was amazed by the number of — let's be blunt — black people at Osgoode. "How *nice*," I thought, having been out of Canada for several years, "Toronto's really changing!" Then, I learned that what had changed was Osgoode's admissions policy. . . .

    Imagine you are a student at an institution that has lowered its standards to admit you. You know you do not deserve to be there. There's no hiding it. You know it. Everybody knows it — the other students, the teachers. What do you do? How can you hold up your head? It's easy. You go around finding racism everywhere! Making accusations. Bullying the faculty. Making unreasonable demands that go unheeded so you can then charge the administration with being racist.

I pity the poor student of colour who *does* deserve to be at Osgoode. He's got "affirmative action" stamped on his forehead. He's lumped in with these self-serving fools. . . . Congratulations, you've just created another black neo-conservative!

Imagine the white student who qualifies but does not make it on account of his colour. You've just created another conservative—or maybe a bigot. Remember, you've done him an injustice. Let's just hope that he's mentally stable. Remember [Montreal school shooter] Marc Lepine? . . . Contrary to the manipulation of this terrible tragedy by the women's movement, Lepine was not out to shoot "women" but "feminists." ("You're all a bunch of feminists," he yelled, as he opened fire.)

Name and Address Withheld

(Yeah, I am a white male. Big deal!)

The *Obiter Dicta* layout volunteers wrapped the text of the letter around an ad in the lower left corner of the page for the Equality Committee's upcoming "Equality Eve" pub night.

The author of the anonymous letter was Kirk A.J. Rintoul, Osgoode Hall Class of 1988. His graduation photo shows a grinning, somewhat chubby fellow with a Beatles-style haircut. Rintoul would later become a college professor at Toronto's Humber College, teaching professional ethics. He would also work for the Law Society of Upper Canada as a teacher for the Bar Admission Course.

The "Bigot?" letter was denounced in a letter to the editors from the Osgoode Hall dean, Jim MacPherson, who denied that standards had been lowered for black or any other minority students and stated that all Osgoode students were chosen on the basis of excellence.

Many Osgoode students and faculty were upset by the "Bigot?" letter and the fact that the editors had allowed it to run anonymously. There were meetings of the Legal and Literary Society, meetings of other groups, a blizzard of letters to the editors, protests, petitions, demands for a referendum, and many intense debates in hallways and classrooms. Finally, two of the *Obiter Dicta* editors were fired by the Legal and Literary Society (which arguably did not have the authority to do so), and the other two quit. Even Toronto's mainstream media outlets reported on the story.

With the help of the Legal and Literary Society, the Osgoode Hall Black History Month Collective (which included Miguna Miguna) took editorial control of *Obiter Dicta* for the next issue. Ninety percent of the content in the February 24 issue of *Obiter Dicta* dealt with racism, colonialism, and social justice. The right-wing bias of the student newspaper was suddenly replaced by an equally hard-left bias. The cover featured, in large print, the words "THEY FAILED TO ASK MY NAME, SO THEY CALLED ME NEGRO—Alexander Dumas." Surrounding this unusual headline, the rest of the cover consisted of hundreds of repetitions of the phrase "black African nigger negro black" in small print.

Any student who had somehow missed the controversy over the previous week's "Bigot?" issue was unlikely to fail to notice this.

Due to the firings and resignations of the *Obiter Dicta* editors, the election of the next year's editors was held early, on February 26. Only regular contributors or regular volunteers were allowed to vote. Three new editors were elected: Gil Cornblum, Christine Blair*, and Tim Bartkiw.

Why did Stan not put his name forward? It was probably because he knew that doing so might provoke Miguna Miguna and his Pan-Afrikan supporters into further anti-*Obiter Dicta* protests. Besides, only three of the four spots for editors for the next year (and the rest of 1992) were filled, leaving one spot that Stan could fill later.

Gil did not have much time after the election before leaving on a school trip to Boston, with the 25 other members of the International Law Society, to participate in the Harvard National Model United Nations. The Osgoode delegation was assigned to represent Iran. Although Gil's group did not win any awards at the model U.N., members of the club would later write about the good time had by all. For someone planning to specialize in cross-border law, this trip to the United States would look good on Gil's resume.

7 | ALL THE WORLD'S A STAGE

At the end of the 1991–92 school year, after the last issue of the student newspaper, Stan was elected to fill the fourth editor's position. He was, from the start, the guiding force of *Obiter Dicta*. Tim Bartkiw was accused by Stan and Gil of being "too lazy" and was, in Stan's later words, "squeezed out." His name would not appear again in the student paper. Much later, he would become a professor at Ryerson University, teaching employment law.

Gil and Stan came up with a smart idea. They contacted a bunch of different Toronto-area entertainment outlets, offering to write reviews in *Obiter Dicta* in exchange for free tickets. The plan worked perfectly. They scored pairs of free tickets to various cultural events, including (best of all) tickets to several plays at the famous Shaw and Stratford festivals.

Gil and Stan were both unemployed that summer. This was during the start of a deep recession that hit youth employment especially hard. The friendship between Gil and Stan deepened that summer, largely as a result of the plays and musicals they went to see together at Shaw, Stratford, and elsewhere. Christine (the other editor) got a few of the tickets, but Stan and Gil used most of them.

On June 20, 1992 — an unseasonably cold day — Gil and Stan saw two plays at Stratford. The first, at 2:00 p.m., was Shakespeare's *The Tempest*, in a largely empty theatre. Later they had tickets to an adaptation of Robertson Davies' novel *World of Wonders*. Before it started, they ran into another "theatre critic," who had disliked the play. Despite the warning, Stan loved it, raving that it "illustrates how all our lives, no matter how obscure or isolated, are all interconnected and interdependent." After seeing *World of Wonders*, Gil and Stan "came to a conclusion that shaped our viewing summer. We may not know theatre, but we know what we like. And we liked *World of Wonders*."

On the last day of July 1992, Gil and Stan went to see their first play at the Shaw Festival, a one-hour lunchtime production called *Overruled*.

Before getting to the theatre, Stan wanted to buy a lunch to eat during the performance. (He often carried around cans of tuna to eat for lunch, but not this day.) A deeply frugal person, Stan was hoping to find a low-budget, fast-food joint. But he was disappointed to find that all of the restaurants near the theatre were priced for the "well-established" set, and none had anything substantive for less than five dollars.

His review of *Overruled* mainly discussed the time he spent prior to the play on a desperate, doomed search for an A&W or Taco Bell. His review barely mentioned the play, describing it only as "OK, nothing special. . . . [D]on't sever an artery if you miss it."

Gil and Stan very much enjoyed seeing *Ten Minute Alibi* at the Shaw Festival in August—a play about a man who gets away with the perfect crime: the hero kills a gigolo who seduced his fiancée. The hero is almost caught at the end but manages to cleverly trick the police and ensure a happy ending.

o o o

Gil, obsessed with self-improvement, read a book in the summer of 1992 called *30 Days to a Better Vocabulary*. He was struck by one obscure foreign word: *weltschmerz*.

In German—a language Gil could read—it means the "sorrow which one feels and accepts as his necessary portion in life; sentimental pessimism; world-pain."

8 | AUTHOR'S ENTRANCE

As Gil was starting the third year of his four-year program and Stan was starting his last year, I showed up at Osgoode Hall Law School for my first year.

My plan was to get a law degree but not become a lawyer; being a writer was my goal even then. I was 23 years old — a year older than Gil, a year younger than Stan.

One of the first things I noticed about Osgoode Hall was *Obiter Dicta*. The cover of the first issue of the year consisted of a confusing joke: over a large photo of a doughnut store called Mister C's Donuts, the editors placed the headline "Osgoode Privatizes First-Year Bell Curve." As a first-year student, this made zero sense to me. Later I learned that Osgoode students were graded on a "C curve," meaning that, in any given class, the average student would get a final grade of C. (This was a constant source of irritation to Osgoode students, as other Ontario law schools graded on a B or B+ curve, making it hard for Osgoode grads to compete for jobs against students from law schools that gave out inflated grades.) The fake news article claimed that Osgoode Hall's administration, desperate for money, had contracted to let Mister C's Donuts sponsor the bell curve.

What I found most baffling about the article was the byline:

By S.J. Grmovsek
Kwisatz Haderach

I vaguely remember reading this and wondering what it meant. I would not find out until much later, during the research for this book. "Kwisatz Haderach" has two meanings.

First, it is the name of a prophesied messiah in the science-fiction novel *Dune*. Kwisatz Haderach is a man (it cannot be a woman) who undergoes a "ritual spice agony" to obtain "organic mental powers" that "bridge space and time," giving him the ability to be in many places at once and to read the future. The hero of *Dune* becomes a Kwisatz Haderach, rules the universe for a while, then kills himself.

There is a second meaning to the phrase. In ancient Hebrew, *kwisatz haderach* (sometimes spelled *kefitzat haderech*) literally means "the act of jumping from the road." Like the ability to teleport in *Star Trek* — Gil's favourite TV show — *kwisatz haderach* refers to the ability to jump instantaneously from one place to another. There are Hasidic folktales in which God gives a righteous rabbi the gift of *kwisatz haderach*, which enables the rabbi to "jump" into the treasure room of the emperor, steal bags of gold, and then jump back to his small village without being noticed. The rabbi uses the gold to help poor and persecuted folk, never for his own personal benefit. Later, when the emperor is planning to pass laws harmful to his community, the rabbi again uses the power of *kwisatz haderach* to teleport into the emperor's throne room and, taking on the power of invisibility, beat the emperor with a stick. When guards rush to help the emperor, the righteous rabbi uses *kwisatz haderach* to escape from their clutches and return to his grateful village.

I believe Gil and Stan knew both of these meanings — they were fans of science fiction, and Gil had studied Jewish history and folklore while growing up — and one of them stuck the phrase into the byline as a private joke between them. Or maybe it was a deliberate, playful clue to the world about their intentions — a clue that, they assumed, nobody would ever figure out.

o o o

The *Obiter Dicta* masthead soon anointed Stan as editor-in-chief. Gil and Christine were senior editors. Previous and later editors, such as me, did not feel the need to puff up our job descriptions like that.

Stan picked a fight with the Legal and Literary Society in the first issue of 1992–93, claiming that most school clubs "engage in nothing more than intellectual masturbation: getting-off on their own ideas as they preach to the converted." He demanded that funding be cut off for any clubs that did not enhance Osgoode Hall's reputation or serve the entire school population. Basically, Stan wanted other clubs to get less money so that *Obiter Dicta* could get more. His proposal met with almost zero support, unsurprisingly. His follow-up proposal to the society—that all Osgoode students be forced to pay an extra dollar a year in student fees to support the paper—also bombed.

Gil also took a strong stand in the year's first issue on the issue of national unity. During the summer, a University of Montreal Law School student representative named Patrick Beuger contacted Gil, inviting him to an exchange of letters to be published in both the Osgoode Hall and the University of Montreal student newspapers. Gil agreed; his letter began thus:

Dear Patrick,

Like you, I am excited about this project. I firmly believe that communication between individuals is an important step towards understanding the differences in our societies and cultures. . . . I would disagree with your assertion that there is something "circus-like" in the evolution of the constitutional debate. I do believe, however, that there are clowns in attendance, but I suggest that they are from Quebec and are led by Premier Robert Bourassa. . . . [H]e has acted more like a spoiled child than a leader. He clearly seems to believe that Quebec holds all the cards. I think the opposite is true. . . . What is insulting to English-Canadians is the aloofness of Mr. Bourassa and Quebec, particularly in their "all or nothing attitude." . . . If push came to shove, as none of us hope it will, I have no doubt that Quebec would swallow its pride and, as a matter of survival, remain a thriving part of Canada. . . . [T]he hostile attitude displayed by many towards Quebec is directly attributable to Quebec's own isolationist attitude towards the rest of our country. What is needed is more trust. . . .

Like Stan's writings, but to a lesser degree, this letter was designed to be deliberately provocative. With its chest-thumping majority nationalism, its insults against Quebec politicians, its threats of civil war and genocide, its simple-minded slogans, its final line of "P.S. My Canada includes Quebec"—the tone and style of Gil's argument were not what one would expect in a constitutional discussion by a law student, especially one like Gil, who had lived in Quebec for two summers. Much later, Stan would admit to helping Gil with the letter but would point out that the joke about Quebec politicians being "clowns" was Gil's idea.

Beuger did not respond to Gil's letter, and the letter exchange died.

Under the banner of the next *Obiter Dicta*, the editors placed the words "RECENTLY VOTED THE BEST WEEKLY NEWSPAPER ON CAMPUS." That was not true.

Several of the articles by Stan had implied that he was willing to break laws or engage in unethical behaviour; on September 8, 1992, he was explicit. He returned to his "Goldwater the Konservative Kommentator" persona to write a detailed how-to guide on how to steal copies of *Now*, a left-wing newspaper, from a coin machine. The copies were priced at a dollar each at certain machine locations at that time, but Stan advised his readers to

simply pull out the small latch at the right of the box. Continue this act as you pull the main handle towards you—this should lock the small latch in its extended position. While continuing to pull out the main handle, release the small latch with your right hand, take a breath, and smack it back into place with your right palm. If done correctly the NOW magazine box is now a free NOW receptacle. . . . Those who can afford must pay, those who cannot can steal. . . .

Sometime that week I found my way to the *Obiter Dicta* office and met Stan and asked him if I could write a regular column. The office was just a single long room, with long tables along the walls, a single computer, and stacks of papers and shelves of books, all under fluorescent tubes that buzzed slightly. Beige-painted brick walls, no windows. All I can remember of our first meeting is that he agreed to my column idea and that he was, I think, wearing a baseball cap. I seem to recall that he usually wore one, along with jeans and gym shoes and T-shirts with the logos of U.S. college football teams. I remember how he liked to put his feet up on tables and grin while talking.

Starting in September, and continuing throughout the year, various items belonging to *Obiter Dicta* — such as computer software and an old typewriter — started appearing "for sale" in the personal ads. This had not been done in previous years. It is not known where the money from the sale of these items went.

Gil returned to the constitutional debate on September 14, when he wrote an editorial about the Charlottetown Accord titled "Why I'm Voting No":

At risk of sounding more arrogant than usual, I must add that I see no compelling reason for anyone (unless their life philosophy is appeasement) to vote in favour. . . . [Regarding Senate reform,] I don't see how electing another layer of inept politicians would solve anything. There is simply nothing in this Accord that puts a smile on my lips or a twinkle in my eye (and those who know me know how easy that is). . . .

The following Thursday, Gil was at the Osgoode Hall pub night. He sat near some students who were discussing his recent editorial on the Constitution. After listening to the contentious debate for a bit, Gil said, "I wrote that. I'm Gil Cornblum."

Shocked, one of the women said, "Really? I thought it was just Stan using a pseudonym!"

The September 14 issue also featured a theatre review by Gil and Stan. They had spent another summer seeing plays and other performing arts with free tickets from publicists. This play, which Gil and Stan did not like, was called *Counsellor-at-Law* and dealt with a 40-year-old Manhattan lawyer who, in his youth, had engaged in some unethical behaviour to help a client. Years later, at the peak of his professional success, a rival lawyer learns of the long-ago offence and threatens the protagonist with exposure, scandal, disbarment. The protagonist lawyer becomes suicidal and climbs onto the windowsill of his skyscraper office to jump to his death—but, at the last second, his secretary bursts in and confesses her love for him. He decides to live and fight. He blackmails the rival lawyer into keeping the unethical conduct secret—a happy ending.

Gil very much liked *The Secret Garden* at the Royal Alexandra Theatre:

> I was ten years old when I first read *The Secret Garden*, Frances Hodgson's 1911 classic. What struck me then, and what has made it timeless, was its honest portrayal of a nine-year-old girl who survived tragedy. . . . The central theme of the novel [is] rebirth. *The Secret Garden* is a story of new beginnings, healing, and of hope rising from tragedy. For this reason, I had some misgivings as to the ability of a musical to capture the flavour of the novel. The production I saw fully caught the full range of emotions the novel generated and is revered for. Having read the book so long ago, and having very vivid pictures of some of the characters in my mind, I was a bit disappointed by some of the actors. . . . While *The Secret Garden* has historically been labelled a children's story, the themes and subtexts are relevant for all audiences. . . .

The main character is a depressed orphan girl who, after a bird leads her to the key to a walled-in garden, goes into the forbidden place and discovers, for the first time, beauty and happiness. She keeps the garden a secret, except from her closest friends; at one point, her "secret garden" is referred to as a "stolen" garden. This secret transgression gives her a reason to live.

The September 14 issue featured the first appearance of my column, titled "Whatever." It was in the back pages and began with "If you want relevant information about Osgoode, stop reading right now. I'm in first year & I don't know much about anything. But I have this column to fill, so I'm going to ramble on about whatever. . . ." I went on to crack a bunch of jokes about being in first year.

The following week my column was not so funny. For some reason, I decided to attack the York Federation of Students. My second column began with deliberately overblown rhetoric — "The budding flower of reform in the YFS has been brutally crushed by the ruthless jackboot of oppression" — followed by a too-harsh personal attack on the YFS leaders.

Looking back, I think the main reason why I wrote this overly harsh article was because I knew that Stan (the only editor I had then dealt with) would like it. He did, placing it on page 4. (*Obiter Dicta* had the best stuff at the front and the dregs at the back.)

My next article pleased Stan even more, making it onto the front page. It began thus:

> I seem to have become a bit notorious among the staff at Osgoode's cafeteria. They think I'm a total fool, perhaps even deranged, but that's unfair. Let me tell my side of the story.
>
> You see, I really like the spinach-puffs they sell down there. (Have you tried one? They're crispy pastries with a filling of melted cheese & spinach — & in my opinion they're better than orgasms, because after having one you don't have to rest 15 minutes before having another.) . . .

The part of my third column that Stan liked best was about him: "I don't want to seem like a butt-smoocher, but I'd like to take this opportunity to say that Stan — despite having a major cocaine problem and a savage hatred of ethnic minorities & an unnatural lust for Canada geese—is almost one of the finest persons I've ever met." Stan liked that part so much that he made a subheadline in big, bold letters: "UNNATURAL LUST."

Writing my column quickly became more important to me than my classes (which I soon stopped attending almost completely), and I worked harder at "Whatever" than my homework. I worked hard to please both my editors and my readers. My column became very popular among Osgoode students—I was notorious as the "spinach-puff guy"—and this gave me my first tiny taste of fame.

This part of the book revolves around *Obiter Dicta* because, when I went to Osgoode, my life revolved around it—as did Gil and Stan's. So, to write about our lives at that time is largely to write about the all-consuming school newspaper.

Looking back, I see that some of the outrageousness and obnoxiousness of the persona I developed at Osgoode Hall was partially inspired by Stan. During my first year, Stan was sort of a role model to me. His journalism reminded me of that of Hunter S. Thompson, author of *Fear and Loathing in Las Vegas*. Stan was always nice to me. He did not seem to be racist (I have dark skin).

I remember hanging around in the office with Gil and Stan at this time. I don't think anybody else was there then. Gil said something to me like, "I was talking with Stan the other day, and we think that you're the fastest writer in *Obiter* history to go from the back of the paper to the front page. You were on the front page with your third article. We don't think that anybody has ever done that before."

I said something like, "But do the readers like what I'm doing?"

I don't remember their words, or if they just nodded, but Gil and Stan both indicated yes.

Without the "Whatever" column and the encouragement of my editors, I might not have become a full-time professional writer, and this book would not exist.

o o o

At the start of October, the three *Obiter Dicta* editors found a mysterious package of papers in the office recycling bin. It was a computer printout listing the names of all first-year Osgoode students (including me), along with our undergraduate grade point averages, our Law School Admission Test scores, and our student numbers.

Gil, Stan, and Christine knew that this information was confidential. They knew that they could get in trouble for looking at it.

They looked at it anyway, then published a front-page article about it, headlined "What a Scoop!" The article described the documents in vague, general terms and did not reveal confidential information. They did not get in any trouble over it.

o o o

Gil was strongly affected by the opera *Werther*, based on the classic German novel *The Sorrows of Young Werther* by Goethe. This short novel, written in his youth in 1774, is famous for inspiring countless suicides. Generations of young men and women have been fatally seduced by this romantic book.

Gil and Stan saw the opera together, though it did not make a deep impression on Stan, who would soon forget everything about it.

Gil, much more deeply affected, wrote in his *Obiter Dicta* review that

> ... No other word [other than *weltschmerz*] could better describe the feeling of tragic gloom that hangs over the Canadian Opera Company's latest production ... a tragedy from start to finish. ... From the moment Werther declares his love for the unattainable Charlotte, the inevitable conclusion is in sight. ... Werther finally chooses death over a life without Charlotte ... one of the best operas I have seen in a long time. ... [It deals with] the ambivalence between a sense of responsibility (represented by Albert) and attraction to impulse and temperament (Werther). ...

Gil's gloomy heart thrilled at the opera's most famous aria, sung by love-sick Werther when he has decided to die:

Why do you awaken me,

O breath of spring?
Why do you awaken me?
On my forehead I feel your caresses,
and yet very near is the time
of storms and sorrows!
Why do you awaken me,
O breath of spring?

In his review, Gil claimed to have read the novel in the original German. We can imagine his reaction to lines in the book such as

That man's life is only a dream has occurred to many, and this feeling constantly accompanies me everywhere as well. . . .

Human nature, I went on, has its limits. It can bear joy, sorrow, pain up to a certain point, but buckles as soon as that point is passed. So the question here is not whether one is weak or strong but whether he can endure the extent of his suffering. It may be moral or physical: and I find it just as strange to say that the person who takes his life is a coward as it would be out of place to call someone a coward who dies of a malignant fever. . . .

Werther describes a woman who

comes upon a man to whom an unknown feeling draws her irresistibly, on whom she casts all her hopes, forgets the world around her, hears nothing, sees nothing, feels nothing but him, the only one . . . and her beloved deserts her. Numb, senseless, she stands before an abyss; everything is darkness around her, no prospect, no comfort, nowhere to turn! . . . Blindly, driven to desperation by the horrible need in her heart, she jumps off in order to suffocate all her torments in an enveloping, embracing death. . . .

o o o

In the same issue of *Obiter Dicta*, Stan published a theatre review of Verdi's opera *Rigoletto*. This is how it began:

Of late, I have received quite a bit of criticism for my reviews. I have been told that I focus far too much of my review on the occurrences before, during and after the performance; and not on the performance itself. . . . [So] I have decided not to write about the Orchestra strike that almost scuttled the performance, the argument I had with my date about Jim Nabors, the high cost and low quality of the expresso sold within the O'Keefe, the sequined tuxedo that I saw hanging in the men's washroom, and the "stoned" woman, who blessed each seat in my subway car on the ride home. . . .

The play revolves around Poetic Justice, or what can be interpreted colloquially as "Everybody, sooner or later, gets what's coming to him," or if we prefer a more classical phrase: "Be not deceived; God is not mocked: for whatsoever a man soweth that shall he also reap."

Rigoletto chose to serve an evil master and paid the price. At the end of the opera, when Rigoletto discovers that his daughter has been murdered—due to a miscarriage of his own vengeful plans—we realize that the curse has been fulfilled. . . .

[Rigoletto is] both the centre of mocking attention and, at the same time, alone within his own personal torment . . . isolated, pitied, mocked, and damned. . . .

o o o

Stan liked to make fun of Hamilton, Ontario, my hometown, which then had a reputation as a grim, polluted backwater. But there were nice places in Hamilton, and I liked even the so-called grubby parts of the city where I was born and grew up. So I would defend Hamilton and mock Toronto, Stan's hometown.

I remember sitting in front of the computer in the *Obiter Dicta* office, typing something, with Gil and Stan leaning on the table near me. For some reason, Stan started making fun of rap and reggae music. He started imitating a Shabba Ranks song, grunting to the beat in a vaguely hip-hop way and chanting, "Girls, girls / Pick-up truck full of girls, girls / Baseball bat full of girls, girls," and jerking his arms in a "funky" way.

Just as Stan had wrongly assumed that I liked rap because of my brown skin, I jumped to the false assumption that he must like country. So I started a moronic-sounding impression of a country singer: "Ohh, my dog just died / My pick-up truck just broke down / And my woman's long gone. . . ." As I started singing, Stan was still babbling and did not hear me at first.

Gil, always very observant, poked Stan and said, "Listen. Mark's making fun of country." They both laughed when my "honky-tonk" song was done.

I remember sitting in the *Obiter Dicta* office one afternoon with Gil when Stan was not around. Due to his absence, it was much quieter and calmer in there than usual. I said something to Gil that clearly suggested that I was a radical environmentalist. He looked at me in his usual calm, thoughtful way—a hint of a smile fluttering around his lips—and suggested that stronger property rights could help to protect nature. I had spent the previous summer going door to door for Greenpeace, engaging in thousands of debates about the environment with people who answered the door—and I had never really considered the idea of strong property rights as a tool for conservation. I sensed that this was an argument Gil had given a lot of thought and study to. I responded by raising the example of a man who buys the entire Amazon rainforest and decides to turn it into a giant parking lot.

"If property rights are really strong," I said, "then he'll be allowed to do that."

Gil refrained from tearing apart my weak argument. But it was obvious to both of us that he knew more than I, the tree-hugging Greenpeace guy, did about environmental legal theory. I felt humbled.

Much later, Stan would write,

It was the first day of the last term of my last year at Osgoode Hall. I was a bit of a keener, so I arrived early for my Tax Law class and took a seat in the middle of an empty hall. A few minutes later, Michael Bryant [who would later become the attorney general of Ontario] and an associate of his walked into the room before moving towards me. As I turned to look at them, Bryant indignantly shouted, "That's my seat!" Since I had arrived to an empty classroom before sitting down, I did not know what he was talking about. "Everyone knows I always sit in the centre in every class I take," he continued before he or his friend reminded me that he was our graduating class's "Silver Medalist" and deserved the seat that I was sitting in. Unfortunately, Clint Eastwood's epic western—"Unforgiven"—had not been yet filmed, or I would have answered in my best gravelly voice "Deserves got nothin' to do with it." Instead, I recall saying something like, "Well, this is one class where you won't be sitting in that centre seat, award or not" before turning away to hear him snort and storm out of the room. That incident and his sense of entitlement so turned me off that I committed then and there to beating him in that class and, if I could, taking away his Silver Medal.

Under the banner of the January 11, 1993, *Obiter Dicta*, the editors placed the words "RECENTLY SHORTLISTED FOR BEST CANADIAN NEWSPAPER (circ. under 5,000)." That was not true.

In my "Whatever" columns, including the notorious "spinach-puff" one, I had occasionally mentioned that I was a vegetarian. Stan "Goldwater" Grmovsek's January 11 "Konservative Kommentary" went thus:

As I was biting into my venison-burger last week (killing the meat yourself makes the meal cheaper than a Taco Bell Tuesday scrape-the-grill special) and getting drunk on smuggled American rye, I came to the incontrovertible earth-shattering conclusion that vegetarians are not human.

Certainly, every good, red-blooded, bacon eatin', puck shootin', soldier salootin' Canadian out there knows that if God (that's with a big G) did not want us to eat meat, He (that's with a big H) would not have given us the ability to trap or house other living creatures, kill them, and then enjoy the taste of their flesh. . . .

As a perfect example of a good guy "meat-eater" gone bad, I give you the *Obiter*'s weekly "Whatever" columnist, Mark Coakley.

Has there ever been a more irreverent, obnoxious, dumb-assed and disrespectful first-year to walk the halls of the Hall than the tree-hugging, asparagus-sucking, cucumber-fondling, wheat-germ injecting Mr. Coakley. The answer is NO! . . .

What is the cause of this behaviour? Is it too many childhood games of hit-Mark-in-the-head-with-a-heavy-ceramic-object-until-he-bleeds? Too many Saturday nights spent with PAM, a bag, and a hankering for the ultimate under-a-dollar high? Or is it the horrific bet-your-tongue-won't-stick-if-you-put-it-up-against-that-steel-bumper incident of last winter? NO!

After analyzing the data, consulting all the sources, and poking Mark in the eye with a pencil, I have come to the conclusion that his problem is that his diet consists of too much roughage and not nearly enough carnage. In short, he needs to start eating things that once had a pancreas. . . . If God wanted us to be vegetarians, He would not have made meat so darn tasty, particularly when you are drunk. . . .

For the sake of humanity and all things good, decent and pure, Mr. Coakley, kill something and eat it—before it's too late.

The next week my column referred to "the mob of right-wingers who dominate the *Obiter*. . . ."

Stan fired back with an editorial cartoon the following week in which one character asks, "What do you think of Mark Coakley?"

The second character says, "I think he's a goof."

The first character says, "Yah, me too!"

On February 1, I wrote a letter to the editor complaining (in what was supposed to be an ironic, joking tone) that the editors had not given enough publicity to an environmental meeting that I had helped to organize.

Under my letter, Gil wrote, "Editor's reply: We didn't publicize this pathetic event, Mark, because you are a knob."

∘ ∘ ∘

In early February, Stan accused the Legal and Literary Society of a scandalous breach of ethics.

As the only graduating editor of *Obiter Dicta*, Stan was supposed to be included in the group pictures for student government. He got his photo proofs in the mail in January, chose the picture he liked, and mailed back to the photography company an order form and payment cheque. A few weeks later he got a phone call from a company rep asking him to choose a free photo package. Stan asked why it was free. The rep explained that all members of student government were entitled to get a photo package of their choice for free.

Stan had not known about that. He quickly wrote and published an outraged editorial, calling it a "kickback. . . . How can the students of this school trust the decisions of their student government if they do not know what influenced them?"

The society responded with a letter stating that it had decided to decline the offer of free photos for student government officials as a result of the controversy created by Stan's article. However, the letter went on to criticize Stan for the tone of his article and the damage it did to the reputations of the executive of the society: "The more serious question to be raised concerns the ethics of Stan and the editors of the *Obiter.*" The Legal and Literary Society quickly started organizing a referendum to allow it to take over control of the paper.

In the next issue, I wrote a "Whatever" column urging a "no" vote in the *Obiter Dicta* referendum and praising Stan's courage in exposing the "sleazy photo-kickbacks" scandal. I also made some unfair, inaccurate arguments against the Legal and Literary Society. Even though I was secretly annoyed at Gil and Stan for their recent attacks on me in the paper, I still rushed to their defence and imitated their smear tactics.

I argued that allowing the society to control the paper would "create yet another layer of expensive bureaucracy." This was a misleading argument—but when I ran into Gil near the *Obiter Dicta* office a while later, he praised my column in general and that phrase in particular. I said "Thank you" and thought no more of it until I started researching this book. Then, when I reread his "Why I'm Voting No" editorial, I saw that it contained the phrase "electing another layer of inept politicians."

Gil had assumed that my wording was a rip-off of his previous, similar wording. His praise was a subtle way of telling me that he had noticed my apparent imitation and was flattered.

The Legal and Literary Society lost the referendum, and *Obiter Dicta* stayed independent. In revenge, the society removed Stan's photo from the student government composite picture.

Gil and Stan used their free theatre tickets to entertain girls on dates. For example, Stan wrote of taking "the lovely Kristina" to see *Don Quixote* at the O'Keefe. In an echo of his "Green Card" letter, he explained to his readers that Kristina was a Bulgarian waiting for a decision of the Refugee Appeal Board. Stan coughed from his date's cigarette smoke outside the theatre and coughed inside the theatre from the dry ice used for the performance. Gil would write of taking a young lady to Gershwin's *Crazy for You* and looking at her face to see her reaction to the sentimental song "Someone to Look over Me."

Toward the end of the school year — the last for Stan — he wrote an article on crime titled "Young Punks" that was published in *Obiter Dicta* and the *Toronto Sun*, a trashy, right-wing tabloid. He wrote that, while taking the bus to law school one morning, he overheard a "fat-headed 14 year old" bragging to another youth about stealing hats and car radios. The youth said "Y.O. [the Young Offenders Act] can't do shit."

> This punk has lost all respect for authority and our society. For that I blame the liberal bleeding-heart treatment that he has been receiving. . . . I'm of the school that if you do the crime, you should do the time. I don't care if you are poor, were beaten as a child, fell in with a bad crowd, or are mentally deficient. Too bad. It's time society stopped looking for excuses and scapegoats and started finding people like this young punk responsible for their actions.

For the final issue of 1993, a few days before his 23rd birthday, Gil wrote an article called "Last Words."

So, the editors that came in with a bang are finally leaving without so much as a whimper. If this was my last year at Osgoode, I would be really brutal at this point — names would be named, egos crushed, tears flow and careers ruined. But I've got one more year to spend in this hole. . . . I've always found it strange that people who have never put pen to paper stop me in the hall and complain about what is in the *Obiter*. . . . Some of the things that actually made the year bearable: melted wax fights on Thursdays; writing obnoxious editor's replies; and, kicking Legal & Lit.'s butt in the referendum. . . . [Gil described his regularly occurring] urgent desperation to have anything [for *Obiter Dicta*] finished before CorpFiSecReg [a law school course called Corporate Finance and Securities Regulation]. . . . I did actually enjoy being an *Obiter* editor. Thanks go out to my co-editors Christine and Stan, for letting me goof off most of the time. . . . You get no credit, you get no cash (mind you, the kickbacks aren't bad if you like operas and graduation photos). . . .

In May, Stan graduated from Osgoode Hall Law School with excellent grades. In addition, he had won the F.W. Minkler Scholarship as the best graduating student in tax law (beating out Michael Bryant) and the Smith, Lyons, Torrance, Stevenson & Mayer Prize in Corporate Finance and Securities Regulation as the best graduating student in corporate law.

Stan would later point out the irony of being honoured for his knowledge of the same laws that he would later break on a massive scale.

In his graduation photo, Stan stares at the camera with a look of utter confidence. Something about this black-and-white picture is reminiscent of pictures of Hollywood actors from the silent-movie era.

After graduation, Stan started his articling year at the prestigious, high-power Bay Street firm of Osler, Hoskin & Harcourt — where he would catch the insider-trading bug.

Also in the summer of 1993, Toronto lawyer Garry Hoy was working at the Bay Street firm of Holden Day Wilson. His office was in a TD

Centre tower, on the 24th floor. Garry liked to show off to articling students by running at the floor-to-ceiling glass window of his office and then jumping at it, only to safely bounce off. On July 9, Garry again tried this trick. This time the articling students (one of whom was a recent Osgoode graduate) watched in shock and horror as the window-pane popped out of its frame. Garry fell out and down to Bay Street. Soon after the tragedy, news of which soon spread across North America as a true urban legend, the partnership of Holden Day Wilson was dissolved.

Gil and Stan talked about Garry.

Stan said, "That was dumb."

Gil asked, "What was he thinking about on the way down?"

9 | FREE CAKE

Along with three other Osgoode Hall Law School students, I was elected editor of *Obiter Dicta* for 1993–94.

Gil, in his final year of his LLB/MBA program, stayed on as theatre critic, which meant that he kept getting the free tickets. Gil also liked to call himself the *Obiter Dicta* archivist, as a joke. He did not hang out in the office nearly as much as he had as editor.

With Stan gone, and me an editor, the tone of the student newspaper changed. Kirk A.J. Rintoul, author of the "Bigot?" letter from the year before my arrival, wrote to us to complain "how boring the *Obiter Dicta* is now that it is a 'politically correct' paper."

One day one of the other editors mentioned that he had spoken to Stan and told me that Stan was having problems in his articling year at Osler, Hoskin & Harcourt. I heard that Stan had been criticized by senior lawyers for wearing black gym shoes to work and for writing legal memos in the style of the *National Enquirer*.

Still annoyed by Gil and Stan's name-calling in *Obiter Dicta* the previous year, I wrote an article titled "Osgoode's Shame and Disgrace":

> . . . The mental collapses of Stan & Christine & Gil & their resulting antisocial behaviour have already caused irreparable damage to the reputation of our once-proud Osgoode Hall.

Stan Grmovsek is today the most embarrassing of last year's *Obiter* editors. Once this young man was a polite, accomplished student & a guiding inspiration behind this newspaper. Now he is articling at Osler's & apparently behaving in a highly eccentric manner. Recently he phoned the *Obiter* office to tell us about his shoes. He claims to find dress-shoes uncomfortable, so he bought some "sport-shoes" & started wearing them to work. His employers apparently told Stan not to wear them, so he stopped for a while, but by the time he phoned he had started wearing them again.

After some investigative work, I found out that Stan's so-called "sports shoes" are actually a pair of white Nike high-top basketball shoes with air-pumps & little red lights that flash under his heels when he walks. Now, this is highly inappropriate footwear for anyone working at a law firm, as any sane person would realize. It's impossible to understand this behaviour — especially from a guy who's already been almost fired for writing sarcastic memos in the style of the *National Enquirer*. I doubt if many Osgoode students are going to be hired at Osler's now, after their experiences with this lunatic. Thanks a lot, Stan.

Then, more gently, I poked fun at Christine, a nice person, for her obsession with the soap opera *The Young and the Restless*.

I ended the column with Gil.

I've saved the most pitiful mental victim for last. In his third year at Osgoode, Gil has slipped into a fantasy world of delusion and hallucination. He is tragically convinced that he holds the non-existent position of *Obiter* "archivist." We tried to explain it to him — Hey, Gil, we said, there is no such thing as an archivist for this newspaper. You can go home if you want. He refused. Then we challenged him to show us some archives. Gil looked uncertainly inside his briefcase for a while & then, failing to find anything there other than tattered pornographic magazines, he threw himself onto the floor & started to bawl, "But I am the

Obiter archivist! I am, I am, I AM!" To this day, Gil continues to reject all evidence of reality & remains deep inside his weird fantasy. Sometimes, seeing him, it is so hard not to weep. . . .

The co-editor who had told me about Stan's problems at Osler, Hoskin & Harcourt tried to convince me not to print "Shame and Disgrace" in the paper. "Your stuff is usually funny," he said. "But this is just vicious."

But I insisted.

Gil was not pleased. He showed up in the *Obiter Dicta* office and demanded a full retraction and apology. He told me that Stan had told him that one of the lawyers at Osler, Hoskin & Harcourt had read the article and advised Stan that it was defamatory. Gil said that he and Stan and Christine could sue.

I said, "Go ahead. I don't care."

That was true. I was 24 years old, with no assets and lots of debt. I had no plans to become a lawyer and was indifferent to my reputation in the legal community. I believed in free speech. I believed that the insults from Gil and Stan justified anything I hurled back at them. And my article was obviously not meant to be taken seriously. For all those reasons, I doubted that they would sue. And if they did, I imagined it would be an interesting experience. I could write about it for *Obiter Dicta*.

But Gil kept showing up at the school newspaper office, complaining about the article, and demanding an apology. The other editors were becoming uncomfortable with the situation. Finally, Gil's pestering wore me down enough to agree to print the following in the October 18 edition:

CLARIFICATION

The article "Osgoode's Shame & Disgrace" in the Oct. 4 *Obiter* was a work of humour, not journalism.

It seemed to satisfy Gil; he never raised the subject again.

○ ○ ○

Gil published this on November 8, 1993:

> You have to be in the right mood to enjoy or even tolerate
> [*Nunsense II*]. . . . I wasn't in the right mood when I saw this play.
> Since no one except my mother is really concerned with my per-
> sonal problems . . . suffice it to say that I had an ABLW [Advanced
> Business Law Workshop] paper due, and while the goofy nuns
> were singing their goofy songs, I was contemplating minority
> shareholder squeeze-outs, amalgamations, liquidations and
> takeover bids. . . . I was sinking lower and lower into my seat as
> the evening wore longer and longer. . . . I especially enjoyed the
> free cake at intermission. . . .

○ ○ ○

In May 1994, Gil graduated with an LLB degree from Osgoode Hall
Law School and an MBA from the Faculty of Business. He had an arti-
cling job waiting for him at the prestigious Bay Street law firm of Fraser
& Beatty.

In his graduation photo, Gil is not smiling. He looks tired. There
is a slight stubble on his upper lip and cheeks. He has a cold-sore on
his lower lip. He does not look celebratory. He stares blankly at the
camera.

After graduation, I would never see Gil again.

PART THREE

....

1994-98

Few [law firm partners] seemed happy. In fact, having succumbed to the pressures of practice over the years, most seemed bitter, frustrated, impatient, and even hostile. I often sensed this even from passing senior attorneys in the office halls, where the tension on even an average day could be palpable.

from *Proceed with Caution*, by William Keates

10 | (INSIDE)

After getting a law degree, the next step toward becoming a lawyer in Ontario was to take Part One of the Bar Admission Course, run by the Law Society of Upper Canada out of old Osgoode Hall in downtown Toronto. As in law school, students attended classes and wrote assignments. Part One was easy: it lasted only a few weeks, and it dealt with soft, non-technical subjects such as professionalism and ethics.

After that came Part Two—"articling." In the United States, this was called "interning." This was when you worked at a law firm for a year, under the supervision of an approved lawyer, gaining hands-on experience.

After the articling year came Part Three of the course, which consisted of more courses at old Osgoode Hall downtown. Part Three lasted for three months, with students spending about 10 days on each of eight areas of substantive law; each section of the course was followed by an exam. Fail one exam, and you failed the entire course.

Part Three was difficult and demanding. Attendance was mandatory. Many soon-to-be lawyers learn more about the law from the three months of Part Three than from the entire three years of law school.

At big firms such as Osler, Hoskin & Harcourt and Fraser & Beatty, articling students were put into a "rotation" to give them exposure to several different areas of legal practice. A Bay Street law student with an interest in corporate law could expect to spend a series of two-month periods working for different supervisors with different specialties. Fraser & Beatty's system of rotation offered Gil a chance to gain experience in corporate and commercial law, litigation law, employment and labour law, administrative law, and insolvency, anti-trust, and construction-lien law.

At Osler, Hoskin & Harcourt, where Stan articled a year before Gil's term at Fraser & Beatty, Stan's rotation included litigation, corporate, and insolvency law. The litigation part of the rotation would involve Stan in a big court case between Air Canada and a company called Gemini, giving him insight into the realities of Canada's corporate culture. During the insolvency portion, Stan would later say, he often had "nothing to do" and used to waste time staring out a window. At least once he snuck away from the office to see a matinee movie — *Pulp Fiction*. (It became his favourite movie; Gil was a big fan too.)

Stan wanted to become a litigator — to argue with people for a living and often go to court — whereas Gil was heading for a career in corporate deal making — to make deals for a living, never having to go to court.

Osler, Hoskin & Harcourt was a big firm, with hundreds of lawyers in offices in Toronto, New York City, Montreal, Calgary, and Ottawa. Its advertising claimed that "our domestic and international clients rely on Osler to provide strategic, innovative advice on the most complex M&A transactions, significant labour and employment developments, intricate taxation issues and precedent-setting litigation matters."

The firm's founder, Britton Bath Osler, was from Hamilton. (He was the older brother of William Osler, the founder of modern medicine.) Britton became famous across Canada in 1885 for being the prosecutor who sent Métis-rights activist Louis Riel to death by hanging and for his involvement in the Canadian Pacific Railway corruption scandal that forced Canada's first Conservative prime minister out of office.

The firm's advertising also boasted that "almost from the start, the firm's clients included many of the country's largest concerns: the Canada North-West Land Company, Canadian Pacific Railway, banks and insurance companies, manufacturers and resource companies. It attracted the best and brightest: ambitious young barristers and solicitors as well as former Supreme Court judges and prime ministers."

One hundred and fifty years later, not much had changed.

On his second day at Osler, Hoskin & Harcourt, waiting in the lobby for the start of an orientation seminar, Stan was sitting beside another new articling student—a tall, slender brunette named Natalie. Also hanging around in the lobby were 10 or so other new articling students. A student who had spent the summer working for the firm approached Stan and Natalie and started to chit-chat with them.

Stan would later write, "I distinctly remember [the summer student] prancing around in white leather driving shoes."

Natalie said to the summer student that his shoes seemed inappropriate for wearing to the office.

The summer student—brazenly and bizarrely—responded by telling Natalie and Stan, two strangers, that the shoes were an accessory. He confessed that they went along with an expensive car he had just bought "with the money I made from a deal I was working on."

Summer students did not get bonuses for working on corporate deals. This loose-lipped law student had just admitted to Stan and Natalie that he had used secret information about an upcoming takeover transaction to make tens of thousands of dollars of illegal profit on the stock market.

Stan, a long-time legitimate investor, looked at the summer student in shock at this reckless confession. To Stan, this moment would be a life-changing revelation—a signpost pointing to his true calling. The next time he talked to Gil, Stan told him all about the summer student's driving shoes. Over the course of his articling year at Osler, Hoskin & Harcourt, Stan became convinced that other law students and lawyers were trading on inside information as well. It seemed common on Bay Street. Stan did not trade on any information he gathered at the firm, but he never forgot the lessons learned there. And the cafeteria gave free food to employees; frugal Stan really appreciated this.

The rumours I'd heard about Stan were true—he did wear inappropriate black running shoes to work (inspired by the white driving shoes of the summer student), and he did write a social memo about "pub night" claiming that the law firm was suffering from an epidemic of "the suck-up virus," which caused people to "kiss ass."

At this and future law firms, Stan would give his name as "S. Joseph Grmovsek." People (like me) who knew him before he became a lawyer would call him Stan; people who met him after he became a lawyer would call him Joseph or Joe. And many of the people who called him the latter names didn't know that they were using his middle name or that his real middle name was Jose. (Just like those of us who called him Stan didn't know that his real first name was Stanko.) Stan made this change to help his career; he thought that S. Joseph sounded less ethnic, more WASPish, than Stan.

To make things even more complicated, Stan's many gambling friends called him "the guru." Online, Stan was "kingcityguru" or "anhonestsecretary" or "nightcrawler1" or one of dozens of other temporary usernames. He switched names like masks.

∘ ∘ ∘

Stan found his articling year extremely stressful. He often worked seven days a week, with many hours of work packed into each day. His stress at Osler, Hoskin & Harcourt was so bad that, at night, he could hear the blood pumping in his neck so loudly that he could not sleep without turning on a radio to drown out the noise.

Once, walking to work, Stan heard a car with a noisy engine driving along the street behind him, approaching. Without thinking, he turned and stuck his leg into the street. In his stress-crazed mental state, he hoped that the noisy car would hit his leg and break it. Going to the hospital with a bone fracture seemed, to Stan, the only way to escape the hell that was inflicted on him daily at the firm. He was disappointed when the car passed by, missing his leg.

So Stan went to work and endured more stress, more time measured by the hour and the tenth of an hour, more unnatural suffering. He would always hate lawyering, especially how particular files would take over his life.

○ ○ ○

In late 1994, when Stan was finishing his articling year at Osler, Hoskin & Harcourt, Gil was about to start his own at Fraser & Beatty. (This firm would later merge with other firms and change its name to Fraser Milner Casgrain.) Fraser & Beatty was as big as Osler, Hoskin & Harcourt, with hundreds of lawyers in Toronto, Montreal, Ottawa, Edmonton, Vancouver, and Calgary. And, at 160 years old, it was older — older even than Canada.

Fraser & Beatty's advertising boasted of "acclaimed expertise in litigation & dispute resolution, financial services, professional liability, mining, public-private partnerships, securities / corporate finance, as well as strengths in energy, employment / labour, mergers & acquisitions (M&A), real estate, and tax." To its clients, Fraser & Beatty said, "We know that to serve your needs effectively, we must understand your business and objectives in a broad context. . . ."

Fraser & Beatty's clients included casinos, gold miners, investment banks, oil companies, the Royal Bank of Canada, Goldman Sachs, and J.K. Rowling, author of the Harry Potter books.

Two lawyers from Gil's time there would later become successful federal politicians in the Stephen Harper Conservative government. Peter Van Loan (Osgoode Hall Law School, class of 1987) practised municipal and planning law at Fraser & Beatty for 16 years, also serving as the president of the Ontario Conservatives from 1994 to 1998. Later, as government house leader, answering the questions of the opposition, Van Loan became famous as a nasty and giggling "cheap shot specialist"; he also tried a sneaky trick to reduce the house representation from Ontario (a Liberal-leaning province) while increasing representation from Alberta (a Conservative-leaning province). The other lawyer from Gil's era at Fraser & Beatty to later serve in the Conservative federal government was Jim Prentice, who, as federal environment minister, would bring Canada into international disrepute by defending the grossly polluting tar sands and denying the threat of climate change. In late 2010, at around the same time that Prentice quit politics for a job at a Bay Street bank, the British Columbia Securities Commission would investigate allegations that a secret environmental assessment report about a Canadian mining company had been illegally leaked from the Harper Cabinet, profiting certain well-connected tippees.

The Harper Conservatives would claim power in Ottawa in 2006 through election finance fraud. According to Elections Canada, "the Conservatives overspent on election ads by disguising national ads as local expenses in an elaborate plan that involved the participation of 67 candidates, including four cabinet ministers." A Federal Court judge in 2010 found that 10 Conservative candidates in 2006, including three cabinet ministers, exceeded spending limits—a form of political cheating.

Gil was working at Fraser & Beatty, along with ultra-successful lawyers like Peter Van Loan and Jim Prentice, when his insider trading activity began. It was all Stan's idea. But Gil did not resist much, if at all, and they agreed to split everything 50–50.

Stan agreed to supply the "seed money" and to hold on to the proceeds of crime until split day. Gil would trust him with the money.

Using the $310,000 Stan had earned on the stock market after defrauding the Ontario Student Assistance Program, Stan started to buy stocks based on inside information that Gil stole from Fraser and Beatty clients. At the start, Stan traded through discount brokers, using his own name.

Gil and Stan's first trade with inside information involved a corporation called Slocan Forest. It was based in British Columbia, operating saw mills and pulp mills for the logging industry there—an industry notorious for the greedy and unsustainable clear-cutting of old-growth rainforests, often on Native-owned land. Another BC-based tree-grinding company, Canfor Corporation, made an offer to buy all of Slocan's shares.

While preparing a memo on anti-trust law, Gil learned of the offer before it was made public and tipped Stan, who bought a few shares in Slocan Forest. When the deal was announced, the value of Slocan Forest shares jumped, and Stan sold his shares for a profit of $181.

Slocan would eventually reject Canfor's offer, but by then Stan had already cashed out. (In 2004, Canfor would again try to take over Slocan, this time with success.)

Gil and Stan's second illegal trade involved Onex's hostile, $2.3-billion attempt to take over Labatt's. Onex, controlled by Gerry Schwartz, was a corporation that specialized in strategic investments, also known as "arbitrage," and takeovers. Schwartz was a Canadian version of Henry Kravitz, the Manhattan takeover specialist who seized control of R.J.R. Nabisco in the 1980s (as described in the book and film *Waiting for the Barbarians*).

Labatt's was one of Canada's two megabreweries, marketing the bland but popular Blue lager. Labatt's also owned TV stations, Toronto's SkyDome sports stadium, and the two-time World Series champion Toronto Blue Jays.

Tipped by Gil, who had learned of the deal from one of his supervisors, Stan bought 200 options for Labatt's. A week before the options were to expire, Gil showed up at an Onex shareholders' meeting.

Somebody in the audience asked Gerry Schwartz, "Will you be taking over Labatt's?"

"No," Gil heard Schwartz say.

Gil phoned Stan and told him the news and said, "Well, just sell them for whatever you can get."

Schwartz's statement caused the value of Stan's Labatt's options to drop dramatically — from $2 to 10¢.

When Stan had managed to sell half of the options, he noticed that many others in the market were still interested in buying them, despite the Onex announcement, and he began to wonder why. The only person who would want to buy these options, Stan decided, was someone who knew that Schwartz's statement of non-interest in Labatt's was a lie. On a hunch, Stan decided to hold on to his remaining 100 Labatt's call options.

A day before they were due to expire, Onex announced that it planned to take over Labatt's after all. The value of Stan's options rocketed up to $7 each, helping Stan to recover his initial investment and make approximately $10,000 in profit.

Labatt's would resist Onex's hostile takeover attempt by calling in a "white knight," Belgian-based Interbrew, also known as InBev, which eventually became the master of Labatt's.

The timing of the two Onex announcements—first that the company did not want to buy Labatt's, and then that it did want to buy Labatt's—led Stan to believe that Labatt's share prices had been manipulated. He was bitter and convinced that Schwartz had dishonestly tricked everybody, including him.

Stan had been planning to buy a sports car with the profits from inside information about Onex, but the $10,000 he ended up with was not enough for the car he wanted. Stan often complained, "Gerry Schwartz cost me a Miata!" Stan never forgot the lesson. He would operate on the assumption that the stock market was full of trickery and abuse of position.

Insider trading was a ticket to easy wealth, Stan saw, so he started a systematic plan to steal a fortune for himself and his best friend.

After his articling year at Osler, Hoskin & Harcourt, Stan wasn't asked to return to work there as a lawyer after Part Three of the Bar Admission Course. He had not impressed his supervisors with either his attitude or his work.

So Stan started looking for a job. He applied to Wall Street's dominant investment bank, Goldman Sachs. After the 2008 Wall Street collapse and George Bush's massive cash bailout of the big banks, Goldman Sachs would be famously described by Matt Taibbi in *Rolling Stone* as "a giant vampire squid sucking the face of humanity."

When the SEC charged Goldman Sachs with securities fraud in 2010, the company would be represented by a partner at Sullivan & Cromwell. The firm had a long-standing and profitable "special relationship" with Goldman Sachs. Also, in late 2010, the *New York Times* would allege that several Goldman Sachs employees were under investigation for involvement in an insider trading ring.

Stan made it through the Goldman Sachs hiring process to the final interview. There must have been something about him the company liked. But, in the end, it rejected him. Years later Stan would try to explain why. "Maybe they saw a darkness in my soul," he wrote, "or maybe they saw one that was not dark enough."

(If Stan had aced the final interview and been hired at Goldman Sachs, would he much later have been one of the Wall Street bankers called to testify at the U.S. Senate in 2009 about the mortgages and derivatives scam? Would Taibbi have savaged Stan in the pages of *Rolling Stone*?)

Stan was also looking for work closer to home. He soon started working for a small, "boutique" law firm, Bratty & Partners. It was in Vaughan, Ontario, just north of North York (which was just north of Toronto). Bratty & Partners was in the same neighbourhood as Osgoode Hall Law School. The firm specialized in real estate law and municipal law.

The senior partner, Rudolph Bratty, a graduate of Osgoode in 1957, also operated a major land development corporation. As a lawyer with strong Conservative Party connections, he specialized in dealing with the legal and political obstacles to land development. Bratty helped to transform Vaughn, Brampton, Markham, Mississauga, and other municipalities around Toronto, convincing the local politicians of the day to allow many thousands of acres of fertile farmland and wild places to be turned into car-centred, near-identical subdivisions and shopping malls and big-box power centres. More than anyone else, Bratty encouraged and got very rich from Toronto's unsustainable sprawl.

Bratty & Partners' advertising boasted that "although Bratty and Partners occupies a unique niche in the real estate and land development areas of law, we offer a full range of services, including lawyers who specialize in municipal, corporate, commercial and estate law. . . . We represent many of the Greater Toronto Area's most prominent construction firms, developers and financial institutions."

After being hired at Bratty & Partners, Stan moved out of his parents' house. He moved into his first apartment, near the corner of Yonge Street and Eglinton Street.

While working at the firm, Stan represented clients in court three times. He argued a contempt of court motion and a collection matter. He argued a mortgage matter before the Court of Appeal. Those were the only times that Stan ever went to court as a representative.

11 | THE TWO TOWERS

When Gil finished his articling year at Fraser & Beatty, he wasn't asked to return to work there as a lawyer after Part Three of the Bar Admission Course. This must have been a disappointment.

In early 1996, Gil felt desperate to find a job that was good enough for him. So he did a very risky thing, which he and Stan referred to as "pasting." Gil photocopied his transcript of grades from Osgoode Hall, then cut out some of the A's. He put glue onto the backs of these A's and stuck them onto another copy of his transcript, covering up three B's, one C+, and one C. When this sheet was photocopied, the quintet of forged A's looked just like the real ones.

With so many A's and A+'s on his transcript, Gil managed to score a high-paying and prestigious job in New York City. He was hired as an associate at Sullivan & Cromwell, a famous Wall Street law firm. It paid for Gil's expenses in moving from Toronto to Manhattan.

Regarding the legal issue of working in a foreign country, Gil would later explain, "Under the NAFTA treaty, there are, I think, some number of professional designations . . . to work in the other NAFTA country without the need for—you have an automatic visa. It's called a TN visa, a 'Treaty NAFTA' visa. So all I needed to do was go to the border with a letter from Sullivan & Cromwell saying I had a job offer and a copy of my diploma from law school." He started work in Manhattan in March 1996.

The mayor of New York City in 1996 was the widely feared Rudolph Giuliani, who first came to fame as a high-profile prosecutor, crushing Wall Street inside traders Mike Milken, Ivan Boesky, Martin Siegel, and Dennis Levine. (Mike "The Junk Bond King" Milken was fined $600 million plus 10 years in prison, while Boesky got off lightly with $100 million and three years in prison.) Gil and Stan often joked about Milken and Boesky. Stan read and enjoyed Levine's memoir, *Inside Out*.

Gil took the New York Bar exams over two days at the end of July 1996. The test consisted of 200 multiple-choice questions on the first day and six essay questions on the second day. Seventy percent of those who wrote it passed—including Gil, who was soon afterward called to the New York Bar.

Although a Canadian citizen, Gil became an American lawyer.

One of the largest and most elite law firms in the world, a dominant force in banking and securities law, Sullivan & Cromwell had a fascinating history. It had been involved in the creation of Thomas Edison's General Electric Company in 1882 and U.S. Steel in 1901. It had been the driving force behind the digging of the Panama Canal. It had represented Rockefeller's corporations, including Standard Oil and United Fruit. It had also represented German firms I.G. Farben (which would later make chemicals for the death camps) and Fritz Thyssen (which would later make the steel used for barbed wire around the death camps).

Until 1935, Sullivan & Cromwell drew profits from its law office in Nazi Berlin, advising clients on how to comply with Nazi laws and working to bring much-needed U.S. capital investment to Hitler's projects.

In 1937, a young Richard Nixon unsuccessfully applied to work at Sullivan & Cromwell as a lawyer; without this rejection by the eastern establishment, the future U.S. president probably would not have bitterly returned to California to enter politics.

Allen Dulles, boss of the CIA in the 1950s and responsible for the Bay of Pigs planning errors, was a Sullivan & Cromwell lawyer. Dulles would later serve on the commission investigating the killing of President John F. Kennedy.

In the 1970s, Sullivan was the only major "white-shoe firm" (i.e., one that mainly employed white, Anglo-Saxon, and Protestant lawyers) in New York City to embrace a controversial new field of corporate law: hostile corporate takeovers. The field was otherwise dominated by firms of mainly Jewish lawyers.

Sullivan & Cromwell was deeply immersed in the wild consolidation of the commercial banking industry in the 1980s.

In the 1990s, the firm handled high-profile assignments from multinational corporations such as Exxon, Eastman Kodak, British Petroleum, Diageo, Philips, France Telecom, InBev (the Belgian brewery that took over Labatt's), British Airways, Scottish Power, Endesa, and Vodaphone. Other prominent clients included Bankers Trust, Microsoft, Disney, First Union Bank, United Healthcare, Oxford Health Plans, Kansas City Power and Light, Wells Fargo, Pearl Jam, President Bill Clinton (during Whitewater), and Conrad Black.

At the time of Gil's hiring, Sullivan & Cromwell was suffering from a major public embarrassment—one of its litigators, Steven Holley, had leaked sealed, confidential documents to a *Business Week* journalist. A huge kerfuffle erupted in court, with the law firm obtaining an injunction preventing *Business Week* from publishing the documents. This unfair and unconstitutional injunction was soon overturned on appeal. As a *Wall Street Journal* article at the time noted, the scandal "focused a spotlight on lax practices on the part of 119-year-old Sullivan & Cromwell that could alarm its other clients. . . . [T]he firm didn't file the sealed papers in a secure place, contrary to the law firm's policy. . . . [T]he document wasn't stamped *confidential*. . . ." It was reported that, in conversations with the *Business Week* journalist, Holley had insulted the personal appearance and questioned the sanity of a top female Justice Department prosecutor. Sullivan & Cromwell issued a standard apology.

Gil was officially in Sullivan & Cromwell's "general practice" section, but he often worked with lawyers from the mergers and acquisitions department. An associate in Sullivan's M&A department at this time, Michael Kimelman, would years later be accused of involvement in a Wall Street insider-trading conspiracy led by Raj Rajaratnam.

Gil would work at Sullivan & Cromwell with banking and finance specialist Carlos Spinelli-Noseda. Soon after Gil's hiring, Spinelli-Noseda started secretly overbilling Sullivan & Cromwell's clients. The overbilling went on for almost a decade, bringing in more than half a million dollars before the fraud was caught and Carlos was fired and disbarred. He admitted that another Manhattan-based Sullivan & Cromwell associate had been involved in his client rip-off scheme; the identity of this associate has been kept secret by Sullivan & Cromwell.

The firm had a main office in Manhattan and other offices in Washington, Los Angeles, Palo Alto, Paris, London, Melbourne, Tokyo, Hong Kong, Frankfurt, Beijing, and Sydney.

Three years before Gil's arrival, Sullivan & Cromwell bought part of the Manhattan office building at 125 Broad Street, for a bargain price from the bankrupt Canadian real-estate developer Olympia & York. This grey, 40-floor skyscraper on the East River, a short walk south of Wall Street, became Sullivan & Cromwell's headquarters. It was near the New York Stock Exchange (at the corner of Broad Street and Wall Street) and the Federal Reserve Bank.

60 Broad Street had been the headquarters of Drexel Burnham Lambert in the roaring 1980s, ruled by "Junk Bond King" and inside trader Mike Milken.

85 Broad Street was the headquarters of Goldman Sachs, Sullivan & Cromwell's biggest client. The two firms enjoyed a special relationship. Sullivan & Cromwell lawyers would often work out of Goldman Sachs' offices for months at a time, getting to know the people, philosophy, and techniques of Goldman Sachs in a way that went far beyond the typical attorney-client relationship. Goldman Sachs would later move its headquarters to 1 New York Plaza, a building directly across Broad Street from Sullivan & Cromwell's offices.

The law firm shared the 125 Broad Street property with insurance giant Johnson & Higgins, Saloman Smith Barney (an investment bank owned by Citibank), the National Association of Securities Dealers, the American Civil Liberties Union, and the Vietnam Veterans' Memorial Plaza.

Sullivan & Cromwell's advertising boasted that

the results we achieve have set us apart for over 125 years and become a model for the modern practice of law. Our success is the result of the quality of our lawyers, the most broadly and deeply trained collection of attorneys in the world. . . . We hire the very best law school graduates and train them to be generalists within broad practice areas. . . . The result is a partnership with a unique diversity of experience, exceptional professional judgment and a demonstrated history of innovation. . . .

Gil worked in Sullivan & Cromwell's 40-floor office tower near Wall Street and lived in a dark, 57-floor apartment tower on West 57th Street, just south of Columbus Circle and Central Park.

322 West 57th Street (a building also called The Sheffield) had 845 units and was fancy, with a concierge, a laundry room on every floor, valet service, a health club with a swimming pool, a rooftop tennis court, and a nice ground-level outdoor courtyard/garden. Gil's apartment was near the top. His apartment window, like his office window, faced north—toward Central Park and Canada. He bought a treadmill and put art prints on the wall. The rent was $2,700 a month—almost triple rent in Toronto.

Also renting an apartment in the building was musician Steve Van Zandt, guitarist for Bruce Springsteen, later to play a gangster in *The Sopranos.*

Across the street was a vampire-themed disco, Le Bar Bat, popular for a while in the early and mid-1990s with young professionals.

For a culture-loving man like Gil, living in this part of Manhattan must often have felt like a dream. His building was only a block from Carnegie Hall. Broadway, less than a block away, was the shortest route to his job. He was living on a road famous for prestigious art galleries, ultra-exclusive fashion and jewellery stores, jazz and classical performances, fancy restaurants, opulence, glamour, elitism. The most expensive things in the world were sold on the most expensive real estate in the world.

Gil lived at the northern end of a neighbourhood called Hell's Kitchen. It had often appeared in arts and literature. In the movie *Taxi*

Driver, Robert DeNiro works out of a garage at the west end of 57th Street, near Gil's apartment. *West Side Story* loosely deals with the history of Hell's Kitchen and was filmed nearby. Most of the locations in *Seinfeld*—a TV show that Gil enjoyed—are based on places a few blocks north of his apartment. The snobby love interest in Ayn Rand's *The Fountainhead* (one of Gil's favourite books) lives in Hell's Kitchen. Patrick Bateman, the hero of Bret Ellis's *American Psycho* (who specializes in both "mergers and acquisitions" and "murders and executions"), leaves some of his tortured-to-death victims rotting away in a Hell's Kitchen bathtub. The blind comic-book superhero Daredevil bases his crime fighting from there.

Tiffany's jewellery store, as in Truman Capote's *Breakfast at Tiffany's*, was at the corner of 57th Street and Fifth Avenue. The Ritz Tower on 57th Street inspired the story "The Diamond as Big as the Ritz" by F. Scott Fitzgerald.

Composer George Gershwin—whom Gil adored—often partied at a friend's 57th Street home, along with Charlie Chaplin and Harpo Marx. Another of Gil's musical heroes, Cole Porter, often visited 57th Street as a young bachelor, courting a young woman who lived there; the pair would later get married and move into a house on the same storied street.

There was also some tragic recent history on 57th Street that Gil probably heard about. Jerzy Kosinski, Holocaust survivor and author of *Being There* and *The Painted Bird*, killed himself in his 57th Street apartment in 1991. Also in 1991, classic rock musician Eric Clapton's four-year-old son fell out of a skyscraper's window, to fall down to 57th street and inspire Clapton's song "Tears in Heaven."

At its east end, 57th Street joined the Queensboro Bridge. This old iron bridge features prominently in Woody Allen's movie *Manhattan*. Simon and Garfunkel sing about it in "Feelin' Groovy." F. Scott Fitzgerald put it best: "The city seen from the Queensboro Bridge is always the city seen for the first time, in its first wild promise of all the mystery and the beauty of the world. . . ."

Every day in Manhattan, Gil imagined killing himself.

12 | IT'S BETTER IN THE BAHAMAS

In 1996, Stan left Bratty & Partners to join a small new Toronto law firm, Johnstone & Company, which was really a one-man operation before his arrival. This "boutique" firm in downtown Toronto served small corporations, often ones involved in Canada's controversial mining industry. According to Stan, Johnstone used to like to say, "If only half of this is legitimate, it is still worth a fortune."

Sixty percent of all the world's mining companies were Canadian-controlled. These companies committed uncountable human rights violations around the world in southern places most North Americans had never heard of. The mining industry was the world's largest source of toxic pollution and the second-largest cause of deforestation. Gold mining was especially filthy, creating more waste per ounce than any other metal—mainly massive amounts of cyanide and mercury. Much of the toxic waste-water at gold mines was pumped directly into the ocean. According to the No Dirty Gold campaign, "Producing a single gold wedding band leaves behind 20 tons of waste at a mine site." The waste rock was piled onto land that had once been rainforest. Much gold sold in North America was "blood gold" from the war-torn Democratic Republic of the Congo, where gold profits fuelled the work of jungle warlords and mineral traders—who often engaged in mass killings, mass rapes, mass mutilations, and other profitable activities.

Perhaps the most disturbing part of the harm caused by the gold-mining industry is the fact that gold (which the primitive Egyptians called "the flesh of the gods") has few practical uses. It is purely decoration, a useless jangle of vanity.

At Johnstone & Company, Stan put a screensaver on his computer that scrolled a quotation from the movie *Conan the Barbarian*: "Conan! What is best in life?" "To crush your enemies, see them driven before you, and to hear the lamentation of their women!" Stan soon met another lawyer, Carl Dahomey,* who worked in the same building. Carl specialized in helping Canadians to trade stocks through accounts and corporations based in the Bahamas.

For a total fee of $30,000, Carl helped to set up Stan's first offshore company, which Stan named Dobro, which means "good" in Slovenian. He was understandably feeling patriotic about his parents' homeland at that time; Slovenia had just recently gained its independence from the former Yugoslavia.

Stan went to the Bahamas to sign the paperwork. He did not get a copy of the paperwork. His ownership of the Bahamas-based corporation was hidden; he had a "beneficial interest" in the corporation but was not listed on any paperwork as an officer, director, or shareholder. Officially, Stan was just an "adviser" to Dobro, giving "advice" to its executives (whom he never met) through Carl; Stan's peremptory "advice" would indicate the shares to buy or sell, the price at which to buy or sell, and the timing of such purchases or sales. The executives would place his orders through a brokerage house, such as A.G. Edwards.

Only once did the Bahamian executives of Dobro contact Stan directly. After noticing that he had invested in advance of several corporate takeovers, they wanted to know how he had chosen his stocks.

Gil and Stan went to the Bahamas, taking separate flights. Gil stayed at the hotel when Stan met the Bahamian bankers.

Stan told them that his success was due to "tracking the movement of options" and their "relationship to the share price." It was a convincing lie. The Bahamian executives seemed satisfied by it. Annoyed by their curiosity, Stan soon asked Carl to make a new corporate structure involving a different group of Bahamian executives.

Gil and Stan took separate flights back to Toronto.

Stan's second offshore company was named Wolverine, after the ferocious and claw-fisted and Canadian-born superhero.

Stan would later say,

For all these trades, if it involves Carl Dahomey, I would always go through him. Like, I didn't know who to call on the offshore. So I would call him, I would tell him the order, and he would call—sometimes it would be on a conference call, most times not, and he would say, "The adviser to Company X," whatever the name of the company is now, if it's Dobro or Wolverine or whatever it is, "has advised you to buy 10,000 shares of X at $20 or better, good for the day." And then they would—the directors down there would approve that advice, and then they would execute the trade through whatever brokerage house they were using, and they would skim their own fee for that phone call to the broker, and the broker would do his fee. So it was actually relatively expensive. . . . Every time you called them, they would bill you for another call, so if you changed the order they would bill you another $500. . . . A lot of these brokers who use the offshore stuff, they were charging, like, way too much commission, and a normal client would not pay this, but an offshore client, you know, is worried about other things, so you're paying, like, $4,000 or $5,000 on a stock purchase of a million dollars when you could do it at a discount broker for $100 or $200. . . . The difficulty, because I'm using Carl as a conduit, is that you had to call him at a specific time for an order, so you can't be changing your mind all day. You make a decision to put an order in, I got to get him at the office, he's got to get the guys down south on the phone at the same time. So a lot of the times it's hard to do these deals. . . . I remember at least one deal where I wanted to do it, and we couldn't get in touch with Carl, and then the deal happened the next day, so we didn't buy it. . . . None of these offshore structures ever had [any paperwork]. There's a trust element, I guess, you know—is it trust between thieves or something? — that no one questions the other person, just assume he's not going to rip you off or do anything else, or if he's going to rip you off it'll be a small rip-off, not a big rip-off. So that's the assumption. If they're not stealing a little bit from you, you assume they're stealing a lot. So you're almost happy the brokers were overcharging you because you go, "That's what they're stealing right there, they're getting their $5,000 commission on some nothing trade."

Until 1999, Stan paid Carl approximately $100,000 for Carl's unwitting help in concealing Stan's illegal and very profitable trades. In all these trades, Stan went by the alias "Mr. Phillips."

Around this time, Stan took a vacation to Portland, Oregon, with his fiancée Jennifer to visit her mother. (Jennifer was the woman who allegedly enjoyed rough sex and liked to "steal things and call it art.") While they were in Portland, she became angry at Stan because he had broken some promise he had made to her. To demonstrate his remorse, Stan went to a Portland tattoo parlour and had the Latin phrase *Vir Honorabilis Sum* permanently inked onto his right buttock. Translated into English, his new tattoo stated, "I Am an Honourable Man."

13 | SULLIVAN & CROMWELL

Three years before Gil was hired, a young tax lawyer at Sullivan & Cromwell named Terence Campbell—during just his second week at the firm—was hit by a bullet from above while walking across a Manhattan bridge. It almost killed the Columbia Law School graduate. The shooter and gun were never found; police speculated that a random stray bullet had hit the unlucky Terence. Most young lawyers hired by Sullivan & Cromwell had less traumatic starts to their careers, but none found it easy.

During his time at Sullivan & Cromwell, Gil would have heard about the recent tragedy of an associate lawyer at another Wall Street firm who could not handle the stress. He tried to open a window at work, but they were sealed. This young lawyer went home to his skyscraper apartment's balcony and jumped off.

Also just before Gil's arrival in 1994, a second-year associate named Charles Ford McKenzie at the Wall Street law firm of Cleary, Gottlieb, Steen & Hamilton jumped in despair from the roof of an 18-storey hotel. His grieving parents sued the law firm, blaming the suicide on stress and overwork; their claim was dismissed.

Sullivan & Cromwell employed about 700 lawyers in 12 offices around the world. Most of the lawyers were in Manhattan.

Gil had a tiny office on the 29th floor of 125 Broad Street. He made little attempt to decorate it; there were legal papers piled in heaps on his desk and on the floor. His window faced north; looking out from the tower, Gil could see across five miles of Manhattan to the tower he lived in. Canada and home were over the distant horizon.

Gil would later say, "At Sullivan & Cromwell, I was not in the M&A group. I was in what they called the general practice, meaning I represented issuers and underwriters in financing activities, raising equity, mostly debt work, mostly high-yield debt work, public and private financing, some bank transactions, some corporate structuring and corporate governance."

After Gil's friend Will Meyerhofer quit Sullivan & Cromwell to become a psychotherapist, he wrote this: "It was hell working there. They expected you to be on-call 24 hours per day. We worked until late at night all the time, and weekends, too. A call from a partner at 5 p.m. on Friday, and you were there all weekend. That happened a lot. And they never said anything nice to you, either. You were always 'screwing something up' and getting frowned at and made to know you weren't any good."

Wall Street law firms were stressful places to work. Associates at Sullivan & Cromwell were regularly expected to work 60 to 100 hours a week, at least 11 hours a day, to reach the firm-wide minimum goal of 2,000 billable hours per associate a year. Every month the firm gave Gil an individualized summary of his billable and non-billable hours from the prior month, along with a running total of his hours since the start of the year. Every day, all day, Gil had to keep track of everything he did and how long he did it for. It was a constant burden to keep track of what work had been done for what client, then to put that information onto a detailed time-sheet — every single day. His salary and future promotions depended on filling in those time-sheets. The longer it took him to finish an assignment, the more hours he could bill, so the system encouraged overwork, inefficiency, and exaggeration. At work, Gil measured his personal value by the tenth of an hour — that is, six minutes was noted as ".1," while an hour and a half was noted as "1.5." It generally took a lawyer between nine and eleven hours of actual time spent at work to achieve eight billable hours. The non-billable time would be "wasted" on things like eating, getting a coffee or Diet Coke (the trendy soda among professionals back then), going to the bathroom, office meetings and staff management, general legal education, office politics, and switching from one file to another. Also not billable was time spent daydreaming, banging a head onto a desktop, or silently weeping behind a closed office door.

Cameron Stracher, who also worked at Sullivan & Cromwell around this time, would later write in a memoir titled *Double Billing* that

> partners had the corner offices, the ones on the higher floors, the large southern exposures. Associates [such as Gil] had offices with windows and played a frantic game of musical chairs when colleagues departed and their offices became available. Paralegals dwelled in the interior offices, two to a room. Secretaries were grouped in threes and fours in "stations" near their bosses, their faces visible to all who passed in the hallway, a four-foot wall obstructing only their computers. And in the inner circle, airless and lightless, clanking with the machine drone of copiers, smelling of toner and grease, crowded with boxes and files, dwelled the messengers and file clerks. . . . The gender and complexion of [the firm] changed too, as one moved inwards. Almost all the partners were male and white. Associates were mostly white with a sprinkling of Asian, a dash of Latin, and several African Americans. Men still outnumbered women, especially among the senior associates. The secretaries were evenly divided between white women who tended to live in the outer boroughs of New York — Staten Island, Queens, Brooklyn — and black women who lived in the Bronx. The inner circle [messengers and file clerks] was composed almost entirely of young, black men.

The Sullivan & Cromwell cafeteria had a class-based apartheid system. Staff were not allowed to eat in the section of the cafeteria where the lawyers ate. In the lawyers' section, associates were not allowed in the subsection used by the partners.

Gil's starting salary in 1996 was $80,000 (U.S.) a year, with a bonus of around $3,500. (In today's inflated dollars, the amounts would be much higher.) Second-year associates were paid between $86,000 and $102,000, third-year associates between $89,000 and $117,000.

Gil got three to four weeks of paid vacation, although most new associates were too busy to take much or even any vacation. There were generous benefits: insurance for health, life, accident, disability, and dental work; a 401(k) retirement plan; paid parental leave; payment of bar association dues; and payment of continuing education. While Gil was studying for the bar exam to be allowed to practise law in New York State, Sullivan & Cromwell paid his salary, the cost of the bar exam courses, and the $1,500 fee to write the exam.

All Wall Street firms started associates at approximately the same salary, but subsequent yearly increases were not the same. After five years, salaries would range from $110,000 at some firms to as much as $170,000 at firms such as Sullivan & Cromwell. Associates generally either became partners after seven or eight years or felt pressure to quit. Partners at Sullivan & Cromwell in the 1990s always earned at least $600,000 a year.

The hefty salaries and benefits at Wall Street firms were sometimes called "golden handcuffs" because they had the effect of preventing many associates from leaving, knowing that they would be paid less elsewhere. But if, a few years down the road, you did decide to leave, having a famous international megafirm like Sullivan & Cromwell on your resume would make finding future employment easy.

There was an attraction to representing big corporations with famous names in deals and litigation that sometimes made it onto the front page of the newspaper or on the TV news. Another benefit of working at a huge firm was access to the best research materials. Online legal databases of laws, cases, and commentary (such as Lexis/Nexis and Westlaw) cost hundreds of dollars an hour in the mid-1990s — too expensive for many small and medium-sized firms but not for Sullivan & Cromwell. The firm also had an excellent, comfortable legal library.

Paralegals are to lawyers what nurses are to doctors, handling routine matters under a lawyer's supervision. Only at a huge firm like Sullivan &

Cromwell would a first-year associate have a paralegal to whom he or she could delegate the most tedious and time-consuming tasks.

Gil became friends with two other young lawyers at the firm: mergers-and-acquisitions lawyer Will Meyerhofer, who worked in an office two doors down the hall from Gil, and tax lawyer Chris Kippes. All three of them shared a passion for classical music.

Will would later describe Gil as

> short and rather owlish. Dressed in kind of a homey, Canadian way. I seem to recall a casual cardigan that he'd wear. He wasn't a flashy dresser. More like rumpled knits for Gil. . . . It was amazing, working with Gil, since he was so pleasant and relaxed. He smiled and chortled to himself. . . . Gil was small, and he always seemed to be perched behind his desk in his chair, contentedly perusing some document or other. . . . He was quiet, a bit eccentric. . . . He sort of chortled and smiled his way through the day. . . . He had a bustling busy-ness about him but an easy smile. He was a very likable guy. . . .

Stan would later say that Gil "chortled" so much at work because he was laughing at his colleagues — first Gil got hired with fake grades, and now he was making secret millions from Sullivan & Cromwell's clients.

Gil and Will worked on a few corporate deals together, doing what Will would later describe as "the most mundane standard stuff"—shuffling the paperwork for corporate debt.

Gil and Will and many other young lawyers were supervised by a Sullivan & Cromwell partner named Bob, who would handle dozens of these kinds of routine transactions at a time. Bob had the unusual habit of keeping his office dark except for a single lamp over his desk, a habit that some young lawyers reporting to him found eerie, even creepy.

Young lawyers like Gil and Will found the partners at Sullivan & Cromwell to be distant, scary figures — not mentors at all. The partners at most Wall Street law firms pitted lawyers against each other in a struggle for partnership, isolated lawyers in tiny offices or the library, demanded an excessive degree of "dedication," and tended to weed out the most sociable and friendly associates.

Clients were viewed not as people needing help but as continuing sources of business revenue in a highly competitive market; clients paid sky-high fees and had just as high demands and expectations.

Having paralegals and secretaries and others to delegate work to was helpful in some ways but a major source of stress in other ways; lawyers in their mid-20s with no management experience were suddenly made responsible not only for their own mistakes but also for those of subordinates who could be much older than them.

The cooperative spirit of law school was replaced with competitiveness when a young lawyer started at Sullivan & Cromwell. Frequently used expressions such as "sink or swim," "eat what you kill," and "survival of the fittest" showed the attitudes prevalent at all big Wall Street firms and suggest the levels of personal sacrifice (a.k.a. "dedication") that were expected and required. Associates often felt lonely and isolated—especially Gil, in a foreign land far from home. Office politics were subtle, confusing, and central to survival.

Although Gil was higher in the Sullivan & Cromwell hierarchy than the staff—the office managers, paralegals, secretaries, word processors, librarians, proofreaders, accountants, recruiting coordinators, and computer techs—he was far below the partners (who owned the firm) and below any other associate with more seniority. As Gil was at the bottom of the pecking order of lawyers, it was harder and more stressful for him to get his work done—staff would give his work the lowest priority, and senior lawyers would often suddenly shanghai him to work on their own projects. Asking a senior lawyer for help or advice could be seen as proof of incompetence.

In Gil's first year, his job performance was twice reviewed by all of the senior lawyers Gil had worked for that year. In future years, he would be reviewed once a year.

Stracher explains big-firm economics:

A first-year associate, who billed at $150 an hour, multiplied by 2,000 hours, minus his salary of $85,000, cleared $215,000 for the partners, less overhead. Every hour that the associate worked, once the firm had covered its expenses, went directly into the partners' pockets. Each year, as the associate's billing rate increased, so did the partners' take. Like a giant Ponzi scheme, profits depended on an unending source of associates entering at the bottom of the pyramid, funnelling cash up the chain, and departing before making partner. The greater the ratio of associates to partners, the greater the profits. No one forgot the simple equations. That was why the partners told us to bill clients for the time we spent thinking about their cases in the shower, on the subway, while jogging. Our thoughts were money in the partners' pockets.

Stracher sums up his Wall Street experience thus: "Most of all, I remembered the coldness of law firm life. . . . What I didn't remember were any close friendships I had forged, any attempt among the lawyers to connect. . . ."

William Keates, a young Wall Street lawyer at the same time as both Cameron and Gil, would later write in a memoir titled *Proceed with Caution* about the day-to-day routine of young attorneys:

Document reviews are the bane of a new associate's existence. First-year associates are inevitably called on to pore through documents in connection with government investigations, or civil suits, or corporate transactions. These reviews consist of scrutinizing a sometimes towering collection of documents to determine the relevance and importance of each document in your case. Most new associates consider document reviews the worst and most undesirable assignments. Such reviews are virtually always tedious, boring and completely unfulfilling intellectually. . . .

Large firms often handle cases that call for tens or even hundreds of thousands of documents to be reviewed — in a single case! And it's not just a matter of reading the documents. There are the administrative hassles associated with collecting, reviewing, organizing and shipping documents. . . .

You have to carefully examine each potentially relevant document, even if that means rummaging through paper for hours or days without finding anything really significant. . . .

As the most junior associate on a document review, you'll typically be called on to prepare a memorandum documenting the search. . . .

Keates also noted that "Practicing law in the pressure-cooker environment of a large firm can cause a stress that makes your facial muscles tense, ties your back muscles in knots so tight you got backaches and made you snap at people you work with. . . ."

And, "Surrounded by other professionals who routinely put their personal beliefs aside, and surrounded by plush offices, expensive artwork and state-of-the-art technology, I found it depressingly easy to overlook any distaste I harboured for certain clients and cases."

Finally,

with little opportunity to develop a life outside of the profession, over time, lawyers often begin to define themselves *solely* by their work: "I'm a litigator" or "I'm a corporate lawyer." The prospect of giving up their career is tantamount to giving up the only identity they know. . . .

Some feel trapped, believing that they just don't have viable options. Others blame themselves, feeling inadequate because they aren't living up to their career potential. And others believe that they have invested too much time and effort to leave. . . .

Finally, the way senior attorneys treat junior associates can contribute to depression. . . . Cut out of the decision-making loop, [associates] are left feeling emasculated, dominated and possibly even humiliated by seemingly omnipotent partners who tolerate little input. According to psychologists quoted in the *Wall Street Journal*, this "infantilization" by partners may connect young associates' work experience with childhood memories of parents, as well as with their childhood desire to please their parents and quell fears of abandonment.

o o o

Sullivan & Cromwell had some procedures to protect client information. For example, the firm had separate work stations for Internet access that were not connected to the firm's internal document-sharing network. There were security guards in the lobby making sure no unauthorized people could wander in from the street. All the firm's lawyers were reminded regularly of their ethical responsibilities.

None of that offered any protection from Gil.

He tore into the soft underbelly of Sullivan & Cromwell, invisibly clawing deep into the biggest vulnerability of that or any other law firm — its trust of its own employees.

o o o

To maintain a cover story, Stan researched the companies involved in takeovers in case he was asked (as he had been by the Bahamians) to explain why he had bought a particular stock. Another way to disguise the criminal conspiracy was sometimes to buy stocks for which Gil had provided no inside information. Most of these stocks declined in value, enabling Stan to claim that not all of his investments were suspiciously successful. If a broker asked Stan too many questions about his trades, Stan would replace the broker.

Gil did not see the account statements from Stan's offshore accounts. Gil trusted Stan to tell him what profits they had made. Gil also trusted that his best friend would be careful and discreet in how he handled the trading.

As time passed and Gil's paranoia increased, they adopted new security measures. One was stopping the use of his home phone for conversations. Gil later said that Stan

discovered the use of these calling cards that you could get in every street corner in New York, that for 10 bucks you'd get a hundred minutes or whatever, some number of minutes, and you could use a pay-phone coupled with a calling card. . . . The calling card has a 1-800 number. You then type in the unique code that's on every calling card and then type in Grmovsek's number. . . . [In addition to tips about deals,] we'd talk about the weather. Talk about, you know, girls we were seeing. Talk about, you know, the Jays, the Mets, whatever, President Clinton, politics, you name it, you name it.

And they started to use their own code names for deals. Stan would later write,

> While we would often discuss stocks of all kinds and the movement of commodities, Gil would signal that a particular phone conversation would be about a coming material event or change by how he introduced the topic or how he would describe the stock in a way that I could determine what it was but without mentioning its name. . . . After that first discussion we would try not to mention the name of the company again, but would make reference to whatever code word we gave to it. . . . [I]f time was of the essence and we had to mention the name of the company in a phonecall, we would often say the wrong name of the company or reference the buyer rather than the target, all in a way that we both understood who the target really was but might confuse anyone listening in on the phonecall. Of course, this was only used when Gil was certain a deal was to occur and he was certain he wanted me to buy it. If he was not or was not yet certain, he might muse about it and other stocks during our general conversation without any real regard to what he would call "tradecraft." While we used calling cards when he was living in New York, this was more because of costs than camouflage. . . .

o o o

Gil and Stan's first deal using information stolen from a Sullivan & Cromwell client was the 1996 proposed merger between Staples, North America's biggest office supply store, and Office Depot, North America's second biggest. Sullivan & Cromwell provided legal advice to Staples on this deal, with Goldman Sachs providing the financing.

Gil tipped Stan to buy shares in Office Depot.

On September 4, 1996, the executives of Staples and Office Depot announced that the two corporations were planning a stock swap valued at $3.4 billion, which would create a combined company, to be called "Staples the Office Depot," with yearly revenue of $10 billion and more than 1,100 superstores across the world.

Staples chairman Thomas Stemberg said, "In deals like this, one group usually wins and another loses. In this particular transaction, every single stakeholder wins." He added, "This is a logical and rational attempt to put these two growth machines together into one even bigger growth machine."

Office Depot chairman David Fuente denied that the merger was anti-competitive: "We see this as an opportunity for more rational pricing," and "We're thrilled with this transaction. We're a lot happier to be together with Staples than competing against them."

Executives compared the deal to the previous successful merger of Price Club and Costco.

At the announcement, Office Depot shares jumped in one day from $15 to over $20. Stan usually sold his shares within half an hour of the announcement, when the price of the target company would usually hit its peak.

The Staples and Office Depot merger was popular with its executives, with investors, and with Wall Street players. But it was not popular with the U.S. Federal Trade Commission, which agreed with Ralph Nader that the merger would break anti-trust laws, reduce competition, and raise office-supply prices.

The FTC asked a judge to shoot the deal down; the judge did. Staples and Office Depot were ordered to stay apart. The wedding was off. The proposed near-monopoly was dead. Office supply consumers (such as writers and law firms) had reason to celebrate.

Disappointed, the Staples chairman complained that, in pursuing the denied deal, his company had wasted "countless hours" over a 10-month period.

Gil and Stan made $180,000 in illegal profit: a large amount, but much less than the $20 million in legitimate fees enjoyed by Sullivan & Cromwell and Goldman Sachs for their work on this failed deal.

○ ○ ○

Stan was at work at his desk at Johnstone & Company when he learned how much money he had made from Staples and Office Depot. Without thinking, he triumphantly yelled, "One hundred and eighty thousand!"

His boss, William Johnstone, was in the office and heard this outburst. "Why did you say that?" William asked.

Stan said, "I just made one hundred and eighty thousand dollars trading stocks."

His boss said, "So, does that mean you are going to quit?"

"No," Stan lied. "Why would I do that?"

○ ○ ○

In early 1997, Gil and Stan used stolen information to profit from the announcement of H.F. Ahmanson's hostile takeover bid for Great Western Financial.

H.F. Ahmanson, the holding company for the largest savings and loan bank in the United States, had assets of about $50 billion and was based in a Los Angeles suburb and mainly served customers in California and Florida.

Great Western Financial, the second largest savings and loan bank in the United States, had assets of $42 billion. It was also based in a Los Angeles suburb and also mainly served customers in California and Florida.

Sullivan & Cromwell represented H.F. Ahmanson. Gil stole information from H.F. Ahmanson. Stan bought lots of shares in Great Western Financial, then sold them after the bid announcement for a fast, easy, and big profit.

○ ○ ○

The profits from inside trading were so fast, so easy, and so big that Stan decided that it was not worth his while to be a legitimate lawyer anymore. In the spring of 1997—a few weeks after Gil's 27th birthday—Stan quit (or was fired from) his job at Johnstone & Company.

He stopped paying insurance fees to the Lawyer's Professional Indemnity Company and stopped paying membership dues to the Law Society of Upper Canada. As a result, his licence to practise law was suspended. He remained a lawyer, though.

Stan became a full-time stock trader based out of his apartment. Some of his trading was legitimate; most was not. As a cover story, Stan sometimes described himself as a "consultant" employed by a non-existent company called Punta del Diamante. Other times he called himself a professional investor. Occasionally, he claimed to be a professional gambler, with a talent for counting cards at casinos. He would never practise law again.

The name Punta del Diamante was based on an obscure character in the movie *Barcelona*: a masochistic, disco-loving pervert who likes to wear painful leather bands under his clothing, which somehow leads to the character getting the nickname "The Point of the Diamond" or, in Spanish, "Punta del Diamante." Stan designed and had printed business cards with S. Joseph Grmovsek and Punta del Diamante on them. The main point of the business cards, Stan would say later, was "to look respectable to chicks."

With a lot of free time suddenly on his hands, Stan decided to temporarily move to Manhattan and live in Gil's 57th Street apartment. For several months, Stan slept on a pull-out sofa in Gil's living room, right beside Gil's treadmill. Gil used this machine to relieve stress and keep his weight under control; he also liked jogging in Central Park or walking the five miles to his office, trying to take a different route each time. Gil did not own a car in Manhattan.

They often joked about the fact that Gil had never seen the chairman of Sullivan & Cromwell, Ricardo Mestries. Ricardo was Gil's ultimate boss (everybody at the firm seemed to be afraid of him), but Ricardo had never bothered to introduce himself to Gil, who had never seen the chairman in the hallways of the firm or at meetings. When Gil and Stan were walking down a Manhattan street, Stan would notice a homeless man sleeping in an alley or someone equally disreputable looking and point the character out to Gil, saying something like, "Hey, look! There's Ricardo Mestries!" Sometimes Gil would be annoyed by these jokes—the fact that he had never met his boss showed just how low he was on the Sullivan & Cromwell hierarchy—but often he would make the same kind of joke himself. "There goes Ricardo, heading into that porn theatre!" There were many odd-looking characters roaming Hell's Kitchen who could have been Mestries, man of mystery.

There was little food in the fridge—usually just bread and apples. Stan would buy the apples. Gil did not keep much food at his apartment because the Sullivan & Cromwell cafeteria was free. He ate almost all his meals there or at restaurants on an expense account, billing the chow to a corporate client.

Stan—a TV and film enthusiast—enrolled in a summer filmmaking workshop at the New York Film Academy. The program lasted a few weeks. The school was just west of bustling, tourist-filled Union Square in a large, historic building called Tamanny Hall. The NYFA emphasized hands-on training, offering little in the way of theory. There were no admission requirements other than payment.

Gil would later say, "You have to understand this was not, you know, New York University Film School, which is where Spielberg went or whoever went. This was . . . kind of a market for, you know, lack of a better word, dilettantes. . . . Some people take art appreciation classes. This was the film version of those classes."

Stan was trained to use 16mm, 35mm, HD, and 24p digital video cameras. "I had a lot of fun," Stan would later say, "though I knew I had no chance at a career as a filmmaker."

At the end of the workshop, he participated in a graduation ceremony and a final presentation of student work. A short movie made by Stan titled *Men Lie, Women Break Promises* was shown to the rest of the graduating class. The "star" of the movie was a pretty young woman Stan had approached on the streets of Manhattan, saying, "Do you want to be in a movie?" She had agreed to play the female lead. In addition to directing, Stan also played the male lead. The plot? Stan's character meets and falls in love with the pretty girl. She has a boyfriend. She kills her boyfriend and, as proof, shows Stan's character the severed testicles of her dead boyfriend. Stan's character and the pretty girl have a relationship for a while, until she decides to kill Stan too.

The final scene of *Men Lie, Women Break Promises* shows Stan's character dying as the pretty girl holds out her hand to him. He (and the audience) realize that she is holding Stan's severed testicles. Then he dies. (Judging from this film and other clues, Stan had an obsession with castration.) He would later claim that the plot was Gil's idea.

Occasionally, Stan used his cell phone to call a broker to make illegal trades while at film school. He would later say, "I'd always watch CNBC [the investment channel] when I wasn't going to film school." Stan became a fan of the channel's pundit James A. Watt, who was also a famous hedge fund manager. When asked about a trade Stan had made on a tip from Gil, Stan would sometimes say, "Well, that was one of James A. Watt's top three picks last week, and that's why I bought it."

One day they were talking about how hard it was to get tickets to see the Blue Jays play when the team visited New York City. Offhandedly, Gil said, "I wish we could get options on Blue Jays tickets." Then a lightbulb went on in both of their heads. They both said at the same time, "Let's buy options!" They had until then in New York avoided buying options based on inside information, thinking that regulators might monitor options sales more closely than regular stock sales. It suddenly seemed ridiculous to take such a precaution; they would start going for maximum profits on each trade.

Gil didn't think that it was fair for him to have to work long hours at Sullivan & Cromwell and do all of the spelunking while Stan just went to film school and did the trading. Gil's part of the conspiracy was much more difficult and risky than Stan's part. Gil was envious. He wanted the arrangement to be more fair, so he suggested that Stan get a job at a Wall Street law firm too—as a janitor. Either at Sullivan & Cromwell or at another mergers-and-acquisitions firm. That way Stan could spelunk at night too. To Gil, that seemed more fair than the current arrangement. But Stan refused, not wanting to be a Wall Street janitor, and Gil could not force him.

Over the summer, they did illegal trades at least every week, sometimes more often. Stan would later say that he and Gil ripped off Sullivan & Cromwell more than they ripped off any other law firm.

During this time, Gil and Stan both invested in art — prints of dollar signs, made by Andy Warhol. Stan bought three of them for $4,000 each. (Years later, looking at a newspaper photo of Conrad Black, Stan noticed that Black also owned a Warhol dollar-sign print, which hung on the wall of Black's Toronto office.)

In 2004, Stan would sell his Warhol prints for $10,500 each: $31,500 in total. He would use this money to buy gold wafers, which would subsequently double in value. Gold is easy to hide.

o o o

Soon after Stan moved in with Gil, they used information stolen at Sullivan & Cromwell to profit on the announcement of Dime Bancorp taking over North American Mortgage. By this time, their illegal profits were almost $2 million.

A month later they bought shares of Equitable of Iowa just before it was taken over by ING, a client of Sullivan & Cromwell. Gil had learned about the deal during one of his spelunking expeditions from a draft press release left lying around in the fax room. In his later words, the document described "not price but, you know, kind of the usual press release items, *combinations of two great businesses*, you know, *leveraging*, you know, *platforms*, kind of the usual bumph you find in press releases." Gil was already familiar with ING, having worked on a different deal for the company a few months earlier.

He told Stan about it when he came home from work. Soon more secret money flowed into the Bahamian accounts.

Later, in July 1997, Gil found another press release at Sullivan & Cromwell indicating that Nellcor Puritan Bennett Inc. was to be taken over by Mallinckrodt Inc. Gil and Stan gave this deal the code name Fat Chick because the word *Nellcor* reminded them of Nell Carter, the name of an overweight actress from the 1980s. Stan bought lots of Nellcor Puritan Bennett shares. In fact, he invested all of his and Gil's illegal capital into buying securities in the company.

Some of the securities he bought were regular shares, but others were bought "on margin." Margin buying is when you borrow money from your broker to buy shares, using other shares as collateral for the loan. This is a way of magnifying the profit or loss made by the share price going up or down.

A second part of buying on margin is the feared and loathed "margin call." This is when the value of your collateral shrinks compared with the value of the debt owed to your broker, to a point where the broker is required by law to demand more money to meet the "margin requirements"—the 1:1 ratio between loan and collateral.

Anyway, the important thing is that, after Stan bought his margin shares in Nellcor Puritan Bennett, negative news about the company's earnings appeared in the media. It put the merger at risk; the terms had to be renegotiated; the deal might not happen after all.

The value of Nellcor shares plummeted. The value of Stan's shares sank almost enough to trigger a margin call. The broker contacted Carl Dahomey and told him to warn Stan (or "Mr. Phillips") that, if the stock continued to sink, the broker would have to demand more money to satisfy the margin requirements.

The problem was that Stan had no more money to pay the broker. A margin call could wipe out all of his and Gil's profits to date—and more. It could ruin Stan financially and, maybe, force him into bankruptcy.

Annoyed, Gil and Stan started calling the deal Fucking Fat Chick.

Luckily, the stocks rallied a while later, giving Stan a chance to dump all of his shares at a small, acceptable loss.

A few weeks later Gil told Stan, "Well, the deal's back on. It's going to happen for sure." The two corporations had worked out their problems. Stan bought shares in Nellcor again, at a higher price than what he had just sold them at. After the announcement, the Canadian conspirators cleared about $200,000 (U.S.) in profit.

Soon after that and soon after graduation from film school, Stan moved back to Ontario.

Around this time, he learned a valuable lesson about how the stock market worked. As he later wrote,

> On the morning before a takeover was to be announced, I would often see a considerable number of shares in the company set to be acquired sold down in price or dumped on the Market for

reasons that I couldn't understand. Only after seeing the pattern repeat itself in deal after deal did I finally realize that institutions or large investors that knew about a coming takeover and that wanted to take advantage of that inside information would use the first few trades of the morning to drive down the price of the target company's shares. The aggressive selling that they initiated would lead to a further drop in prices as regular investors that did not know about the coming takeover sold to cut their losses. In conjunction with those sales, selling would also come from others that did have inside information about the deal, but were not sufficiently well-connected to its source to be certain that the morning sales were not a sign that the deal was now off. If done properly, a "shake down" would create a situation of continued selling throughout the day that would feed upon itself and result in more shares than normal being put up for sale and at lower prices than one would expect for stock in a company hours away from facing a takeover. Those that initiated the "shake down" would then use the opportunity that they created to quietly buy all the shares they wanted, without pushing up prices.

o o o

In the summer of 1997, the U.S. Supreme Court released a final decision in the case of *U.S. v. O'Hagan*. This case had started in a lower court in 1990, the year Gil and Stan met at Osgoode.

James H. O'Hagan was a senior lawyer and a partner in Dorsey & Whitney, a huge, Minneapolis-based law firm with branch offices around the world. He had defended Drexel Burnham Lambert, Shearson Lehman Hutton, and other top securities-trading corporations.

In 1990, O'Hagan was arrested. He was accused of many secret crimes, including stealing trust money from the Mayo Clinic and other clients. He was also charged with insider trading, one example being how he abused information about a plan by the British-based Grand Metropolitan corporation to take over the Minneapolis-based Pillsbury corporation — the seller of baked goods with that cute and giggling dough-boy mascot. In that one deal, O'Hagan scored $4.3 million.

At trial, he was convicted. But at the Court of Appeal, he successfully argued that he should not have been convicted of insider trading because he had not personally worked for Grand Metropolitan and so had not owed it any legal duty.

The Supreme Court overruled the Court of Appeal, finding in the summer of 1997 that O'Hagan had indeed "misappropriated" information from Grand Metropolitan despite the lack of a legal relationship between the lawyer and the corporation. O'Hagan had taken something, information, that did not belong to him; his secret use of the information was an act of fraud on Grand Metropolitan and all investors. The majority decision was in favour of conviction, with the neoconservative activists Clarence Thomas and William Rehnquist dissenting.

If this U.S. Supreme Court decision had gone the other way—if the Republican-leaning Thomas and Rehnquist fringe of the court had been in the majority—then most of the secretive acts committed by Gil at Sullivan & Cromwell would not have been crimes under U.S. law.

But it did not go the other way. The U.S. Supreme Court, in *U.S. v. O'Hagan*, confirmed that what Gil and Stan were doing was illegal and wrong and a form of stealing. The length of the disgraced lawyer's sentence—41 months in prison—should also have been a warning.

14 | ESCAPE ATTEMPT

On November 11, 1997, a media release announced that First Union was pursuing Corestates Financial.

Gil and Stan made a lot of profit from the deal. Stan would later write this:

> I remember in late 1997 placing a trade to buy over a million dollars worth of a particular stock because of a tip I received that it was going to face a takeover the next week. Although I had done trades like that many times in my "career," that one stood out because of what happened next. About three hours after my buy order was filled, a friend of mine—completely unconnected to the source of my inside information and from another city and walk of life entirely [Donald Berlusconi*]—called to recommend that I buy the stock that I had just purchased because he had heard from someone working in a brokerage company that it was about to face a bid. Unknown to him, someone in the same brokerage that I had used was monitoring my trades, obviously saw a pattern of success, and then not only copied it but was confident enough to tell his friend in another city about what an unknown client was buying. Needless to say, I closed that account immediately. . . .

On March 4, 1998, the engagement of First Union and Money Store was announced (creating the largest home-equity lender in the United States, loaded with sub-prime mortgage debt). Gil and Stan made a lot of profit from the deal.

On March 9, 1998, the world learned that Alcoa was trying to seduce Alumax. (Stan gave Alumax the code name Metal Head.) Gil used a pay-phone to call Stan with the tip. They made some more profit.

On April 7, 1998, Household International and Beneficial Corp. announced plans to get into bed. Gil and Stan made more money.

Ameritech and SBC Communications told everybody of their mutual attraction and future plans.

More.

More.

More.

Soon Gil could not handle it anymore. Stress, depression, dread. *Weltschmerz.* (Gil used this word often, in a joking way, at this time.)

The pressure on Gil became, as he would describe it later, "painful and debilitating. . . . Not being able to sleep at nights, weight gain, chewing my fingernails, nervous habits. . . . There was a desperation in my life that I had to leave."

Another nervous habit was using the fingernails of one hand to scratch at the knuckles of his other hand. Stan would later say,

> He was always scratching his knuckles from the stress of finding information. So back then people will tell you he always had bloody knuckles like a bar [or] street fighter, like a bare-knuckle fighter. . . . When he would walk around from office to office in the morning, he was stressed out; he said he did this. It's I guess a sign of guilt. . . . I know at the Sullivan & Cromwell period he hated working there because he was working very, very long hours, so he was resentful.

o o o

At around this time, the issue of law school graduates in Canada falsify-ing their grades was getting more and more attention. I played a small part in this—during my last year at Osgoode, I wrote a front-page story for *Obiter Dicta* headlined "Doctoring Marks." It told the story of Osgoode graduate Rebecca Snapple,* who had been caught submitting a transcript with altered grades to a Bay Street law firm. My story helped to raise this issue in public consciousness enough that, eventually, concerns about transcripts from Canadian law schools made it to Wall Street.

The partners at Sullivan & Cromwell asked Gil for an official transcript, sent directly to them from Osgoode. They would compare it to the unofficial one Gil had been hired on. That would reveal his "pasting." He would be fired, disgraced, and probably disbarred in New York State.

How to escape?

Gil quit. He told his bosses at Sullivan & Cromwell that he was leaving the firm. After that, of course, there was no more mention of Gil providing official transcripts. He started looking for a new job.

His salary at Sullivan & Cromwell then was around $110,000. Gil wanted the same or more at his next job.

During his third year at a Wall Street firm, Gil would have been contacted many times by headhunters, who went after third-year associates particularly and persistently. These associates had enough experience to be valuable, but their salaries were still "low" (compared with those of partners). After three years, many megafirm lawyers were sick of their firms and wanted a change, something that the headhunters understood well. Between their third and fifth years, over half of Sullivan & Cromwell's associates would leave.

A law firm in London, England, showed interest in Gil. He didn't really want to work in England, but when the firm offered him a free airplane ticket and a free hotel room for him to come to London for an interview, he accepted, just for the free travel and hotel. Gil and Stan both loved the idea of getting things for free. Gil persuaded Stan to join him on the trip. They arrived in London on September 6, 1997, which happened to be the day of the funeral for Diana Spencer, Princess of Wales, at Westminster Abbey.

Stan had often ranted on his theory that, "If you wear a suit and look like you know where you're going, you can get in almost anywhere."

To put this theory to the test, Gil and Stan put on their suits and went to Westminster Abbey. It was a bit before 11:00 a.m. They weaved their way through the emotional crowds and the piles of flowers. There were security guards at all the doors of the ancient church. The guards did nothing as Stan and Gil, in nice suits, walked right inside.

There were 2,000 people inside, with another 2.5 billion people watching the event on TV. The funeral began with everybody singing "God Save the Queen," followed by performances of classical music. The crowd in the cathedral included the British Royal Family, Nelson Mandela, former Prime Ministers Edward Heath and Margaret Thatcher, the son of Winston Churchill, Hillary Clinton, Henry Kissinger, various members of various other royal families—and Stan and Gil, who stood discreetly at the back, watching and listening. They were present when Prime Minister Tony Blair, standing by Diana Spencer's coffin, read from the Bible, 1 Corinthians 13:13: "And now abideth faith, hope, love, these three—but the greatest of these is love." Toward the end of the ceremony, Gil and Stan heard Elton John sing "Candle in the Wind."

o o o

In his third-to-last theft of client information at Sullivan & Cromwell, Gil discovered that United Health Group was planning to take over Humana Inc. The next time Stan called Gil at 4:00 a.m. to wake him up, Gil told Stan the news about the coming together of two of the largest health care insurers in the United States. Gil said, "When are you coming back? We have work to do!"

At the time of the phone call, Stan was in France, where he had just finished a photography course. One month of the course had taken place in the south of France, and one month of it had occurred at Arles, home of Vincent Van Gogh. Stan would later say that the most moving art experience of his life was at this time, when he saw the "Cathedral of Images," famous paintings displayed on a cave wall, to music.

(Gil—jealous of Stan's carefree lifestyle—had tried to talk Stan out of taking this trip, and he had agreed not to go, but then he went anyway, telling Gil to call his cell phone if he needed to reach him.)

After getting Gil's call, Stan quickly phoned Carl Dahomey (his offshore-account lawyer) and told him to start buying shares in Humana.

When Stan was flying from Paris back to Toronto, he phoned Gil from the plane. Gil told him that the deal had just been officially announced. Still in the airplane, Stan phoned Carl and told him to start selling the Humana shares.

The second-to-last time Gil stole information from a client of Sullivan & Cromwell was during his last week at the firm, after he happened to come across a PowerPoint presentation while spelunking. The presentation told him that Tellabs was planning to take over Ciena. On the day before the official announcement, Stan bought a large number of options in Ciena. While monitoring the activity of the stock market, he noticed a peculiar trading pattern with Ciena securities. While the price of Ciena's regular shares was staying stable, the price of its options had more than doubled. Stan spoke to Gil on the phone about this, saying that it seemed to indicate a large amount of insider trading being done by people other than Stan. Inside traders often preferred buying options to regular shares because the profits were greater and because the inside information nullified the additional risk normally associated with options. Despite this worrying realization, which made them wonder if the obvious pattern would attract the notice of the Securities Enforcement Commission or another securities regulator, Gil and Stan decided to hold on to the shares. They reasoned that, if Stan was ever questioned about why he decided to suddenly buy Ciena options, he could just point to the unusual pattern of trading as a reason. The next day the takeover was officially announced. The Tellabs and Ciena deal earned them, as Stan would later say, a "ton of money."

The last time Gil broke the law at 125 Broad Street was in regard to Norwest's attempt to take over a client of both Sullivan & Cromwell and Goldman Sachs: Wells Fargo. It was to be a $34 billion deal.

After the June 8 announcement, Wells Fargo's shares—unusually—sank in price. Investors didn't think that this deal was promising. Not all companies fit well together. The stock market frowned at the engagement notice. Wells Fargo shares stayed down, down, down.

Gil and Stan lost almost half a million dollars.

∘ ∘ ∘

Gil got a job as an associate at a smaller (around 400 lawyers) but quickly expanding Manhattan firm called Shulte, Roth & Zabel. As he would later say, it "had a reputation for being a more—I think the phrase was 'a lifestyle firm'—that it was more of—the hours were not as extreme. The lifestyle was not as extreme. . . . [We only worked from] nine to nine." The salary was the same as at Sullivan's, but the Christmas bonus was smaller.

Many if not most of the lawyers at Shulte, Roth & Zabel were Jewish, and many were Orthodox. Not all were Jewish, however. During Gil's time there, the firm also employed an interning law student named Wafah bin Laden, the niece of the Al Qaeda leader.

Shulte, Roth & Zabel specialized in working for the financial services industry, helping to create highly complex structured funds and derivatives. The firm described itself in its advertisements as "the hedge fund industry's 'iconic brand.' . . . Our handling of such 'Deals of the Year' as the Chrysler, GMAC and Albertson's acquisitions—all extremely complex matters involving multitudes of lawyers working across practice areas—speak to our wide-ranging capabilities. . . ."

Schulte, Roth & Zabel represented clients who controlled assets valued in the trillions of dollars. Most of these clients were hedge funds with names unfamiliar to the public. "That was really their bread and butter, representing hedge funds," Gil would later say. Other clients of the firm included Lehman Brothers, NBC, Ernst & Young, Toys "R" Us founder Charles Lazarus, Golden Books Family Entertainment, author Michael Crichton, radio shock-jock Howard Stern, tough-guy actor Stephen Seagal, and investor George Soros. (In 2002, a French court would convict Soros of insider trading and fine him $2.3 million.)

Schulte, Roth & Zabel would later gain a high media profile when many of its individual and institutional clients were revealed to be victims of the massive Bernie Madoff fraud.

Many of the firm's lawyers would describe themselves on the firm's web page as experts on insider trading, boasting of presentations at conferences and published articles on the topic. The senior partner, William Zabel, wrote a best-selling book about investing titled *The Rich Die Richer and You Can Too!*

o o o

Gil told Stan about a fancy new car called the Jaguar xk, a convertible. Stan was so intrigued by Gil's description and his own research that he ordered one by phone, paying by credit card. The car was blue, with an oatmeal-coloured interior. Stan loved it. He also loved the fact that he was, he believed, the only person in Toronto to own one.

But that illusion was soon shattered. One day, when Stan was out driving his Jaguar xk, he saw another xk being driven down the street — by Garth Drabinsky, the musical theatre tycoon and close friend of Conrad Black. Gil had written a glowing review in *Obiter Dicta* about Drabinsky's musical *Showboat*. Years later, Drabinsky would be convicted of corporate fraud and sent to prison for seven years.

When Gil visited Toronto, he enjoyed driving Stan's Jaguar xk. Later, Gil would buy his own.

o o o

After the disastrous Wells Fargo trade, Stan tried a few trades without the advantage of inside information. His own research led him to a takeover of Snyder Communications by France-based Havas; his research indicated that the shares of Snyder were undervalued. Stan bought a lot of Snyder shares.

Soon afterward, Havas made a change to its takeover bid. Snyder shares started to drop. Stan held on to the shares in the hope that they would rally, but they did not.

Stan and Gil lost $1 million.

Later, again without the benefit of inside information, Gil was convinced by his independent research that the shares of online retailer eBay were overvalued. Gil met Stan at the Starbucks on Queen Street in Toronto across from the City tv building and told Stan of his idea. Stan phoned his offshore account lawyer, Carl Dahomey, to short-sell eBay, but Dahomey could not handle that kind of transaction. So Stan found a real stockbroker named Grover Bismarck* and shorted 10,000 eBay shares. But rather than sinking in price as he had bet, shares in eBay more than doubled in value by the time Stan had to cover his short sale.

They lost another $1 million.

o o o

Schulte, Roth & Zabel did not do nearly as much mergers-and-acquisitions work as did Sullivan & Cromwell. Gil provided Stan with only one tip from this firm, regarding CIT's takeover of Newcourt Credit.

Gil had been assigned to this file because he was a Canadian and Newcourt was a Canadian company. Later he would say,

> I remember a lot of drafting sessions on the offer document which was a joint CIT & Newcourt document. And I think I did some of the due diligence work. I remember going to [giant U.S. law firm] Skadden's offices in New York to work on the diligence. . . . I knew a deal would be announced. I didn't know the price. It was a share-for-share deal. I didn't know the price. I knew the two companies were talking to each other. I saw information being passed back and forth, you know, exhibits, material, agreements, you know, Newcourt's biggest agreements with their biggest clients. . . . So, you know, we looked up those agreements to see if they terminated or, you know, whether if something happened if there was a takeover.

It was not long after Gil changed jobs that the two best friends decided to quit the crime biz while they were ahead. They were both rich. They decided to cancel the insider-trading conspiracy forever. All that was left to do was to move their profits out of the Bahamas and to divide them equally.

Gil and Stan travelled to the Cayman Islands, along with Gil's younger brother, who knew nothing of the conspiracy and spent most of his time snorkelling or relaxing on the beach.

At this time, according to allegations by SEC, Sam Wyly and Charles Wyly (the owners of Michael's Crafts and other big companies) were also using the fraud-friendly laws of the Cayman Islands to hide the proceeds of crime. The SEC would claim that these conservative tycoons (who started out as newspaper publishers) and their lawyer, Michael French, reaped $31.77 million in a single insider-trading transaction on February 14, 2000. The SEC would claim that "French utilized his roles as the Wylys' lawyer . . . to cover the Wylys' scheme with a false cloak of legality that was essential both to its concealment and execution. . . . Michael French had over twenty years' experience as a federal securities lawyer." French worked for Jones Day. (We will encounter that law firm again later.) The total fraud of the Wyly brothers, channelled through their Cayman Islands accountant, was estimated at $550 million.

Gil and Stan met with either Barclays Bank or the Bank of the Caymans. They also met with a man there named Lewis Rowe, who worked for a company called Zephyr International. Lewis asked Gil and Stan if they wanted to get in on a special investment that would guarantee them 2% interest a month. The Canadians were not interested in that (being able to make much more inside trading). All Gil and Stan wanted was for Lewis to help set up accounts for each of them at a Cayman Islands bank. Gil and Stan were to be the "beneficial owners" and "informal advisers," but, as was the case in the Bahamas, the names on the paperwork would be those of local banking executives. As Gil would later say, "That way the assets would be sheltered from taxes and authorities looking at them because they would be owned by a Cayman institution instead of a Canadian or American institution or person." They paid Lewis by handing him a newspaper with $2,700 (U.S.) in cash hidden inside.

Lewis would later be convicted and jailed for money-laundering offences. He was also convicted of running a Ponzi scheme — into which he had tried to suck Gil and Stan with his offer of a high-interest investment. Scammers are always a target of other scammers.

Stan named Gil's account INM for "I Need Money." He named his own Cayman Islands account TGATAP for "Through God All Things

Are Possible." Stan would later say that he chose this name because it sounded "cool," comparing it to the Bible quotation that one of the gangsters in the film *Pulp Fiction* recites before killing somebody. According to Gil, however, Stan copied the phrase from the professional boxer Mike Tyson.

Each account held approximately $2,750,000 (U.S.).

PART FOUR

··

1999-2003

And, forsaking all others, be faithful to her
as long as you both shall live?

Standard wedding vow

15 | LOVE AND MARRIAGE

In 1999, Stan went to Pamplona, Spain, to run with the bulls. Gil was supposed to go too, but (according to Stan) Gil "chickened out at the last minute." So Stan ran with the bulls alone.

During his time in Manhattan, Gil had started a long-distance romantic relationship with a young woman, Susan Bliss Richler.* Susan lived in Toronto. She also was a lawyer, working in house for a large Canadian telecommunications corporation. She was cute, slightly shorter than Gil, curly haired, and slender.

Stan had introduced them two weeks after the Cayman Islands trip. He was living in an apartment near the intersection of Yonge Street and Eglinton Street in Toronto. Susan lived in the building too, one floor above him, and they began chatting when they met in the elevator. When Stan realized that she was single and Jewish, he decided to introduce her to single and Jewish Gil. When Gil came to Toronto one weekend, Stan took them both out to dinner. Sparks flew, and soon Gil was flying from Manhattan to Toronto almost every weekend.

Gil would later say,

I met my wife and for a variety of reasons decided I would rather move to Toronto than have her move to New York. Toronto is a better place to raise a family, that type of thing. My parents are here. My brother is here, and she was here, and I was really quite sick of New York. You know, it had nothing but bad memories for me. It made me ill just to be there. So I met her in November of 1998, and by February of 1999 I was looking for a job in Toronto.

Gil got a position with a mid-sized Bay Street firm, Meighen Demers, and moved back to his hometown.

Although Gil was firmly convinced that his days of inside trading were over, Stan would still pester Gil sometimes to give him some inside information from Meighen Demers. Gil would always refuse or change the subject. He would later say that, at this time, he considered the criminal conspiracy to be completely over; Stan was just a "loud, amusing friend." They still spoke on the phone almost every day, also meeting weekly for lunch and socializing. But Gil kept his firm's secrets.

"One of the advantages of a small firm," Gil would later say,

> is you do know what every single person is working on. And, you know, we worked on the Ranger Oil takeover, worked on the Indigo and Chapters transaction. I didn't tell him, but we did work on transactions. . . . [When Stan asked for tips,] I'd say something like this and that, you know, stuff. I would be non-specific. . . . I didn't say go to hell, which I should have said. I didn't say leave me alone. I didn't say none of your business, but I responded in a, you know, unspecific way.

Keeping over $2 million U.S. each offshore, Gil and Stan each transferred $600,000 Canadian to Canada, with the help of Carl Dahomey. Gil got his money first — Stan delivering a cheque from Dahomey to the apartment Gil and Susan were sharing, handing the cheque to Susan when she answered the door. This money — plus some of his savings and some of Susan's savings, as well as a tiny mortgage — would buy an $879,000 house, registered to both Gil and Susan. They lived in Rosedale, downtown Toronto's most elite and expensive neighbourhood, on Icarus Avenue.* Although just half a block west of Yonge

Street, the city's main commercial strip and transportation artery, their street was quiet, tree shaded, and very nice to stroll along.

Gil and Susan lived a few blocks north of the University of Toronto, one block east of a Hare Krishna temple, and one block south of two cemeteries. The forested Don Valley was a short walk to the east. Gil often walked the three miles between his office and his home.

Stan fell in love too, with Rochelle Landry,* whom he met in January 1999 through the Telepersonals, a phone-based dating service. She had been at York University for a year when Stan was there, but they had not met then. Rochelle left university without a degree and now worked in cosmetics sales. She was 5'9", pretty, of French Canadian descent, with straight brown hair. Stan would later say, "She was a good person, and I was not."

Their first date was on a Friday, at a place called Coffee, Tea or Me? There was a lot of snow on the roads, and much of it had been piled up at the entrance to the parking lot. Stan had a hard time getting his blue Jaguar XK over the snow ridge and into the lot. He tried and tried, backing up and accelerating forward, for over five minutes before he had the idea of trying an indirect approach. He managed to sort of slide his car over the snow bump and get it into the lot and meet Rochelle inside Coffee, Tea or Me?

She was sitting by a window and said, "I saw you trying so hard to get in. You seemed so determined out there. . . . You could have just gone home, you know."

Stan said, "That's not how I do things."

He (and his car) charmed her.

Stan and Rochelle were engaged in October 1999. The following month she quit her job in cosmetics sales, and Stan borrowed $40,000 from Gil for a deposit on a $614,900 house in King City, a small town a 30-minute drive north of Toronto. Stan had been storing some furniture at Gil and Susan's house; Stan and two of his in-laws—Philip Zahir* and Achilles Zahir*—showed up at Gil's house one day to take the stuff to Stan's new house. Gil and Stan and the Zahir brothers got to work. Gil's wife warned them that dropping furniture on a concrete surface might break the concrete. Philip Zahir said, "It's already cracked." After taking Stan's furniture to his new house, the Zahir brothers talked about Gil and agreed that he was, as one of them put it later, "a little bit of a peculiar fellow."

When Stan eventually transferred to Canada his own $600,000 (Canadian) in proceeds of crime to pay the rest of the price of the house, he did not pay Gil back the $40,000 loan. Stan would never repay this debt to Gil.

They had their only real argument at this time. Gil did not want Stan to marry Rochelle, thinking that they didn't have much in common. Susan didn't like Rochelle either, and Rochelle didn't like either Gil or Susan. After some harsh words flew between Gil and Stan, Gil dropped his objections to Stan marrying Rochelle.

Around this time, Stan decided to stop using Carl for stock trading. One reason was because Carl had not been able to help him short-sell eBay stocks. (Carl was a lawyer, not a broker with all the resources of a brokerage house.) The other reason was because Carl was going through a divorce at the time, which affected his mood. Stan was worried by what he considered "irrational" behaviour by his offshore-account lawyer, who was apparently "freaking out."

(At around this time, top Wall Street banker James McDermott was convicted of repeatedly tipping a Canadian porn actress — a case that amused Stan and inspired jokes and puns linking inside trading to sex.)

At a neighbourhood party in King City, Stan met Paul Borges,* who lived in the area and described himself as "pretty much retired." Stan and Rochelle soon became friends with Paul and his wife. Over dinner one day, Borges was complaining about all the money he had lost in a "highly leveraged mutual fund scheme" recommended by his investment adviser. Stan mentioned his financial expertise and said, "I can invest your money if you want." Stan explained that he invested based on doing "lots of research" and that he was an expert in the commodities sector. Borges agreed. On Stan's advice, Borges opened an E*Trade online account and gave the username and password to Stan (which meant he could control the trading but not take money out for himself). Paul left all of the investment decisions to Stan. Later, despite Stan's success with the investments, Borges questioned whether Stan really knew what he was doing. Stan replied, "This is what I do. I'm an expert in this area. Mind your own business. Let me do what I have to do."

In early 2000, Gil helped senior Meighen Demers lawyers Nicholas Williams and Mark Convery on Petrobank's $1.6 billion bid to take over Ranger Oil, representing Barclays Bank. He would later be part of the team of Meighen Demers lawyers representing Borealis Infrastructure Trust's $290 million bond issuance. He worked on several other deals for the firm, never giving any of the secret information he learned to Stan—despite Stan's pestering him to do so. Gil had always been a skilled lawyer, and now he was, for the time being, an ethical one too.

Shortly before they married, Stan made a confession to Rochelle. He told her that he had problems with Revenue Canada, which had reassessed his 1997, 1998, and 1999 income and capital gains related to stock trading. He had failed to report hundreds of trades. The tax-man was now demanding $300,000. Stan told her he would take care of the tax debt. He paid half the debt using money from selling his Jaguar XK and importing some offshore proceeds of crime. The other $150,000 came from Gil, by means of a cheque written "in trust" to Stan's tax accountant. Stan would later write that Gil was "acknowledging his half interest in those capital gains [i.e., proceeds of crime] by paying towards my tax liability."

Also shortly before their wedding, Stan looked out his kitchen window and saw what he believed was a wolf in his backyard. He mentioned seeing the "wolf" (probably a coyote) to some of his gambling buddies. One of them sold Stan a pistol, a cheap semi-automatic, for protection from the "wolf." He kept it at home. He told Rochelle about it.

On May 27, 2000, Stan and Rochelle were married in King City. Gil was Stan's best man. Gil met many of Stan's friends and family at Stan's wedding but did not seem to make much of a memorable impression.

Stan had enjoyed alcohol as a young man, particularly wine or cranberry juice with vodka. At least once he did something while drunk that he later regretted: writing that rude "Green Card" letter for *Obiter Dicta*. At his wedding, Stan gave up alcohol and took up drinking plain cranberry juice. He stayed off booze for a long time.

The next weekend, on June 4, Gil and Susan were married. Gil's younger brother was Gil's best man.

Stan was annoyed at not being asked to be Gil's best man. As he had introduced Gil and Susan, Stan thought he deserved the honour, but Gil (confusingly) said that, even if Stan had not introduced them, they would have met some other way.

Gil's friend Chris Kippes, the tax lawyer from Sullivan & Cromwell, flew to Toronto for the wedding and, on his return, spoke with amazement of the lavish arrangements and the obviously high cost. Some lawyers from Fraser & Beatty were there too. Stan discreetly avoided talking to any lawyers Gil had worked with.

Soon after the pair of synchronized weddings, Gil and Susan visited Stan and Rochelle for a barbeque. Although she thought Gil was well-spoken, Rochelle did not like him and did not feel comfortable around him; she told Stan that after Gil and Susan had gone home. Stan theorized that his wife did not like his best friend because Gil, whenever Susan was around, had a tendency to be bossy toward him, and Stan tended, in that situation, to be deferential to Gil. Apparently, Rochelle wanted her husband to act like a dominant male toward Gil.

In his big new house, Stan set up a home office on the main floor, near the back, with a view out the window of his lawn and the forested ravine behind the yard. Rochelle would often see Stan busy at his work, staring at the computer screen or watching a stock market channel on TV or talking on a telephone headset that he always wore around the house. Rochelle considered his business to be mysterious, because he always spoke about it vaguely or not at all. He never received any business letters sent to his home office. She did not pry; all that mattered was that he brought in lots of money, which he did.

Stan thought that a minivan was an appropriate vehicle for them and their future family, but Rochelle didn't like the idea of being seen driving around in a minivan; it clashed with her image. So they ended up buying a pair of his-and-her SUVs. His was a Lincoln Aviator, hers was a Ford Highlander. They were both huge, gas-guzzling, car-crushing, monster machines.

When they were in Mexico on vacation, Rochelle mentioned that she would like to visit often. Stan paid $20,000 for a time-share interest in a condominium in Cancun.

Later in 2000, Stan and Rochelle attended the Gestalt Institute of Toronto for relationship counselling. It offered a "present-centred and experiential approach to personal change. Through living in the present we are able to take responsibility for our responses and actions. To be fully present in the here and now offers us more excitement, energy and courage to live life directly."

Later in the year, the title of Gil and Susan's matrimonial home on Icarus Avenue was transferred to her name alone.

○ ○ ○

Stan decided to test his new gun. He asked Gil to join him. Very late at night, they sneaked into Toronto's Mount Pleasant cemetery to test-fire it. Stan went first. Holding the plastic-handled, metal-barrelled gun fearfully in one hand, he pointed it down at a burial plot. Hesitantly, he pulled the trigger.

BANG! So much louder than expected!

Stan, after he got over his shock and fright, started laughing nervously. He pointed at the grave, shouting at the person buried underground, "I just killed you!"

Gil went next, also firing the 9mm Bryco Jennings into a used burial plot.

BANG! The noise of the blast was almost deafening.

The recoil shook Gil's arm. He shrieked down at the stranger's grave, "You're dead!"

Stan got the gun back.

Then they fled. Gil—fit from all his walking and jogging—was a faster runner than Stan. Laughing wildly, gasping for breath, they ran away.

○ ○ ○

In the summer of 2001, soon after his 31st birthday, Gil quit Meighen Demers. He had accepted an offer from Dorsey & Whitney—the huge Minneapolis-based firm that James O'Hagan had been a partner in—to open a Dorsey & Whitney branch office in Toronto.

"Meighen Demers was a small firm," Gil would later say.

I think including me there were 30 lawyers, and it was just not the atmosphere, the type of law I wanted to practise. You know, in terms of kind of the market for law firms, it was a period of time where either, you know, you go big or you go home. Law firms were getting bigger, and the bigger the law firm the more it was capable of doing, and it was squeezing out the historically mid-sized firms that, you know, used to bat above their weight. They were starting to bat below their weight because they didn't have enough lawyers to do big firm work, and they had too many to do small firm work. In addition, I was passed over for partnership or I was informed I would be passed over for partnership at the end of that year. So it seemed like it would be banging my head against the wall to stay.

The new Dorsey & Whitney branch was at BCE Place (later renamed Brookfield Place), 161 Bay Street, Suite 4310. BCE Place was a complex of tall office towers, connected at their bases by a soaring, cathedral-like structure of glass and steel. The area enclosed by the beautiful roof was warm in winter, cool in summer. Sometimes musicians would perform on a stage to amuse the strolling and cell-phone-chatting and lunch-eating office workers.

An August 1 article in *Business Wire* stated that

in a move that underscores its continuing commitment to serving clients engaged in international business and trade, Dorsey & Whitney LLP announced today that it has opened an office in Toronto. It is the seventh international office for the firm, which now has 22 locations worldwide. . . . Peter S. Hendrixson, the New York-based Managing Partner of the firm, [said], "A base in Canada's financial center bolsters our ability to assist Canadian businesses, as well as their Canadian legal advisors, in southbound financings, M&A, and other commercial activities." . . . Dorsey is the only U.S. law firm with offices in both Toronto and Vancouver. . . . The [Toronto] office will also be supported by Seattle-based Dorsey partner Chris Barry. . . .

"The passage of NAFTA served to deepen and strengthen the already significant economic ties between Canada and the United States," said Dorsey partner and former U.S. vice president, Walter F. Mondale. "The firm's decision to open another office in Canada reflects not only the recognition of this economic integration, but also the importance of providing sophisticated legal resources for our Canadian clients with business interests outside of Canada." Dorsey's senior international advisor and former U.S. Undersecretary for International Trade, Ambassador David L. Aaron, stated, "Canada and the United States enjoy a substantial trading relationship. While U.S. law firms have generally neglected the opportunity to enter this promising market, Dorsey is making a commitment of top personnel in establishing this office. Dorsey has a long and varied history of working to dismantle unfair trade barriers to international trade and assisting in cross-border investments. Our Toronto office will reinforce these efforts on behalf of both Canadian and U.S. clients in the financial services and other business sectors." Dorsey announced earlier this year that it had opened an office in Shanghai, becoming one of the only Midwest law firms with an office on the mainland of China. . . . Dorsey & Whitney had experienced strong growth worldwide — almost doubling in size during the last four years. Dorsey & Whitney has completed more M&A transactions in the U.S. than any other legal advisor. . . . The firm was ranked No. 1 in the world for the number of transactions completed in 1999. . . .

Although Dorsey & Whitney had over 650 lawyers across the world, its Toronto branch was very small by Bay Street standards, with never more than two lawyers and two support staff working there at any time. Gil was not the senior lawyer there at first; an older lawyer named Grant Vingoe was. Vingoe was originally from Toronto, a graduate of Osgoode Hall Law School, but had just spent 15 years at the New York office of Dorsey & Whitney.

"Dorsey was not as regimented as Sullivan & Cromwell," Gil noted. "I was an associate in the corporate group, which was also the securities group, which was also the M&A group, and because I was in Canada I was in the Canada–U.S. group. It's all the same. . . . I was technically the first employee in the Toronto office. . . . A partner from New York was regularly in Toronto at the time." (Gil was referring to Vingoe, who also served on the advisory committee for the Ontario Securities Commission. Eventually, Vingoe moved his office to Toronto full time.)

Dorsey & Whitney's Toronto office, according to its office manager, "had very few actual clients come into the office. Most of the client names are offsite and few." As a result, the "log-in book at their reception desk . . . collected dust."

Gil rarely got to enjoy face-to-face meetings with the CEOs of the corporations he represented, so he communicated with them otherwise, through phone calls, letters, and emails. Gil communicated using a tough-sounding, no-bullshit tone to corporate leaders, which they seemed to appreciate. More than once, Stan overheard a Bay Street corporate executive say something along the lines of "Gil is a little rough, but he does good work."

Gil maintained his Manhattan habit of being the first one to arrive at the office each morning, with occasional exceptions. He was usually in his office working by 8:00 a.m. and continued, except for lunch, until usually 8:00 p.m., every day except most weekends. Almost every day, he carried Dorsey & Whitney paperwork home in his satchel-style backpack. He also often took work home on weekends and would often talk on the phone to other corporate lawyers about corporate law. He organized his time in a paper pocket calendar.

What kind of work did Gil spend the most time on? According to his office manager, "It was a lot of letters, a lot of prospectuses, you know, drafts, anything from that across the board. So conference calls, whatever related to that particular client. Gil did a lot of mining work. . . . Mining and energy."

Gil's practice focused on advising investment dealers about regulatory practices in the United States and about corporate finance, such as how Canadian corporations could raise money in the United States.

The firm also represented corporations in takeover bids; Gil handled such cases, often with the help of lawyers from other Dorsey & Whitney offices, who would come to Toronto to work on particular deals.

Gil worked often with "dirt lawyers" (i.e., mining industry specialists) from Fraser Milner Casgrain, Fasken Martineau DuMoulin (especially John Turner), and Cassels Brock (especially Mark Bennett and Andrea Fitzgerald). Occasionally, he did a deal with lawyers from Osler, Hoskin & Harcourt or Sullivan & Cromwell.

Gil successfully applied to the Law Society of Upper Canada to be certified as a "foreign legal consultant" for Dorsey & Whitney. This meant that, though he was based in Canada, his practice consisted of giving advice on U.S. corporate and securities law. His work straddled the border. He was a Canadian living in Canada but also an American lawyer working for an American law firm. A double-sided man.

In late summer 2001, religious men crashed airplanes into Manhattan's World Trade Center. That was a shocking and sad day for Gil. He had lived and worked close to the disaster site. What did Gil think seeing the TV images of frantic people leaping from the skyscrapers' windows — the collapse of the Twin Towers — Wall Street blanketed by horrible grey dust — and the thousands of people, including 24 Canadians, who died because of where they happened to work?

o o o

Gil had invested his entire INM Cayman Islands account in trendy, media-hyped, high-tech stocks. This was near the peak of the "dot-com bubble." (In the 1980s it was "junk bonds," in the 1990s it was "tech stocks," and in the 2000s it would be "mortgage-based derivatives"— same scam, different flavours.) Predictably, the dot-com bubble burst. The value of Gil's picked stocks plummeted. Gil held on to the shares that he had bought at the beginning even as they collapsed. The stock market decline after 9/11 was another big hit to his portfolio.

His shares in Cisco Systems cost him $831,936. By 2001, they were worth $147,488.

His shares in Exodus Communications cost him $884,380. By 2002, they were worth $0.

When Gil received account statements in the mail (always delivered to him at work), he threw them in the trash unopened. He didn't seem to care about his secret fortune. By 2001, his $2.7 million (U.S.) had dropped to less than $1 million. The losses would continue. By 2003, INM held only $29,383.

$29,383!

That was only 0.1% of the $2.7 million. The rest—gone.

What Gil had taken from the stock market the stock market had taken back. He had stolen a fortune, invested it stupidly, and then done nothing as it drained away to almost nothing. Why?

In Stan's opinion, Gil just did not like "to admit that he's wrong or to crystallize a loss." So he stuck with his falling tech stocks to the end out of pride.

o o o

Stan's wedding had been a week before Gil's. In baby-making, however, Gil went first. His and Susan's baby son, Saul,* was born in February 2002. Two months later, at their home, Stan and Rochelle's baby son, Greg,* was born. Gil met many of Stan's friends and family at Greg's christening, but (as at Stan's wedding) Gil did not make much of an impression. Years later, several of Stan's friends and family would struggle to dig up memories of the only two times that most of them had ever met Stan's best friend.

o o o

At Meighen Demers, as at Sullivan & Cromwell, Gil had worked on corporate deals as an assistant to a more senior lawyer (the "lead lawyer") or as part of a team supervised by a lead lawyer. At Dorsey & Whitney, Gil worked as a lead lawyer for the first time.

His dream was to make partner. He would then share in firm profits and be able to charge his own clients a much higher rate. At this time, Gil charged clients around $300 (Canadian) per hour. Some Dorsey & Whitney partners at this time charged as much as $1,180 (U.S.) per hour. Plus, being a "partner" sounded impressive.

When Goldcorp completed an offering and private placement of its shares in late 2002, Gil was credited with providing advice on U.S.

securities law to the underwriters of the deal: BMO Nesbitt Burns, CIBC World Markets, Merrill Lynch Canada, National Bank Financial, RBC Dominion Securities, and Sprott Securities.

Early in 2003, Gil (assisted by Jonathan Van Horn) provided advice to IAMGOLD on U.S. securities law regarding the merger between IAM-GOLD and Repadre Capital.

Also early in 2003, a few days before Gil's 33rd birthday, Ontario's government toughened up the Ontario Securities Act. The maximum fine for insider trading was increased to $5 million, and the maximum term of imprisonment was raised to five years. The government could also seize a violator's assets for triple the profit made or loss avoided. Stan would later say that he and Gil did not notice this change in the law.

Gil was becoming a leader of the Toronto legal community. Along with senior Dorsey & Whitney associate Grant Vingoe, he joined the Ontario Bar Association's Securities Law Subcommittee. The subcommittee was comprised of 25 lawyers, all from Bay Street. They would send many letters to various authorities, lobbying for changes to securities laws. Most of the lobbied-for changes asked for less regulation of the industry and more freedom for corporations. The subcommittee gave occasional lip-service to small-scale investors but rarely (if ever) mentioned the wider public interest. Since Gil was a member, his name appeared on all its correspondence, even the letters he did not personally write.

Gil and two others from the subcommittee (Aaron Emes and Barbara Hendickson) wrote a letter on May 2, 2003, to the lawyer for the Alberta Securities Commission, commenting on a proposal to standardize securities laws across all of Canada's provinces and territories. Their letter supported this effort "to reshape securities legislation to reflect the realities of today's fast-paced and multi-jurisdictional financial markets."

We are ready and eager to work with the [Canadian Securities Administrators] to ensure that Canadian securities legislation remains up-to-date and continues to serve its dual purpose of facilitating the efficient operation of the Canadian capital markets, while at the same time protecting investors. . . . We strongly support the goal of creating a seamless system of securities regulation which would allow for "one stop shopping" by industry participants. . . . If you have any questions, please do not hesitate to contact Gil Cornblum at 416-367-7373 (cornblum.gil@ dorseylaw.com). . . .

The Dorsey & Whitney office was high up on the 15th floor over Bay Street, with an impressive view of downtown Toronto and Union Station. The office space was shaped like an L—the front door led to a hallway that, after passing the reception desk, extended back to a high-speed copier and a scanner, where the hall made a 90° turn; Gil's room was around the corner; his door could not be seen from the reception area or the main part of the hallway. At the end of the hallway, near his door, was the back door to the office, through which Gil could enter or exit without being seen from the reception area or the main part of the hallway.

Gil decorated the walls of his office with visual art—mostly photographs of mining equipment, mines, and mine workers.

The office next to Dorsey & Whitney's Toronto branch was used by Bloomberg News.

Gil was working almost directly across Bay Street from the building where Garry Hoy had worked before his 1993 attempt to bounce from his office window had sent him plummeting down to the street.

o o o

In the spring of 2003, the Liberal government of Canada introduced a tough new piece of anti-crime legislation to Parliament. This bill would amend the Criminal Code, adding new offences of "illegal insider trading" and "tipping." (This legal change was opposed by several Bay Street insiders, such as ex-OSC enforcer Joseph Groia.)

When Bill C-46 became law, tipping and insider trading would no longer be just a violation of provincial securities regulations. They would be listed in the national Criminal Code, in there with sexual assault, terrorism, kidnapping, and murder. Insider trading and tipping would now be investigated by the Royal Canadian Mounted Police, and the risks would be much higher. Later Stan would claim that he and Gil had not been aware of this change to the Criminal Code.

16 | FAMILY PROBLEMS

Unemployed but for occasional stock trading on the Internet, Stan had lots of free time. He took to fatherhood with an unusual level of intensity. He took charge of most aspects of baby care, reading many books and scholarly reports about how to be a good parent. He told Rochelle that she was not cleaning the baby bottles correctly and soon took over almost all aspects of the baby's care. Although Rochelle was allowed to keep the job of providing breast milk, Stan would supervise her use of the pumping machine and offer suggestions on technique. He often boasted of his parenting skills and criticized those of his wife.

In January 2003, Stan and Rochelle started marriage counselling with Dr. David Clair. They had long-standing problems in their relationship and struggled emotionally as a couple. They attended regular sessions with Dr. Clair for the rest of 2003. During these sessions, Stan would admit that his personality was "critical" and "emotionless" and that he often made "negative comments." He attributed his faults to having been the child of an alcoholic parent.

In June 2003, Stan and Rochelle's son Greg had just turned one. Little Greg was playing with one of the toddler-aged daughters of Stan's younger sister, Helena Zahir.* They were all in a room of Helena's house. While playing, Helena's daughter bumped into Greg, hurting his head. Stan waited for five seconds, hoping that Helena would step up and discipline her daughter. When that did not happen, Stan approached the little girl and said, "Don't bump heads with Greg."

His words to his niece enraged Helena. She struck Stan, then chastised him for his comment and tried to justify her daughter's head-butt.

When he got home, Stan wrote an email to Helena, urging her to discipline her children so that

> they learn to respect others and to behave in a way that will benefit them as teenagers, young adults, and adults. For as long as I can remember, people have tip-toed around you when it comes to commenting on the behaviour of the girls for fear of your reaction. I could show you literature that I have that describes your permissive and exculpatory behaviour (behaviour that I also manifest with my child) as the classic symptoms of how "adult children of alcoholics" often parent. . . .

After adding a complaint about Helena's girls "hitting me in the testicles," Stan admitted that his sister would probably "dismiss this note as the ramblings of your cranky and controlling brother."

A few months later Stan and Rochelle had a "date night," using Stan's mother as a babysitter. When Stan phoned his mother to check on how things were going, he detected that she had been drinking. He rushed to his parents' house. When his mother did not answer the door quickly enough, Stan kicked the door down to get in. He would never use his mother for babysitting again.

Soon after the interrupted date night, Stan and Rochelle started to attend counselling sessions with Dr. Linda Zimmering, a psychotherapist. They attended several sessions together until Stan stopped and Rochelle continued them alone. She complained of "the sheer constant grinding pressure of living with Stan" and noted that "Stan was home all the time (rarely going out of the house)."

o o o

On June 4, 2003, Gil and Susan celebrated their third wedding anniversary. The next day Susan went to see a doctor and was diagnosed with inflammatory breast cancer. This was more serious than regular breast cancer. Ten years earlier, 95% of the women diagnosed with inflammatory breast cancer died. Recent medical advances had improved the odds, but the disease was still extremely dangerous. "There was an 80% chance she would die at that point based on, you know, the treatment history of that type of breast cancer," Gil would later say. "It's a very fast-growing breast cancer as opposed to many breast cancers that form lumps; this was actually a spiderweb-like cancer. So it's very hard to track until it's very developed. . . . The treatment for this form of breast cancer is chemo followed by mastectomy followed by more chemo followed by radiation."

The news hit both of them hard. Stan would later say that Gil was "very devastated" and "completely supportive" of Susan.

As his suddenly ill wife went to doctors and specialists, Gil had to keep going to work. Assisted by Dorsey & Whitney's Charles Patuznik, Gil helped Dundee Realty to reorganize itself into a REIT (a legal manoeuvre used by real-estate corporations to avoid paying income tax). Later in the summer, Gil advised America Mineral in its public offering of shares.

o o o

On July 1, 2003, Stan filled in a form to open a new E*Trade Canada online stock trading account. He listed his email address as king citygur u@aol.com. He claimed to be self-employed, operating Punta del Diamante, S.A. He chose a margin account with short selling and a margin account with options trading, both to operate with U.S. dollars.

Stan prioritized his investment goals as short term 80%, medium term 10%, and long term 10%. Under "Risk Tolerance," he checked the box beside "high 100%." Under "Investment Experience and Knowledge," he checked the box beside "Sophisticated." Beside that, he printed the words "L.L.B.—Securities Lawyer; C.S.C.—Honours."

C.S.C. stands for Canadian Securities Course; around the time he had articled at Bratty & Partners, Stan had passed the written exam with an 80% score.

Where the form asked "Are you an 'insider' of a public company?" Stan honestly wrote "No."

o o o

One of Stan's gambling friends was Donald Berlusconi. Stan had met him in 1993 while articling at Bratty & Partners. Donald was the law firm's process server. Both Stan and Donald were passionate gamblers, and many members of Donald's family worked at Casino Rama north of Toronto—a place where Stan often gambled. Stan got to know Donald and his immediate family on a personal and professional basis.

In the late 1990s, Stan took an illegal tip from Gil and passed it on to Donald, without Gil's knowledge. Donald used the tip to profit on the stock market, then gave some of the cash and a box of golf balls to Stan as a thank-you.

Toward the end of 2003, Stan filed a Statement of Claim against Donald in the Ontario Superior Court of Justice. His claim was for $214,200. Stan alleged that, a year earlier, Donald had borrowed $157,000 (U.S.) from him and that Donald had signed a promissory note agreeing to repay the sum on demand. Stan alleged that he had made a demand but that Donald had not paid him back any of the debt.

On November 12, at 11:00 a.m., Stan and Donald were sitting together at the Molisana Restaurant in Toronto. Stan took out a copy of the Statement of Claim and served it on Donald, handing it to him. Donald took the court papers.

Stan asked him to sign a "consent judgment" admitting that he had no defence to the claim and agreeing to have the case closed against him. Apologetically, Donald admitted to owing the debt, adding that he had no way of immediately repaying it. He signed the consent judgment.

A few weeks later, no defence having been filed, Stan went to the courthouse at 393 University Avenue in downtown Toronto and paid the court fee of $90 to get a default judgment against Donald Berlusconi for $214,200 (Canadian).

None of the litigation paperwork mentioned why Stan had lent Donald the money. The answer? Because Stan had used Donald for smuggling money from his offshore accounts into Canada. Stan would wire money to one of Donald's associates offshore, and Donald (in theory) would give Stan an equal amount of cash. However, Donald often failed to pay Stan the proper amount, and by this means the debt grew.

o o o

When BC Pacific announced that it had completed a secondary offering of shares, Gil was listed as the U.S. counsel for the underwriters of the deal. His clients were RBC Dominion Securities, CIBC World Markets, Griffiths McBurney & Partners, BMO Nesbitt Burns, Scotia Capital, TD Securities, Canaccord Capital, Sprott Securities, Westwind Partners, and Trilon Securities.

Gil was unhappy at Dorsey & Whitney. He had been passed over for a partnership in the firm—unfairly, he thought. He blamed his failure to become a partner on the senior lawyer at the Toronto office, Grant Vingoe. Gil believed that Vingoe had told the Dorsey & Whitney partners that Gil did not want to become a partner. He thought that was a dirty trick, sabotaging his career, and he was bitter that the Dorsey & Whitney partners didn't ask him directly if he wanted to become a partner. Secretly, Gil became a disgruntled employee.

He started seeing a psychiatrist but quit after only two sessions.

Stan often suggested to Gil that he should leave the legal profession too. They could, Stan argued, get into the mining business directly and "stake some claims," like the ex-lawyers who ran Yamana Gold. (Gil got along well with the owners of Yamana Gold, particularly an ex-lawyer named Ian Tefler, but Stan believed that Gil resented them for having a better job than his.)

Gil did not think that was a good plan. He did not think that he would like being a miner any more than he liked being a lawyer for miners. Apparently, there was nothing that Gil really wanted to do. He never spoke to Stan of a job or business that he would prefer to lawyering, even though it was clear that Gil deeply hated lawyering.

Stan kept pestering him for more tips about upcoming deals, at least once a day, sometimes more often. "What do you know? What are you working on? Are you working on anything good? What are people working on? What's going on? What can I use?"

o o o

Stan and Rochelle had used a fertility clinic to conceive Greg. Their next conception was an accident.

In late December 2003, Rochelle was hospitalized with pregnancy complications. During her two-week stay at the hospital, Stan cared for Greg with the help of a newly hired maid, originally from the Philippines. Rochelle had their second baby in February, by emergency Caesarian section. This baby was a girl, Grace.*

PART FIVE

....

2004-06

Judge not, lest ye be judged.

> Matthew 7:1

17 | RISK, LIES, VIDEOTAPE

In early 2004, three days after Gil brought Susan back from her first chemo treatment at the hospital, Stan phoned him to pester him for inside information. Later that day, Gil realized that the roof of his house had sprung a leak and that water was dripping down from the bedroom ceiling, soaking Susan's pillow. The leak was the final blow; something inside Gil snapped at the sight of that wet pillow. "I could feel myself cracking during that whole week, felt myself crack open," he later said.

So Gil asked Stan, "How much money do we have left?"

Stan understood his friend's question to refer to criminal trading. It was Gil's subtle way of saying, "If you supply the money to buy stocks, I will start providing corporate secrets again."

Stan quickly agreed. Rise and shine again!

But this time there was a difference. Without telling Gil, Stan decided to trade stocks not just through the safe offshore accounts but also directly through his own easily traced E*Trade accounts (he soon had five of them) and the E*Trade accounts he ran for many of his friends and family. That was risky; Gil never would have agreed to resurrect the conspiracy if he had known Stan would do that. Almost as risky was Stan's secret decision, despite Gil's explicit instructions to change stockbrokers frequently, to stick with Grover Bismarck at BMO

Nesbitt Burns the whole time. (Stan had been introduced to Grover by Donald Berlusconi, the man Stan had sued for a debt arising from money smuggling into Canada.)

Stan and Gil agreed, like last time, to split all profits 50-50.

Whenever Dorsey & Whitney lawyers came to work at the Toronto office, Gil would wait for them to leave and then go through their garbage can looking at discarded documents with useful information. He often found it. If a lawyer left a laptop unguarded in the office, Gil would snoop inside it. He spelunked enthusiastically on visits to Dorsey & Whitney's head office in Minneapolis. He probably did so on his frequent visits to the New York office and the Seattle office (which controlled both the Vancouver and the Toronto offices).

Gil also developed a habit of fraudulently overbilling his clients, charging them for his clothing, his office art, and his frequent and lavish lunches with Stan. Sometimes Gil would puff up a client's bill by up to 40% as a self-determined "bonus." "There was no oversight," Stan would later say.

Stan got some of the seed money from putting a $400,000 mortgage onto his and Rochelle's matrimonial home. At the same time, he put the title of the house under her name alone, as she had asked him to do. (Stan would later describe the title transfer as a "pre-divorce" move.) He would later claim that during these transactions he discovered that Donald Berlusconi had registered and assigned a fake mortgage on Stan's house without his knowledge, twice, as part of a "real-estate scam" involving "gangster types" and "reputed or known criminal types in Toronto."

When Stan contacted Donald about this, Donald said, "Oh, don't worry about it. That's already been taken care of. I paid them back. It's been discharged already. Just coincidental to your calling me."

The next day the mysterious mortgage was discharged.

In addition to the $400,000 from Stan's mortgage, the rest of the seed money was money Stan had left over from the 1994–99 phase of insider trading—around $1.5 million (U.S.).

In early 2004, along with his Dorsey & Whitney colleagues Jonathan Van Horn and Gabe Gartner (a tax expert), Gil advised Central Fund in its $150 million MJDS (multi-jurisdictions) stock offering. This was the last deal that Gil worked on before his return to insider trading.

Gil tipped Stan about an upcoming takeover of copper-mining company Aur Resources by copper-mining company Inmet. Stan used this information to buy Aur shares with his offshore account. (This deal would fall apart in June and not close. Stan would like the stock anyway and would, after the collapse of the takeover talks, buy Aur shares in his Canadian accounts.)

Six weeks later the executives of Goldcorp announced plans to take over Wheaton River Minerals. Gil had worked on the transaction but, he later said, "not in a very large role. I was busy working on other things at the time. . . . Vingoe and Van Horn were working on that file. It's an office at that point of about three people. Hard not to know about it. . . . I actually went on a meeting or two with Vingoe to Fraser Milner's offices to work on the transaction." Gil tipped Stan; after the news release, Stan sold his Wheaton River Minerals shares for a profit.

Gil worked around this time on another deal involving Wheaton River Minerals, along with his Dorsey & Whitney colleagues John Hollinrake and Gabe Gartner, but did not tip Stan about it.

Also in the summer of 2004, Martha Stewart and her former stockbroker were convicted of lying to government investigators in an attempt to cover up their small-scale insider trading. Stewart was sentenced to five months in prison, followed by five months of home confinement, plus large fines.

After firing his offshore account adviser Carl Dahomey, Stan had replaced him with Grover Bismarck. The money that had once been managed by Carl had been transferred to Grover's control. Grover had set up a new but similar corporate structure for Stan in the Bahamas.

Gil went with Stan to the Bahamas when Stan was to meet with the banking executives. They stayed at the hotel at Paradise Island. (I am half-Bahamian and used to live there; I can remember when Paradise Island was a weed-covered strip of coral sand known as Hog Island.) Gil and Stan did some gambling and smuggled about $12,000 in cash back to Canada.

Stan's offshore trading account was called Pennstate, after the U.S. college football team, and Stan was an "adviser" to the Bahamian executives whose names were on the paperwork. Grover moved the trading account a few times over the years, including once to Switzerland. Eventually, the account settled at a Swiss bank based in the Bahamas called Clariden Leu (at the corner of Shirley and Charlotte Streets in downtown Nassau, my dad's hometown. He once told me an old Bahamian joke: "Thief steal from thief, God laugh"). Stan went to the Bahamas to set up the Clariden Leu account—meeting with a banker named Peter Wirth and another named Antonio—but rarely had contact with the bank afterward; he never received any account statements or documentation from Grover or Clariden Leu.

(A decade earlier the same bank had been used for insider trading by the crooked Wall Street banker Dennis Levine. Clariden Leu's decision to break its promise of secrecy to Levine and share its records with U.S. investigators was the turning point in an investigation that led from Dennis Levine to Ivan Boesky, then to Martin Seigel, and finally to "Junk Bond King" Mike Milken.)

Stan's arrangement with Grover was not connected to Grover's work for BMO Nesbitt Burns, a brokerage firm, though it was conducted out of his BMO Nesbitt Burns office. Grover wished to keep their arrangement secret, so he asked Stan to open a regular account at BMO Nesbitt Burns to justify why he visited so often. Stan used $100,000 to open up a regular account.

On the BMO Nesbitt Burns client account agreement, Stan gave his email address as kingcityguru@yahoo.com (apparently having switched from AOL). He would describe himself as self-employed and working for "Grmovsek Inc." (No corporation by that name existed in Ontario or anywhere else in Canada.) He listed his estimated net worth as $2 million. He described his investment knowledge as "high/expert."

Gil would sometimes remind Stan to switch brokers frequently. Stan would reassure his best friend that he was doing so, but he was lying. He stuck with Grover Bismarck to the end. Stan would lie to Gil about this many times. Stan also betrayed his best friend's trust by trading on tips through his own personal accounts and those of his own family and friends. Gil had no idea what reckless risks Stan was taking. Stan would later call his decisions at this time "moronic."

He supported himself and his family only on money from insider trading, while Gil and his family lived on money from his legitimate salary.

∘ ∘ ∘

In the summer of 2004, Dorsey & Whitney's White Collar Crime and Civil Fraud Practice group hosted a breakfast meeting and panel discussion on the topic "Insider Trading: After Martha Stewart." Three Dorsey & Whitney partners participated—Peter Carter; Roger Magnuson, head of the Strategic Litigation Group and Minnesota Lawyer of the Year, 2003; and Zachary Carter, an ex-judge working in the New York office, also a regular talking head on CBS and CNN. Following are some of their comments.

R. Magnuson: ". . . Let's remember what insider trading is—it is the use of nonpublic, material information, and every executive in this room has access to all kinds of nonpublic information. If you look at every budget committee or every meeting you half paid attention at, or every meeting you've made a little note at, you've got oodles and oodles of nonpublic information. . . ."

Z. Carter: "The general concern I have is that because of the extraordinary leverage that the government has now, due to enhanced sentencing guidelines, and company-busting civil penalties now available, issues of intent are seen through the lens of self-righteous 20/20 hindsight. More and more, I strongly suspect that innocent defendants are pleading guilty solely to avoid the penalties at the harsher end of the guidelines. . . ."

Z. Carter: ". . . One of the things that those of us who have been in law enforcement know is that the government's bread and butter is people and companies being willing to confess. Many crimes would go undetected absent the strong human impulse to either: (a) unburden their souls, or (b) try to convince the person who has power over them that they are not so bad and that they did not do anything terribly wrong. . . ."

R. Magnuson: "[Preventing insider trading] starts with a good compliance program. Companies that don't have really good insider trading policies and educate their executives on those policies are being very, very foolish. Many prosecutors with the Department of Justice and other government agencies look at the kind of policies, the kind of instruction given on those policies, and the culture at the company before making any final judgments."

As part of Dorsey & Whitney's compliance program, lawyers were tested every year on ethics. This test was to determine if a lawyer was ethical or not. Gil passed every year. Did Dorsey & Whitney expect confessions on these tests?

In 2009, a Dorsey & Whitney corporate partner named Andrew Rimmington would be charged in Britain with insider trading regarding a big 2006 takeover. So, in less than two decades, Dorsey & Whitney had at least three partners in the firm who were publicly accused of major-league inside trading: James O'Hagan, Gil Cornblum, and Andrew Rimmington. Thanks to that trilogy of notorious names, Dorsey & Whitney will be associated with insider trading by lawyers for a long time.

o o o

On August 6, 2004, Stan went on a three-day trip to Las Vegas. He went there a couple of times a year, sometimes with his friend and fellow lawyer and "degenerate gambler" (Stan's expression) Marvin Noir. This time, he went alone. Money would have been transferred from his Pennstate account at Clariden Leu to a Las Vegas casino, where he would launder the money. Laundering is when money gained from criminal activity is transferred to someone in a way that makes the money appear to have come from a legal source. One way to do so in Las Vegas consisted of using "dirty money" to buy a large number of black jack chips; after playing cards for a while, Stan would cash in his remaining chips; then, if necessary, he could describe the money as "clean" gambling winnings. He later wrote,

I would wire money into Vegas. When you arrived you would go to the Cage and confirm that your wire had arrived. If it had, you would then sign for it and it would then become your "front money" from which you could draw against with Markers while playing at the tables (When asked once by a host why I did not just take casino credit instead of wiring in my "own" money I said I had covenants in certain loan agreements related to my business that prevented me from doing so). I would then play at the tables—usually taking out 10,000 at a time and playing at a 500 minimum table—for an hour or so or until I was up a decent amount or near that 10,000 mark if I had already put in what I thought felt like sufficient time (remember, I was counting cards at the time so the House edge against me was non-existent or in my favour so I rarely, rarely, lost that entire 10,000 ever). I would then take the chips to the cage and cash out for cash. In the past, they actually let you wire money in and take back what you did not use as a cheque so you could wire 100,000, play 30,000 or so, and then take your cash and the cheque for the 70,000 left home. After 9/11 that all changed and they would only give you back your "unused" front money in the form that it was deposited.

Stan did not believe that he was the only one money laundering at Las Vegas. Once he was sitting in a casino and saw two men dressed, as he put it, "like Mexican gang-bangers" walk into the casino and dump a large duffel bag full of paper money onto a table in exchange for chips. Stan watched them hand out big stacks of chips to some other Mexican-looking men, who scattered throughout the casino to gamble. Stan assumed that the "gang-bangers" were laundering the money.

Although his purpose in Vegas was money laundering, Stan really enjoyed the gambling. (Gil had gone to Vegas with Stan a few times—once they took their wives, who didn't get along with each other very well—but Gil did not have a passion for gambling.) Stan was treated like a big spender in Vegas; he never had to pay for his hotel room. His favourite Vegas casinos were Wynn, Mandalay Bay, and Caesar's.

Stan had trained himself to count cards in blackjack. Although this was legal, casinos would kick out detected card counters and ban them from ever returning. So you had to be subtle. Stan was both subtle and brilliant at card counting. He would later say that "I've always been obsessed with finding an edge in things. . . . I'm really good at seeing holes in the system. . . . Sometimes I'd be counting cards at Binions [a famous casino, once home to the World Series of Poker], and I'd detect other card counters, and I'd let management know what they were doing, get them kicked out." Stan enjoyed exposing other cheats, plus it improved his own chances of winning.

Stan often stayed at the Mandalay Bay hotel. It was a place best known for hosting Ultimate Fighting Championship events. Stan never saw mixed martial arts live, just on TV, but he often saw boxing live in Vegas. He was a fan of all kinds of combat sports. At one point, he even invested money in a top Canadian boxer, Syd Vanderpool.

Stan sometimes met famous people in Vegas. He played cards once with Larry Flynt, publisher of *Hustler* and other pornography. On another occasion, Stan had dinner with wrestler and action-film star The Rock, who was complaining about a contract he had signed with his manager. As they ate, Stan gave The Rock some legal and financial advice.

On one occasion in Las Vegas, after a day spent gambling and money laundering, Stan went back to his fancy and high-ceilinged hotel room and dumped a briefcase full of his winnings onto the bed.

Stan had always been a frugal person. He was still in the habit of eating cans of tuna as a cheap source of protein. He had taken cans of tuna to eat at Osgoode Hall Law School, and, many years later, he took cans of tuna to eat at the Mandalay Bay hotel.

Stan went to the hotel room sink and started using his can opener to prepare his dinner. As he was opening the tuna can, his hand slipped, and he cut it on the sharp edge of the lid. Stan looked at his hand bleeding over the sink for a while; then he looked at the hotel bed. About $50,000 in cash was piled on top of the bedsheet. Stan realized that his frugality had become ridiculous. He was a multi-millionaire, in an expensive Vegas hotel room, with $50,000 in "clean" cash. "Fuck this," Stan thought, tossing the can into the trash. "I'm going to a steak house!"

After using card tables for money laundering for many years, Stan had to change to a new, more complex method of money laundering around this time. One reason was the fact that the Canadian government changed its rules about bringing cash into Canada.

The other reason had to do with casino management, which one day gave Stan a big fright. As he was cashing in his chips at MGM, and the casino teller pushed a big stack of cash to him, Stan heard a deep, intimidating voice behind him saying, "Excuse me, sir." Stan turned to see a huge employee of the casino standing nearby. Stan looked up at the employee's serious-looking face in horror. The giant man said that casino management had noticed the odd pattern of his betting and wanted to know why he was now taking out so much money in cash. It was obvious that Stan was suspected of money laundering. Since his money had come into the casino by a wire transfer, the casino expected that any money he did not spend gambling should be returned to him by a wire transfer.

Thinking fast, Stan explained that he was tired of playing cards and was taking the cash out so that he could bet on sports games at a different part of the casino. He gave the impression that he had already decided on certain teams to bet on.

The giant casino manager, Stan later wrote, said,

"Let me take you there" and walked me over to the MGM sports book where he introduced me to the Manager and said that he wanted to open up a Sports Betting account so that I could get credit for my sports betting toward my Comp rating. I opened the account and then, since they were all watching me, proceeded to bet about $1100/game to win $1000 on every basketball game on the list that night. When done, they left and I was left with a bunch of tickets on games that I knew nothing about. Not wanting to leave that money to chance, I decided to take the other cash I had in my room and bet the opposite side to all those games at other casinos so that I could limit my losses to only the $100 vig on the losing ticket (e.g. you bet 1100 to win 1000 which means I was betting 2200 overall to win 2100 which I would get back from the winning ticket). It never occurred to me that I could make money doing these offlay. In fact, some of my tickets ended up being Win/Pushes which means the spread on one side of the game tied and the spread on the opposite side of the same game resulted in a win which meant I received my $1100 back on the push and $2100 back on the win which meant I ended up laundering $2200 and getting back $3200 in winning tickets that I would mail back to Vegas from home and in a few weeks receive a cheque that said "Sports Book or Sports Book Winnings" on it. Other tickets ended up being Win/Win because the game felt directly in the middle of the spreads (e.g. I would bet the Raptors +3.5 on one ticket against their opponent Lakers; at another casino I would then bet the Lakers at, say, -2 over the Raptors. If the Lakers won that game by 3 BOTH tickets would win because the Lakers would cover on the -2 bet because they won by more than 2 and the Raptors would cover on the +3.5 bet because they lost by less than 3.5). Added to that, I came across a cab driver on my travels in Vegas who saw me sorting through all my tickets in the back of his cab when deciding which ones I would take home to mail back to Vegas and which ones I would discard as losers and asked to buy the LOSERS from me at 3 to 5% on the dollar as Americans can use losers to offset against taxes they must pay on their winning wagers. In short, this type of money laundering came — at worst — at a cost of $1 for every $22 laundered or about 4.1%. Of course, those costs were offset by the profits from Win/Pushes or Win/Wins and from the sale of losing tickets to cabbies or others that wanted to buy them because they could use them to save on their own tax liabilities.

On August 9, Stan returned to King City from his Vegas trip. When he got home, Rochelle told him that she was "not happy" and wanted to separate.

On September 10, Stan and Rochelle separated. The children continued to live in the matrimonial home, while Stan and Rochelle alternated 24-hour periods of living there.

The status of their marriage was uncertain for a while. At one point, Rochelle agreed to give their relationship another chance, on the condition that Stan sell the house in King City and move to Oakville, southwest of Toronto. He also had to attend marriage counselling with her psychiatrist.

In the evening of September 28, Stan and Rochelle were in the matrimonial home at the same time. He said that he was, unilaterally, going to fire the nanny and pull Greg out of his daycare. Rochelle became upset and emotional. Harsh words flew back and forth between the parents. The children were present and in distress. Stan, seeing his wife's condition, ran to grab a video camera. He videotaped his wife's hysterical outburst. As Rochelle wept and raged, Stan kept filming her and the upset children, making comments like "Look at Mommy! She's going into a rage! She's crazy!" Later Stan invited over members of his family, members of Rochelle's family, and some neighbours to watch the videotape.

18 | "COME PICK UP YOUR SHOES"

One day Grover Bismarck at BMO Nesbitt Burns in Toronto told Stan of a new way to smuggle illegal money from the Bahamas to Canada. Grover had clients in Toronto who were willing to give Stan cash in exchange for Stan transferring the same amount from his Clariden Leu account to the offshore accounts of Grover's clients. (Stan would get cash into Canada without a paper trail or having to cross the border with it, and Grover's clients would similarly get their money out of Canada.) Stan never learned the identities of Grover's other money-laundering clients or where his money went.

Stan signed a direction given to him by Grover instructing Clariden Leu to wire the money pursuant to instructions provided by Grover. Grover forwarded the direction and instructions (including the amount to be transferred and the name and location of the recipient account) to Clariden Leu. Sometimes Clariden Leu was instructed to send the money to a Swiss bank, other times to a bank in the Turks and Caicos Islands. Stan assumed that the money was going to one of Grover's clients in the construction or restaurant industry. He recognized some of Grover's acquaintances as having been clients of Bratty & Partners at the time Stan had worked there. The only person whom Grover worked for that he ever mentioned to Stan was Vic De Zen, the Royal Plastics billionaire (who was then being investigated by the OSC for insider trading; De Zen would be charged with fraud in 2008 and acquitted in late 2010). Stan got the cash at the time he signed the direction.

The cash-for-transfer meetings were arranged by Grover, who would call Stan and use code such as "Come pick up your shoes" or "I bought you a new tie." Stan would then go to Grover's BMO Nesbitt Burns office and leave with an envelope of cash. He never saw the instructions Grover sent to Clariden Leu with the direction. Often Grover would put the envelope into a bag from a fashion store so that Stan could walk out with the bag visible, to support the alibi of showing up for shoes or a new tie.

All together, Clarien Leu would make 10 wire transfers from the Pennstate account controlled by Bismarck of $49,000 Canadian each plus seven wire transfers ranging from $1,000 to $39,000 U.S.

The first payment from Bismarck to Stan was in $1,000 Canadian bills. Stan had a hard time finding a place that would accept them. Finally, he managed to get rid of most of them at Home Depot outlets, buying tools or a gift card and getting change in smaller currency. He paid an installment of a loan from Carl Dahomey (who had helped Stan buy an Aviator SUV) with a $1,000 bill, which annoyed Dahomey and led to a "dispute." Later the bills from Bismarck would be smaller — sometimes even as small as $5 and $10 bills — and the envelopes of cash would be correspondingly bigger and bulkier.

Sometimes they met outside Grover's office, such as in the parking lot of a mall near Stan's house; at those times, there was no fashion store bag around the envelope, which Grover would give to Stan while sitting in Grover's car.

When Stan agreed to a wire transfer, part of the arrangement was that he would receive 3% less than what was transferred. However, the actual cash in the envelope would always be even less. Stan later complained, "I would count the money, and I would always be short $1,000, so I assumed [Grover] was taking some extra out of the envelope. He would say — it's like, 'Here's $47,550,' and I'd count it, and it was always, like, $46,000. So then I stopped counting after a while because I didn't want the confrontation. Like, you're shortchanging me, or someone's shortchanging [me]."

The one time Stan complained about the missing cash, Grover said, "Oh, I don't know how that happened."

Stan told Gil of only two such money transfers. Stan showed up at Gil's Dorsey & Whitney office and gave Gil some Canadian cash in an envelope. On both occasions, Stan lied to his best friend and told him that only $9,800 had come from the broker, giving Gil just $4,900 as his "half."

Grover was scamming Stan; Stan was scamming Gil; Gil was scamming Dorsey & Whitney; and Dorsey & Whitney was representing corporations across the planet.

Stan justified himself by rationalizing that he needed the money more. It was to pay his living expenses. He was just coming out of a marriage breakdown. For Gil, the cash was "mad money," used for personal luxuries or expenses he hid from his wife. Gil kept the cash in a drawer of his office at Dorsey & Whitney. During the second phase of insider trading, he would get only $50,000 in total—some from casinos, some from the exchanges Stan arranged with Grover.

In addition to his official cut of the money transfers and whatever else he secretly skimmed, Grover took $3,000 in fees every three months from Pennstate. Clarien Leu's Bahamian executives enjoyed hefty fees too. Gil's tips were feeding an ecosystem of parasites.

o o o

Reconciliation having failed, Stan and Rochelle both hired divorce lawyers. The lawyers started exchanging letters and phone calls, negotiating and racking up billable hours. The main issues were custody of the children (Stan wanted joint custody; Rochelle wanted sole custody) and the matrimonial home (Stan wanted to keep it or wait for a high offer; Rochelle wanted to sell it as soon as possible). Neither of them was interested in the Cancun property, which was in arrears of payment. They abandoned it and let it be repossessed.

In the interim, as negotiations dragged on, Stan and Rochelle alternated living in the house every 24 hours, while the kids lived there full time. Whichever parent happened to be in the house would care for the children. For the first two weeks of the arrangement, Stan spent his off nights at Susan and Gil's house (which made tipping easier).

Rochelle complained about Stan to a Children's Aid Society worker, who opened a file and contacted him, telling him that he was under investigation. Stan met with a CAS worker for an interview. After that, he started playing rough and sneaky. Without telling the divorce lawyer whom Stan had hired to negotiate with Rochelle's divorce lawyer, Stan secretly hired a second divorce lawyer. This lawyer helped Stan to prepare and file an "emergency motion" that was to be brought to court *ex parte* (meaning behind Rochelle's back).

Stan's Notice of Motion and supporting affidavit were filed in Newmarket Provincial Court on November 3, 2004. In the affidavit, Stan swore as to the truth of the following statements.

4. . . . In the last several weeks, Rochelle has acted in ways and has made decisions (detailed further below) which have not been in the Children's best interests. I am most afraid that if the Children are not placed in my care on a full-time basis and if structure and calm are not immediately returned to the Children's lives, the effects, especially for our son, Greg, may be irreparable. . . .

5. I have been both Children's primary caregiver since their births. . . .

6. Not only am I concerned about the Children's physical safety in Rochelle's care, I am also worried that she might remove them from the Matrimonial Home. Her recent defiance and willingness to simply ignore our agreements with respect to the Children . . . causes me concern that she will simply run with the Children, perhaps with the assistance of her mother. . . .

9. . . . Rochelle has a history of psychiatric issues. . . .

13. . . . Rochelle also claimed, with increasing frequency, that she was anxious and stressed. This is despite the fact that she did not have any employment responsibilities and that her care of the Children and our household was minimal at best. . . .

20. ... Image and perception have always been important to Rochelle and played a major role in our marriage. Rochelle was also visibly relieved by not having to look after Greg's needs on a constant basis. She was able to pursue her own interests and when Greg was in daycare, she was out of the house much of the time. I cannot be sure of her pursuits.

27. ... Greg's natural and unprompted reaction was always to run to me and not to Rochelle. That is because I have cared for him all his life, especially at night, and we are very closely bonded. I do not believe he has the same bond with his mother.

31. ... Rochelle's ... increasing paranoia caused me to suspect that she was out of balance, for reasons which were unclear to me at the time. ...

32. I became ever more concerned in September, 2004, when I found various medication[s] in our house all labelled to Rochelle and all dated at or near when she said she wanted to separate. ...

Stan's affidavit then described the videotaping incident.

33. On the following day, September 29, 2004, a prospective buyer was to attend to view the Matrimonial Home at 5:00 p.m. At the last minute ... Rochelle insisted that she take Greg to dinner. ... [An argument began in the driveway; then Rochelle] telephoned 911. ... Three police cars arrived at the Matrimonial Home shortly hereafter. Rochelle told the police, in front of me, that there was a gun in the house. She then proceeded to give the police the key to the cabinet where the unloaded gun was stored. ... I told the police, in front of Rochelle, that the gun was obtained for Rochelle by her ex-boyfriend, for her protection. She did not correct my explanation to the police. ...

35. ... The police refused to review the video I had made the night before of Rochelle lunging at me. No charges or arrests were made. The gun was taken away by the police. ...

Stan's affidavit admitted to lying to the police about who owned the gun. Lying to police officers during an investigation is a crime called "obstruction of justice." Stan also lied, under oath, in this affidavit when he claimed that the gun was unloaded. He also lied under oath when he claimed that no charges were laid by the police. There were other lies in parts of the affidavit not quoted. The whole affidavit was deceptive and depressing to read, even for someone like me who has practised family law. Stan attached to it some photographs of "unexplained bruising on my daughter's arm." Every time I looked at Grace in these pictures — as the cute toddler smiles innocently at the camera while Stan's hand holds up her arm for the camera, collecting "evidence" to use against the child's mother — I felt sad.

Stan claimed that Rochelle's mother's home was "disorganized and unkempt, including mouse droppings in corners, on window sills and under the furniture. . . . I am concerned that Greg's cries for help are to alert me to something happening to him while he is in Rochelle's care. I am worried about his safety and that of my daughter. . . . [T]he anxiety Greg has been experiencing may have irreparable effects on him. . . . "

Stan's material included affidavits from his mother and his brother-in-law, both of whom accused Rochelle of being a bad and possibly abusive parent.

On an "emergency" basis, Stan asked for temporary custody of the children, exclusive possession of the matrimonial home, and that any contact between Rochelle and her children be supervised by someone other than Rochelle or her mother.

Deliberately, Stan brought his "emergency" motion on a day when almost all of the Newmarket judges were away at a conference. Stan knew this and timed his legal move accordingly. The remaining judges in the Newmarket courthouse that day were too busy with other cases to deal with his unscheduled matter. So a court clerk took his Notice of Motion and supporting affidavit and faxed them to Ontario Court Justice Michelle Fuerst (Osgoode Hall, class of 1979). She apparently looked at the materials during a break in the conference and then — without the benefit of seeing any of the people involved first-hand and without having heard any oral arguments—faxed her handwritten decision back to the courthouse.

> Emergency ex parte motion. I am reluctant to make even a temporary order that impacts on custody and access and provides exclusive possession of the home on an ex parte basis. I recognize however that there are concerns about the well-being of the children. I therefore order on a temporary without prejudice basis: 1) A motion for temporary custody and access, and temporary exclusive possession of the matrimonial home and the related relief sought in the Notice of Motion may be brought prior to a Case Conference, but *on notice* to the responding party; 2) In the interim, the children are to reside with AF [applicant father] and are to be in his care; 3) The children are not to be with the RM [respondent mother] alone, or with RM's mother alone, or with RM together with *her* mother; 4) No-one is to remove the children from the Province of Ontario without further Order of the court; 5) Any police force having jurisdiction shall locate and apprehend the children and deliver them to the care of the AF, in the event they are removed from his care without his permission. For further clarity, AF may take the children to reside with him temporarily at a location other than the matrimonial home until a motion is brought, if that is necessary to ensure their well-being in the interim.
>
> [Signed] Michelle Fuerst J.

The judge faxed the order to the Newmarket court and went on with her day. Score: Stan 1, Rochelle 0. Yet again, and not for the last time, Stan manipulated the law like a chess fiend moving his chess pieces.

How could any judge rely on an affidavit in which Stan admitted to obstruction of justice? How could any judge, on reading a self-serving and aggressive affidavit from a man she had never met, strip custody from a mother she also had never met? By fax?

The morning after obtaining the "emergency" order, Stan phoned Rochelle and left a message for her. "Hi, Rochelle," he said. "If you are driving and you are listening to the message, please pull over. It is very important. I don't want you to have an accident when I tell you. Please pull over. The children are fine. Their health is fine. But I have to tell you this. Are you ready? . . ." Stan launched into a long, self-centred rant. Finally, he got to the point:

> I put all these things on paper and went to court yesterday and explained to the judge, and the judge saw all these things and came to the conclusion that you were not acting in the long-term and short-term best interest of the children. You are acting for whatever reason that is clinical or psychological or anger, or it's bad advice. They did not feel you were acting in the best interests of the children.
>
> On a temporary basis, I was given custody of the children at least until the motion is heard next Wednesday at the earliest. Now my children would want me to let you visit them even though I am not required to do so. So I am going to do that. You will be served with documents at 3:30 p.m. today at your mother's house. . . .
>
> This is about the children and only the children from my end, and I tried to be guiding myself by what would the children want me to do to their mother, and that's what I am doing to protect them. Please start doing that. They will be at my sister's house tomorrow; you'll be allowed to visit them. . . . Take a break before you call your lawyer to clear your head, and then we can talk. . . . This is about the children, it really is.

Rochelle responded with court papers of her own, expressing outrage at Stan's tactics. In addition to demanding full custody of the children and exclusive possession of the matrimonial home, she wanted Stan to pay her child support (the amount to be based on the government's child support guidelines), $10,000 a month in spousal support, and "extraordinary expenses." She also requested (and would be granted) a restraining order against her husband.

In her affidavit, Rochelle swore the following.

5. . . . I am fully able to care for my children and make appropriate decisions regarding their safety and well-being. The cruel and misleading allegations in that regard made by the Applicant (which are completely unsupported by any independent evidence) are contradicted by the many professionals who have contact with me and with our children. . . .

6. Secondly, I have never threatened to "run" with the children. . . . I am a stay-at-home mother with no job or resources. I have no place to go, other than to stay short-term with my mother as I have been doing. . . .

8. At the time of receiving the [answering machine message], I had just finished taking my turn in the home with our two children and was returning to my mother's home. I was absolutely devastated and in complete shock. I couldn't understand how the Applicant could have possibly been given custody of the children without notice to me, as I understood that such orders were made only in emergencies where the safety of the children might be in issue. . . .

9. I am alarmed, however, that the Applicant has completely stepped over any reasonable boundary of behaviour. His anger at me has so clouded his judgment that he has disturbed our existing time-sharing arrangement with the children, throwing their lives in chaos and disarray, and embarking on what I believe is his goal to alienate me from our two children. I also fear now that given his bizarre conduct in running to Court while we were in the midst of ongoing negotiations between our two lawyers, he has completely destroyed any possibility of me being able to trust him and co-parent with him.

10. I will not respond in detail to each of the Applicant's false allegations or conclusions, but will focus my evidence on the major issues in respect of which he misled the court to obtain custody of our children without notice to me, which is quite consistent with his past threats to me to make me "look crazy" and "take away the children." . . .

23. While we were living together, the Applicant would upset me, demean me, taunt me and provoke me into becoming extremely emotionally distressed. On one such occasion (which I will describe more fully later in the affidavit) I was worn down and emotionally exhausted, and simply unable to respond rationally and was weeping uncontrollably, he used the opportunity to videotape me to "prove" to other people, like his family, what an emotional wreck I was. . . .

26. . . . The applicant showed the video to his parents, which I found humiliating. My mother-in-law, much like her son, chose to condemn and criticize me rather than try to help. . . .

28. The Applicant did not work outside our home (he trades stocks in his home office). . . . I managed the household and the Applicant tended to his business (which I was never involved with).

46. I am a normal, healthy, well-functioning woman. I am able to care for my children in every way. Since leaving the matrimonial home, and not being subject to the constant emotional abuse of the Applicant, I have grown stronger and more self-assured. I truly believe that is what bothers the Applicant the most—that he can no longer control my every move, every moment of the day.

48. . . . The Applicant became all-consumed with Greg, to the exclusion of everything else, including a normal marital relationship. He left our marital bed and we seemed to have no relationship outside of being Greg's parents.

50. When the Applicant went away on a gambling trip to Vegas from August 6–9, I had more time to think about our marriage. . . . The day the Applicant returned, I told him of my wish to separate.

51. . . . [Stan] asked me to sign a "Personal Agreement" [i.e. marriage contract]. . . . I did not consult a lawyer before signing. . . .

54. On September 28 he presented me with a Separation Agreement which he had drawn up and demanded I sign. . . . [H]e warned me not to make trouble for him.

55. The Applicant has always had mysterious financial dealings, and I was never a party to them. . . .

56. I never questioned his finances, as he always provided very well for us. I do not know how much money he makes or has. I know he has accused me of making an anonymous call to Revenue Canada, but I did not do so. . . .

57. When I refused to sign the agreement without legal advice and financial disclosure, his behaviour escalated in the home, and he became more threatening and menacing towards me.

58. Throughout all of this, I was still attending counselling with Dr. Zimmering. I told her I knew he had a gun in the house, which he got prior to our marriage. I told her that I had locked it in a cabinet, but I was afraid. Although the Applicant never physically harmed me, he was becoming increasingly enraged and his behaviour was escalating. I feared he would snap. . . .

60. . . . When the officer asked me on the phone point blank were there weapons in the house, I said yes, there was a gun. When the police arrived, they asked for the gun, and he lied and told them it was mine. I have never owned a gun and am afraid of guns. . . .

77. It is mind-boggling to me that the Applicant would have continued to engage his lawyer, Mr. Borden, in continued negotiations and correspondence with Ms. Kain [Rochelle's divorce lawyer], as recently as November 3rd, and have been plotting to take my children away, by engaging another lawyer to bring an application without notice to me at the same time. Given that the voluminous material was sworn on October 30th, he must have formed the intention to do so, and met with his lawyer sometime around the 27th or 28th of October at the latest.

78. Given that both of us had lawyers, who were actively engaged in negotiations regarding the children among other issues at the very time he brought this motion, I cannot understand

why the motion was not brought on notice. I believe the Applicant was being underhanded in an effort to obtain some kind of advantage. . . .

83. . . . [A voice-mail] message on October 29th (the day before his material was sworn) talks about us sharing Halloween with the children. The message on October 31 talks only about the possible sale of the house. Although he had just the day before been to a lawyer (not the lawyer who was continuing to negotiate on his behalf and correspond with my lawyer) and sworn an affidavit alleging his fears regarding the children's safety, there is no mention of that issue in that message, and he still suggests shared custody. . . .

105. The Applicant is a lawyer, and understands Court proceedings very well. Despite this, he has not been forthcoming with the court and did not disclose all relevant information. . . .

124. It is hateful and wrong for the Applicant to question whether Greg is being abused by me or my mother. He knows well there is no foundation for these lies. . . .

∘ ∘ ∘

Two days after he read Rochelle's affidavit, Stan served and filed an affidavit in response, claiming that "most hurtful of all is Rochelle's allegation that my proceeding to the court on an ex-parte basis was part of some master plan I had masterminded over a period of time, in an effort to secure an advantageous position in this litigation. Nothing could be further from the truth. I specifically deny Rochelle's allegation in this respect. . . ."

∘ ∘ ∘

By October 2004, Gil's wife Susan had conquered cancer. The aggressive strain of breast cancer was completely gone. She was taking new medications, including an "aromatase inhibitor," that would (according to genetic testing) reduce the odds of the cancer coming back to less than 8%.

Susan wrote in September in their family temple's e-newsletter that "Research into breast cancer has saved my life and continues to preserve it. Now I want to help fund it. I, together with my son Saul and my husband Gil, will be participating in the Run for the Cure on October 3, 2004. Please support me by sponsoring this run."

o o o

Also at around this time, according to allegations made by the OSC in late 2010, another top Bay Street lawyer was stealing a fortune through inside trading. Mitchell P. Finkelstein was a tall, beefy jock. He went to the University of Western Ontario at the same time Gil did, then the University of Ottawa law school. Finkelstein went on to become a well-known partner at the firm of Davies Ward Phillips & Vineberg and (according to the OSC) a crook.

From November 2004 to May 2007, he allegedly passed tips on upcoming corporate deals to Paul Azeff, a Montreal-based broker at CIBC who had been in Finkelstein's fraternity at Western. Like Gil, Finkelstein allegedly passed his best friend tips about his own clients, as well as snooping around the firm's computer network to steal information from clients of other lawyers. Finkelstein and his frat-buddy Azeff were accused of only four crimes—compared to Gil and Stan, they were dilettantes—but they still allegedly made over $3 million.

o o o

Stan and Rochelle's unpleasant family court battle dragged on for a long time, with many depressing details. A few points stand out.

Neither Stan nor Rochelle ever informed the court that they had both been charged with firearms offences related to the handgun that police officers had seized from their bedroom. Both of them deceived the court on that point.

Whenever it was Stan's time to leave the matrimonial home, so that Rochelle could move back in for another "shift" with the kids, Stan would videotape both Greg and Grace. In his written "Transition Reports" (he was not allowed to communicate with her otherwise, except in an emergency), Stan would mention his videotaping to

Rochelle and explain that it was done to "protect myself from false accusations."

These reports also told Rochelle that she was now responsible for her own investments. Stan advised her to "call TD Brokerage and remove me from having trading authority on the account [so that you] can begin managing it on your own." In that message, Stan boasted that, thanks to his investment skills, Rochelle "should end up with about $17,000 in your RRSP [Registered Retirement Savings Plan] from the six or so thousand that you started with about a year ago when I started managing it."

Another note Stan left for her promised that "the house is as you left it and there are no devices of any kind of mine to 'spy' or listen to you (I understand that one of the side-effects of that anti-depressant you were or are taking is paranoia). . . ."

One of Stan's "Transition Reports" would plead this:

> It is unfortunate that you chose not to share Halloween with us. I believe I also have Christmas Eve and Christmas. Your irrational stubbornness . . . is only hurting your children and yourself. Change your ways before all that you have left of their early years is anger and regrets. What do you want? Why? At what cost to your children and their father? Is what you want *over what I offered* worth the bitterness and harm you are creating? Why is shared custody not appropriate?

After learning that Rochelle had signed an agreement of purchase and sale for the house (which was in her name, though Stan as her husband had a legal right to block the sale), he left a rambling message on her answering machine at 8:11 p.m.:

> My God, do you know that you are going to get sued because you can't close without [my consent]? Why would you do that? I have always looked out for you. Now you do stuff to fuck me over. They will sue you! I don't know if you got any legal advice that day; if you did, you could sue your lawyer. Call me back, tonight.

I only look out for you. I am not trying to fuck you, you know. Call me tonight. Let's work it out. This is a big fuck-up! I am going to win [in court], and you're going to lose. No offence, but you will lose. I am telling you quite honestly, I have already discussed it with my lawyer. Ahh, you're shit out of luck. Stop listening to your mother. She does not give good financial advice for herself—look at her debts, look at her line of credit, look at her mutual funds. Call me, it's up to you. I still care for you. Bye.

At 8:25 p.m. (14 minutes later), Stan phoned back, leaving another message:

Ahh, you know I was looking through my file here. For you to go ahead and [list the house for sale] is so incredibly foolish! I'm trying to save your ass, a couple hundred grand. . . . You can't save your ass on this one without talking to me. So talk to me, and I will help you save your ass. We will do this together. You're acting like I was beating and cheating on you. That is how insane you are because you are under [your mother's] nutty spell. Smarten the hell up. We can find a better house or whatever. . . . [I] might sue your mother for good measure, just for fun. Anyway, ha, ha, ha. [Pause.] Apparently, you signed it. My God. Anyway, I'll be here at home. Call me. I'll do what I can think of. Bye.

Another "Transition Report" stated this:

If you are not going to contact me after reading that "Dr. Phil" article I gave you and after your butt being on the line with a sale of the matrimonial home without consent, well, I guess you are just not going to talk to me anymore no matter what. It is very sad that you have adopted the bitterness of your mother's failed marriage and transferred all that hate and bile to me. I may not have been a great husband (although I never quit trying and certainly never cheated, drank, was absent or violent), but I was always someone who greatly loved, cared [for] and protected you and is certainly one of the best fathers around. . . .

A report on November 15, 2004, had a $100 bill stapled to it, along with some advice: "Use the attached $100 to take Greg, Grace, and whomever you are with to dinner. . . . You know that an equal split [of property, including the matrimonial home] is currently acceptable to me and, as such, you control what happens next."

(That happened to be the same day that SEC filed a civil lawsuit against Stan's hero, Conrad Black.)

∘ ∘ ∘

Stan's mind games and legal tricks were successful; such tactics usually were successful in Ontario's dysfunctional, unjust family court. Stan wore Rochelle's resistance down. He got all he wanted.

On January 9, 2005, Stan and Rochelle (in the presence of their lawyers) signed a separation agreement.

Stan got joint custody. The children would live with him four days a week (Saturday to Wednesday) and with Rochelle three days a week (Wednesday to Saturday).

In the future, Stan and Rochelle would have to sit down together and jointly agree on decisions regarding the children's education, religious activities, and health care. Stan had veto power over everything. He had won.

Was Rochelle happy about Stan's continued control over her children and, to some degree, herself? Why did she agree to this instead of fighting for full custody?

Stan was to pay Rochelle $3,000 a month in spousal support for a year, then $2,000 a month for a year, then $1,000 a month for a year. He was to pay $1,500 a month in child support. He was to pay all daycare costs. He was to list his wife as a $200,000 beneficiary on his life insurance plan, with $1.3 million to go to the children. Rochelle got to keep her 2002 Highlander SUV and her own RRSP and bank and brokerage accounts. From the sale of the matrimonial home, Rochelle would get a cheque for $403,000.

She put $324,000 of this money into an E*Trade online trading account controlled by Stan. He could not take her money out, but he could buy or sell stocks without restriction. He would invest his soon-to-be-ex-wife's money very successfully and very profitably — thanks to Gil's continuing tips.

As well, Rochelle continued to have Stan fill in her income tax returns every year. She did not like doing financial paperwork.

At around this time, Stan started managing his sister and brother-in-law's investment money, which they had earned at their dairy farm. Helena and Philip Zahir's investments with Stan also enjoyed an unusually high rate of return.

Stan's usual commission was 20% — usually paid with a cheque made out to both Punta del Diamante and Stan personally; he did not accept any payment from his sister or his parents.

At first, Stan didn't want to accept a commission from his friend from high school and York University, Jimmy DiSantis,* who was a manager of a small Toronto venture capital firm. Stan said he was happy to do DiSantis a favour by increasing the initial $80,000 (in three separate E*Trade accounts) belonging to DiSantis and his wife (a Canadian Imperial Bank of Commerce employee). But DiSantis kept insisting that Stan take payment for his excellent investment results. Stan finally said, "Well, do something for my kids." DiSantis thought that was a good idea. Stan explained how much the fee would have been for his services, then said, "Give it to my kids." DiSantis did, the $17,000 in proceeds of crime going into a Registered Education Savings Plan for Greg and Grace.

DiSantis would later say,

I had no reason to be concerned as to how Stan was so successful because Stan spoke of all the research he did. He would put in emails, "Read this, read this," research, whether it was gold stocks or whatever kind of industry. Charts. As far as I knew, Stan was doing a lot of work behind the scenes to understand the markets and execute based on that knowledge. . . . I knew that Stan looked at industry publications because every once in a while Stan would flip a relevant article to me. There was never any connection between the articles given to me and the trades that Stan would make in my account. Having said that, there may have been a time that I cannot specifically recall that the article and a trade were connected. I didn't really read the material I was given.

19 | FRAUD ON THE MARKET;
OR, CELEBRATE WITH US!

Grant Vingoe left Dorsey & Whitney to start his own practice. Gil was now the most senior lawyer at the Toronto office.

Vingoe had planned to take his clients (most of whom were mining companies) with him. But Gil, who held a grudge against Vingoe for supposedly interfering in his quest for partnership, played a trick of his own called "poaching." As soon as Gil heard that Vingoe was planning to leave the firm, he contacted all of Vingoe's clients (including Goldcorp and IAMGOLD) and told them that he would be representing them in the future. As a result, many of these mining companies did not move to Vingoe's new firm, as Vingoe had expected, and stayed with Dorsey & Whitney and Gil. Soon Gil was billing these clients (and new ones he attracted) up to $6 million a year in total. He soon had many top gold companies as his clients — 80% of his clients were miners — and he was recognized as a rainmaker.

One of Gil's clients was the American Stock Exchange — AMEX — which also happened to be where Stan made many of his illegal trades.

In May 2005 — shortly after his 35th birthday — Gil was made a "non-equity special partner." That meant he could call himself a partner of the firm but wouldn't share in its profits. That did not mollify Gil. He remained disgruntled and kept on doing things that the Dorsey & Whitney *Professional Responsibility Manual* made it clear he was not supposed to do.

(Also in May 2005, Stan's hero, Conrad Black, would be videotaped removing stuff from his office in defiance of a U.S. court order — a moronic act that would lead to later "obstruction of justice" charges against Black.)

Between the early summer and the late fall of 2005, there were over 300 calls made between Gil's Dorsey & Whitney office and Stan's BlackBerry. Most of the calls were dialled by Stan, and most were on weekdays.

Unlike during the 1994–99 phase of insider trading, now they did not bother with pay-phones or codes. They were both confident of avoiding detection. They likely felt safer doing securities fraud in Canada than in the United States since the stock market regulators in Canada (such as the Ontario Securities Commission) were often criticized as ineffectual, underfunded, and generally wimpy. The U.S. Securities Enforcement Commission inspired more respect and fear (though, surely, Gil and Stan realized that, because many of their trades were on the New York Stock Exchange or the American Stock Exchange or NASDAQ, the SEC could still reach north across the border after them).

During one of these calls, Gil tipped Stan that one of his clients, Yamana Gold, was planning to buy back some of its own warrants, in a complex and odd transaction. When the warrant buy-back was announced on June 17, Stan sold the shares he had bought in his parents' trading account (they did not own a computer, leaving everything up to their son) for a small profit.

Gil worked on some deals without tipping Stan, such as when he worked with Dorsey & Whitney's tax expert Gabe Gartner to advise Southern Platinum during its takeover by Lonmin.

On September 19, Starpoint Energy Trust and Acclaim Energy Trust announced their merger. Gil had tipped Stan about this complicated, slow-moving deal a long time earlier. Gil had originally learned about it from a Dorsey & Whitney partner when Gil was in New York;

the partner, who had joined the firm just a week earlier, was bragging at lunch about the $12-billion deal. When Gil phoned Stan to ask "What's going on?" with the announcement and the current price of the stock, Stan and Rochelle were in the middle of a session with a marriage counsellor.

Gil's wife Susan had immersed herself in the effort to raise money for and awareness of breast cancer. In October, she and another breast cancer survivor held a media event in Toronto. To raise money for research, they were selling "thingamaboobs"—keychains made of clear and pink beads of escalating sizes, intended to show women the different sizes of lumps that could be detected through breast screening. Susan and her friend were photographed by the media, each holding up a thingamaboob for the camera. Susan herself bought 50 of the five-dollar keychains to give out at Christmas. She said, "I immediately liked it. I immediately formed the idea of giving it to everyone I know. It's a sweet little thing, pretty and stylish. It's a great reminder to not only rely on one method of detection, in a kind of cute way."

o o o

Later that October Gil spoke at a conference organized by the International Association of Young Lawyers called International Finance Forum 2005: Business Trusts and Similar Financing Structures. It was at the old, classy Royal York Hotel. This seems to be the first time that Gil ever lectured to other lawyers. The organizing committee consisted of Ilana Singer, a lawyer for the Ontario Securities Commission; Brigida Colangelo, a prosecutor for the Ministry of the Attorney General; and six Bay Street lawyers—including Gil.

One participant at the conference was U.S. lawyer Mark Danzi, of the firm Carlton Fields. (We will encounter that law firm again later.) Danzi spoke about "Rationales for Prohibitions on Insider Trading" and "Four Basic Regimes Regulating Insider Trading."

Paul D. Hayward of the Ontario Securities Commission also spoke to the attendees, including Gil, about "Issues Relating to the Prohibition on (Unlawful) Insider Trading." John Humphreys, also of the OSC, spoke on "Issues Relating to Money Laundering and Securities Violations."

A lawyer from France, Silvestre de Marsea, lectured on "The Financial Action Task Force on Money Laundering."

The final speaker — the climax of the event — was Gil I. Cornblum of Dorsey & Whitney. He spoke on "Business Trusts in the United States." After his speech, the lawyers quenched their thirst at "Lunch at Labatt Brewing Company." (That subsidiary of InBev was sponsoring the corporate law conference.)

∘ ∘ ∘

On November 15, Stan's political soulmate Conrad Black was charged in the United States with criminal fraud and obstruction of justice. Black's sidekick David Radler was charged with fraud too — and would cut a deal with authorities to inform on Black to save his own skin.

∘ ∘ ∘

Also on November 15, a staffer working in the office of U.S. Republican Senate Majority Leader Bill Frist tipped stock traders that Frist was about to announce a government fund to settle asbestos lawsuits. In the heavy market trading on that day, the share price of asbestos companies jumped sharply upward. When Frist's announcement was made the next day, big profits were reaped by the Republican-linked tippees.

Frist was not the first and would not be the last Republican politician linked to insider trading — in 1999 and 2000, for example, an employee of House Republican Leader Tom Delay, Tony Rudy, used inside information to profit from about 500 stock trades. In 2006, Rudy would plead guilty to a corruption conspiracy.

At the time of writing, some conservative critics are claiming that abuse of inside information in Washington is as prevalent under the Obama administration as it had been under the Bush administration. Two Democrat senators are now trying to pass the "Stop Trading on Congressional Knowledge Bill" to end this sleazy racket.

∘ ∘ ∘

When not battling with Rochelle or conspiring with Gil, Stan had a lot of free time. Like many of his generation, he became an Internet addict.

He began to spend large amounts of time and energy on various websites. His first online passion was connected to his work. He joined a Yahoo! chat-board devoted to "day traders"—folks who do their own trades online, frequently moving their money from one stock to another. On chat-boards, they would exchange gossip, theories, and boasts of their skill and success.

Stan—now known as kingcityguru—soon got a bad reputation among other day traders on the chat-board, many of whom accused him of "pumping and dumping." This is when you buy shares in company X and then go around convincing everybody you know that company X is great and that they should buy shares in company X too. That is "pumping." If enough folks believe you, the price of company X's shares will go up—and then you can quickly sell, or "dump," your shares for a profit.

One of the Yahoo! chatters published evidence that Stan had pumped and dumped, but it is too technical and complicated for a non-day trader to understand. So let me quote a few of the (oddly nicknamed) day traders. The conversation is jumpy and hard to follow because some parts could not be retrieved from Yahoo!, but the fragmented quotations give a general impression of Stan's reputation among online day traders.

> Copperisnot / RE: buffetology since you asked—Here are the references to the posts and samples of them and the stock price which clearly show kingcityguru was both pumping and spreading rumours of a takeover while selling at the same time. . . .
>
> Buffetology / RE: If I were kingcity—I'd be careful. I agree, he was pumping and dumping, at least so it seems.
>
> Copperisnot / RE: If I were kingcity—. . . No matter how you look at it, that guy's a liar.
>
> Buffetology / RE: If I were kingcity—If he were indeed pumping and dumping, it certainly can be a crime. It is illegal to attempt to influence the stock price. The SEC has previously taken the stance that pumping and dumping on these very stock boards is a crime, at least charges have been filed in some of the

worst cases. It very well may be that kingcity doesn't rise to that level, I don't know. I would still be careful if I were him.

Stan logged on to the Yahoo! chat-board to defend himself.

Kingcityguru / RE: If I were kingcity — What was my offence: I bought in at just under $42, promoted PCU's great story (less than zero cost producer, high yield, increasing production and ore grade, unhedged) everywhere I could and encouraged associates and friends to buy in. It spikes up one day giving me almost a $19 profit (with dividend) on an extremely, extremely large position without the risk of a secondary wiping it out. I tell my associates that I am out and after they are out that day and the next, I disappear. So what?

    Copperisnot / RE: If I were copperisnot — Kingcity, you have no defence, do you. I answer buffetology's request for proof of your pump and dump with your own words and your response, as usual, is to again attack me with a series of lies. For the benefit of anyone new here who might not realize what you are, here are my posts and the dates, demonstrating again your dishonesty. . . .

    Copperisnot / RE: kingcityguru — give up loser / . . . Some of us here seek knowledge, we want to know what's going on in the real world. I align myself with those people. You are not one of them. . . . STOP LYING about me!!!

    Qaydan / RE: kingcityguru — give up loser — Didn't kingcity bail out about 12 dollars ago? After telling about the glories of the stock, he bailed and called people who believed him suckers. That kingcity is back? Looks like the "suckers" got the last laugh now that [PCU shares] are over $60.

Later Stan would admit that he had pumped and dumped on Yahoo! Usually, he did not use his kingcityguru username for this, preferring to create, use, and then discard temporary usernames.

    In one case, Stan learned from Gil that a deal was possible between Wyman Gordon, a machine manufacturer represented by Dorsey &

Whitney, and General Electric. So Stan created a new Yahoo! username, "anhonestsecretary." He would log on to chat-boards with this alias and pretend to be a female secretary at GE. As anhonestsecretary, Stan would start rumours that GE was planning a deal with Wyman Gordon. These rumours made the stock price of Wyman Gordon move upward. Stan dumped all his shares in Wyman Gordon, then logged on to Yahoo! one last time as anhonestsecretary to tell the chat-board folks how he had tricked them. He mocked their gullibility, then abandoned anhonestsecretary forever.

Trading-related chat-boards were useful for another purpose. If Stan was asked by a broker (as he occasionally was) how he managed to make his successful stock picks, he could say that he had come across a rumour on some chat-board that the stock was a good buy. There were so many rumours flying around the Internet that it was easy to find something there to justify almost any transaction.

o o o

Stan used a tip from his law school buddy to profit from the December 5 announcement that Virginia Gold Mines was to be acquired by Goldcorp. (Gil had learned about this deal from Goldcorp's "Canadian counsel.")

The cover of the January 2006 edition of *Martha Stewart Living* magazine shows the blonde convict and homemaking guru holding a birthday cake with candles shaped like a 1 and a 5 on top. Her grinning, airbrushed mug does not show even a sprinkling of remorse. The headlines on the magazine cover were "Sharing the Good Things for 15 Years" and "Celebrate with Us!"

At the start of 2006, Stan and Gil began to be careful again about their communications. There were no phone calls at all between Gil's office and Stan's cell phone from January 2006 until the spring of 2008. However, there were many calls to Stan's cell phone from pay-phones near Gil's office or at the nearby Royal York Hotel or Union Station or at the St. Clair subway station, near Gil's home, or (on weekends) at Gil's gym, also near his home. Gil avoided using the pay-phones at BCE Place, saying, "I never call from my own tower." He knew that it would look strange if someone who knew that Gil owned a BlackBerry saw him at a pay-phone. Using pay-phones, Gil and Stan continued to speak on average once a day.

Some of the calls from Gil to Stan were made before the stock market opened, with Gil informing Stan that the announcement would be coming that day. In other calls, Gil would ask Stan how much money they had made on a particular trade. But the main purpose of the calls was social. They also had weekly lunch dates on Thursdays.

When Stan showed up at Gil's office (always alone) before they went out for lunch, Stan would often chat with Basil Parsnip,* the youthful office manager who helped the secretary with reception duties. Stan usually wore a leather jacket and blue jeans, black leather shoes, never a suit or tie. He carried a BlackBerry. Stan was originally introduced to Parsnip by Gil as Stan. After a while, Gil started referring to Stan as Joseph, which confused Parsnip until Gil explained the deal with Stan's names. When Stan arrived and Parsnip was at the reception desk, sometimes Parsnip would contact Gil on the intercom to ask him to come out of his office; at other times, Parsnip would escort Stan to Gil's room at the back. On the way, Parsnip and Stan often had conversations that Parsnip would later call "jovial" and "cordial" and from which he gathered that Stan and Gil were childhood friends. As Parsnip and Stan had both attended film school in the past, they often discussed the art of cinema. Stan and Gil would then spend some time together alone in Gil's office before leaving for lunch. Parsnip knew that they liked to eat at Taka Sushi on Front Street and, especially, the Swiss Chalet on King Street. (Gil loved the Swiss Chalet dipping sauce so much that he would sometimes order four or five extra bowls of the salty-sweet bird juice.)

Parsnip never asked Stan what he did for a living, and Stan never offered the information; Parsnip was sometimes curious but never felt bold enough to ask. All that he would later remember of Gil and Stan's conversations was that

it seemed pretty jovial, nothing out of the ordinary in terms of two friends who meet to shoot the shit, so to speak. It didn't ever seem business-oriented to me. . . . The amount of time Stan would spend visiting him varied. It depended on what Gil was doing at the time. Sometimes Gil would be wrapping up some work or what have you, and sometimes they would be last-minute, you know, five minutes before they went for lunch and sometimes might be there [in Gil's office] for half an hour or more.

o o o

Gil and Stan realized that most people who traded on inside information did so as a "one-off," meaning that they did it once and then never again. People in that position would try to make the maximum amount of money from the deal. The most efficient way to do that was to buy options instead of common shares. So, to throw off suspicion, Stan rarely bought options during their second phase of insider trading.

Another camouflage technique was to buy the shares in small amounts over a period of time.

A more complicated way to conceal illegal trades was as follows. Say that Stan was told by Gil that mining company X had just found a lot of gold at site A. Stan would do some research to find out which other mining companies were working near site A. If mining companies Y and Z were also operating near site A, then Stan would buy shares in them too. When X announced its big find of gold, and its shares shot up, Stan could (if questioned) explain that he had not picked X because of inside information but because he believed in site A. As well, the proximity of Y and Z to site A would usually mean that the share values of Y and Z followed those of X up.

o o o

In January, the gun charges against Rochelle were dropped. Stan's gun charges were set for trial.

Also in the first month of 2006, Gil finally became a full, "equity" partner at Dorsey & Whitney (though the Toronto office was still, technically, managed by Chris Barry in Seattle). So now Gil had no reason to be disgruntled about not being made a partner.

But his tipping did not stop. Gil was too deep in by this time; he didn't know how to stop.

A month after Gil became an equity partner, Stan used information from Dorsey & Whitney to profit from a media release titled "Yamana Gold Completes Equity Financing."

In February, Gil returned to Osgoode Hall Law School for a professional development program titled U.S. Securities Law: What Canadian Practitioners Need to Know. Once he had studied at Osgoode; now he taught there (though to lawyers, not law students).

His "Faculty Biography" went thus:

Gil Cornblum is a Partner in Dorsey & Whitney's Securities practice group. He is a graduate of Osgoode Hall Law School and was called to the Bars of Ontario and New York in 1996. He joined Dorsey in 2001. He has substantial experience in mergers and acquisitions, corporate governance, and general business counselling, public and private securities offerings, debt and lease financing, tender offers, proxy contests, contests for corporate control and shareholder disputes, new businesses formation and venture capital transactions. A major portion of Mr. Cornblum's practice involves advising Canadian and other non-U.S. clients in accessing the U.S. capital markets, cross-border mergers and acquisitions and investment transactions and U.S. securities law compliance.

Gil had a partner for his presentation, Carl J. Cummings of the U.S. megafirm Shearman & Sterling. The topic was "Continuous Reporting for Foreign Private Issuers." A portion of their lecture dealt with the concept of "Fraud on the Market."

Grant Vingoe co-chaired the event and spoke on "U.S. Securities Regulation: Overview and Comparison to Canadian Regime."

Two weeks after this conference, Stan used a tip from Gil to reap $125,591 on the Toronto Stock Exchange and the New York Stock Exchange when Yamana Gold announced that it would take over Desert Sun Mining (Gil's client).

Stan was also making money from the accounts he managed for several of his family and friends. His father, who did not own a computer, had five separate online trading accounts. At the desk of his home office, Stan kept everybody's passwords and account numbers on a piece of paper; the information was also stored in the web browser of his laptop. He handled his immediate family members' investments for free but collected 20% of the annual profits of each of the accounts belonging to four of his friends and distant relatives. He did not officially charge Rochelle, but he borrowed money from her after his Nova Gold disaster and never paid it back; he viewed this as a sort of fee. One of his in-laws, Achilles Zahir, paid him $8,000 in 2006 according to this arrangement and would pay him $29,000 the following year. Jimmy DiSantis, as described earlier, had paid $17,000 into an education fund for Stan's kids. Stan kept these commissions, and all of the others, a secret from his best friend.

20 | STAN IS BROUGHT TO JUSTICE

COURT FILE 05-00190

SUPERIOR COURT OF JUSTICE

HER MAJESTY THE QUEEN V. STANKO GRMOVSEK

PROCEEDINGS AT PLEA

BEFORE THE HONOURABLE MADAM JUSTICE M. FUERST

on March 9, 2006

AT NEWMARKET, ONTARIO

CHARGE: S. 86(1) C.C.—Careless storage of a firearm

o o o

The Crown prosecutor, John Pearson, began the court proceedings by standing behind his desk at the front of the courtroom and saying, "Good morning again, Your Honour. There was a matter that has resolved, and I didn't want counsel having to wait around. It will be a brief matter, and that's number 2 on our list."

The judge looking down from her dais onto the prosecution and defence desks was Michelle Fuerst, the Newmarket judge whom Stan had earlier tricked into giving him an order for temporary custody and exclusive possession of the matrimonial home. Fuerst's decision had been based on an obnoxious affidavit in which Stan had confessed to lying to police officers about the gun—the same gun involved in this criminal proceeding.

Stan's defence lawyer was Calvin Martin. He had been recommended to Stan by the National Firearms Association, the Canadian version of the National Rifle Association in the United States. Martin charged clients facing gun charges at a rate lower than normal to support the pro-gun movement. He charged Stan less than $5,000 in total.

In the body of the court, sitting on a long wooden bench to watch the proceedings, was Gil Cornblum.

Calvin said, "Yes, I appear for Mr. Grmovsek."

Stan was standing at the defence table beside his lawyer.

The judge said, "Could I just see the indictment, please?"

The court registrar (or clerk) said, "Absolutely," and handed the indictment to the judge.

JUDGE [to Stan]: I'm sorry. It is Mister . . . ?

DEFENCE LAWYER: Grmovsek.

JUDGE: Yes, and for him?

DEFENCE LAWYER: Calvin Martin.

JUDGE: All right. So the proposal is that there will be a plea to which count or counts?

THE CROWN: To count Number 3, Your Honour, then my friend and I have a joint position for the court's consideration.

JUDGE: All right. So count Number 3 is the unlawful storage?

THE CROWN: Yes.

JUDGE: Careless storage, if you like?

DEFENCE LAWYER: Careless storage, yes.

JUDGE: All right. So, Mr. Grmovsek?

STAN: Yes, Your Honour.

JUDGE: The Criminal Code requires me to ask you certain questions directly. Please tell me if you don't understand any of the questions. Do you understand that you have a right to plead not guilty and to have a trial?

STAN: I understand.

JUDGE: Do you understand that by pleading guilty you are giving up your right to a trial?

STAN: I do.

JUDGE: Are you pleading guilty of your own free will without pressure from anyone else and with the benefit of legal advice from your lawyer?

STAN: I am.

JUDGE: Do you understand that by entering this guilty plea you are admitting guilt to the essential elements of the offence of careless storage of a firearm and you are admitting that the Crown can prove those essential elements beyond a reasonable doubt?

STAN: I understand, and I am admitting.

JUDGE: Do you understand that I will listen to the submissions of Crown counsel and to your lawyer and to anything that you wish to say to me about sentence, but I must still sentence you as I see fit?

STAN: I understand.

JUDGE: Then shall we go ahead and arraign Mr. Grmovsek on count 3, please?

COURT REGISTRAR: Thank you, Your Honour.

JUDGE: And I'm not sure, do we need a re-election, then?

DEFENCE LAWYER: Yes.

THE CROWN: Yes.

DEFENCE LAWYER: We filled out the re-election and filed it.

JUDGE: Thank you.

COURT REGISTRAR: Mr. Martin, is that the accused Stanko Grmovsek standing beside you?

DEFENCE LAWYER: Yes.

COURT REGISTRAR: Stanko Grmovsek, you stand indicted by the name that Stanko Grmovsek is charged that on or about the 29th day of September, 2004, at the City of Vaughan in the Regional Municipality of York and elsewhere in the Province of Ontario, he did, without lawful excuse, store a firearm to wit: a 9-millimetre Bryco Jennings semi-automatic in a careless manner contrary to section 86(1) of the Criminal Code. You have given notice of your wish to re-elect the mode of our trial, you now have the option to do so. How do you wish to re-elect?

STAN: By the Judge alone.

COURT REGISTRAR: Thank you. Do you waive the re-reading of the indictment for the plea?

DEFENCE LAWYER: Yes, we do.

COURT REGISTRAR: Upon count 3 of the indictment how do you plead, guilty or not guilty?

STAN: I plead guilty.

COURT REGISTRAR: Harken to your plea, as the court hath recorded you plead guilty to count Number 3. Thank you, sir, you may be seated.

STAN: Thank you.

JUDGE: Mr. Pearson?

THE CROWN: Yes, thank you, Your Honour. Your Honour, the facts here are in respect to September 29th, 2004. Police attended a King residential address. It was in response to a dispute that the gentleman was having with his wife who he was in the process of separating with at the time. There were no allegations of assault. She had contacted 911 just as a result of a verbal argument that had ensued. So police attended and were aware, prior to their attending, that there was a firearm in the home. Upon attending, Mr. Grmovsek took the officers to where it was, which was in a locked drawer, I believe, in the bedroom. It was, as the court's been made aware, a semi-automatic handgun that was simply stored in the drawer. It was loaded with magazine, but there was no round chambered.

JUDGE: Sorry. It was stored in a drawer and did you tell me the drawer was locked?

THE CROWN: The drawer was locked, however, there was a magazine contained within the weapon. There were rounds in the magazine, but one was not chambered and, as a result, the careless storage of the firearm charge was laid and, of course, [the firearm] was seized by police.

JUDGE: Are those facts admitted as being substantially correct?

DEFENCE LAWYER: Yes, they are substantially correct.

JUDGE: All right. Then on those facts as admitted I find Mr. Grmovsek guilty on count 3.

THE CROWN: Your Honour, Mr. Grmovsek does not have a criminal record and, as I indicated, the position being put forward for the court's consideration is joint between my friend and I. We are going to ask that the court discharge Mr. Grmovsek conditionally and that he be placed on a 12-month period of probation. And aside from the statutory terms, I would just ask that the gentleman be prohibited from having a weapon as defined by the Criminal Code for the period of that probation that would be 12 months. There was no, as I indicated, no concern with respect to the dispute that had taken place between the gentleman and his wife at the time. So those are the only conditions that we are asking the court to consider.

JUDGE: All right. Now do I have to impose a reporting condition as soon as I impose any additional condition? I think I do.

THE CROWN: I think he has to report at least once, which would likely be today, and then thereafter as required. I don't know if he will be required to report after that, but he will have to report on the one occasion.

JUDGE: All right. And is there any need for a weapons prohibition order in this case? Is this one of those offences that invokes section 109?

THE CROWN: I'm sorry. I don't have my Code in front of me.

DEFENCE LAWYER: It's not mandatory.

JUDGE: That is what I am just checking. I wanted to make sure it is not mandatory.

THE CROWN: I don't believe it is.

DEFENCE LAWYER: It's not mandatory. Mr. Grmovsek has no interest in firearms anyway in the future, but, in any event, it's not mandatory.

JUDGE: All right. And Mr. Pearson, you see no reason to request it?

THE CROWN: Not outside of the probation period, Your Honour.

JUDGE: All right. Thank you.

THE CROWN: Thank you, Your Honour.

JUDGE: On behalf of Mr. Grmovsek?

DEFENCE LAWYER: I have listened to my friend's submissions and I agree with them and, just briefly, my client has never had a problem with the law. He has been a responsible citizen, had good employment.

JUDGE: What does he do for a living?

DEFENCE LAWYER [to Stan]: You are a computer programmer?

STAN: Your Honour, I am a consultant, assisting companies doing joint jurisdictional listings in the U.S. and Canada. I was a former lawyer, Your Honour.

DEFENCE LAWYER: You may still be one, I think.

JUDGE: All right.

DEFENCE LAWYER: So that's pretty well his life story, so far.

JUDGE: All right. Mr. Grmovsek, before I sentence you is there anything that you would like to say to me directly?

STAN: No, Your Honour, thank you.

JUDGE: Well, as I have heard, Mr. Grmovsek, you have not been in trouble before and you are otherwise, from what I have heard, a responsible member of the community. I am sure you appreciate now the seriousness of keeping a gun with ammunition in a residential location in the manner that you did and I am confident that you are not going to repeat that or any other behaviour that might bring you back before the court. So I accept the joint submission that has been put to me. I sentence you as follows. I impose a conditional discharge. You will be on probation for a period of 12 months. During that 12-month period you will be bound by the statutory conditions of probation which are that you keep the peace and be of good behaviour, appear before the court when required to do so, notify the court or the probation officer in advance of any change of name or address and promptly notify the court or the probation officer of any change of employment or occupation. In addition, I impose the following two conditions. First of all, you will report within two working days in person to a probation officer and thereafter be under the supervision of a probation officer and report as required by him or her. And secondly, you will not possess any weapon as that term is defined by the Criminal Code. Do you understand those conditions?

STAN: I do.

JUDGE: All right. And are you prepared to abide by them?

STAN: I will.

JUDGE: Thank you.

STAN: Thank you.

JUDGE: The other counts? [In addition to careless storage of a firearm (Criminal Code s. 86(1)), Stan and Rochelle had both been charged with possession of a firearm without a licence (Criminal Code s. 91(1)), possession of a firearm while knowing that he or she did not have a licence (Criminal Code s. 91(2)), and possession of a loaded restricted firearm without a licence or authorization (Criminal Code s. 95(a)). During the pre-plea negotiations, the Crown agreed to drop these charges, despite the strong evidence against Stan. He was allowed to pick a single charge he would be convicted on; he chose "careless storage" because it sounded the least serious.]

THE CROWN: If they could be marked withdrawn, please, Your Honour. Thank you.

JUDGE: They will be marked as withdrawn at the request of the Crown.

COURT REGISTRAR: Can I please confirm your address?

STAN: 180 Blue Willow Drive.

COURT REGISTRAR: In what Town or City?

STAN: Woodbridge. It would be unit 62, the address.

COURT REGISTRAR: Thank you. Do you know the postal code?

STAN: L4L 9C9.

COURT REGISTRAR: L4L 9C9. Would you like to address the victim fine surcharge, Your Honour?

JUDGE: All right. What do either of you say about the victim fine surcharge?

DEFENCE LAWYER: I'm in my friend's hands.

THE CROWN: The Crown doesn't have any difficulty with the court waiving that, Your Honour.

JUDGE: All right. Are you content that I waive that, then, on behalf of your client?

DEFENCE LAWYER: I'm content, yes.

JUDGE: All right. The victim fine surcharge will be waived in the circumstances.

COURT REGISTRAR: Thank you.

JUDGE: I have endorsed the indictment that there was a plea to count 3 and a finding of guilt. That Mr. Grmovsek has been sentenced to a conditional discharge with probation for 12 months on conditions read into the record. The victim fine surcharge is waived and all other counts are withdrawn at the request of the Crown.

THE CROWN: Thank you, Your Honour.

DEFENCE LAWYER: Thank you, Your Honour.

JUDGE: Thank you. All right. I think the condition was not to possess any weapons as defined by the Criminal Code?

THE CROWN: Yes, Your Honour.

JUDGE: It says "firearms."

COURT REGISTRAR: Sorry.

JUDGE: All right. So why do I not just change that and initial it.

The case was over. Yet again Stan had successfully manipulated Madam Justice M. Fuerst. His claim that his "good employment" consisted of "assisting companies doing joint jurisdictional listings in the U.S. and Canada" could have been easily disproved, but nobody bothered. His false claim to be a "former lawyer" could have been easily disproved by checking the website of the Law Society of Upper Canada. The judge could have ordered a pre-sentencing report, which would have given her an idea of the sort of man she was sentencing—but she did not.

The prosecutor, John Pearson, also acted questionably in offering to waive the "victim fine surcharge"—a small sum of money that convicted criminals in Ontario were supposed to pay to contribute to a fund to support victims of crime. According to Ontario law, all criminals were supposed to pay it on conviction unless there was a good reason (usually poverty) why it should be waived. Stan's lawyer did not ask for the fine to be waived and offered no reason why it should be waived. Stan's Notice of Assessment for Revenue Canada put his net income for 2006 at $354,265. His net income for 2007 would be assessed by the tax-man at $640,096. The prosecutor did not know that Stan was a multi-millionaire, but it was obvious from his address, education, and purported profession that he was well-off. So why gratuitously give Stan a break on the fine? Just to be nice?

Gil and Stan walked out of the Newmarket courtroom together, the slap barely tingling on Stan's wrist.

Gil said with contempt, "What a waste of time."

Stan agreed, mocking the prosecutor for letting him pick which one charge he would be convicted on and which three charges would be dropped.

This incident increased their disrespect for the justice system and encouraged them to continue with more and more crime.

o o o

Six days after Stan pled guilty to the firearms charge, he used a tip from Gil to hit the stock market jackpot after the announcement that Eramet SA was to take over Weda Bay. Gil had learned about the deal from John Turner, a mining lawyer at a firm called Faskens Martineau—Turner was described by the *National Post* as "one of the best dirt lawyers in Canada, if not the world." Turner had called Gil at home on a weekend to ask him a question about U.S. law.

Shortly after that, Stan opened an account with the investment advisers Canaccord Capital. The form asked him for the name of the person who had referred him to Canaccord Capital. Stan wrote "Gil Cornblum" on the form.

On May 29, 2006, Gil's client Yamana Gold announced that it was planning a takeover of Mexgold Resources. Stan sold his previously bought shares and stashed away yet more unearned money.

Stan and Rochelle's divorce was official on Bastille Day, July 14.

In the same month, Gil and Susan started attending Toronto's Holy Blossom Temple, bringing little Saul to their new place of worship.

On August 16, after the insatiable Yamana Gold announced yet another planned takeover, this time of Viceroy Exploration, Stan scored another jackpot.

Gil was counsel to Addax Petroleum (along with Dorsey & Whitney's Jonathan Van Horn and Shona Smith) on another deal that was announced on the same day — "Addax Petroleum Closes $402M Public Offering." Gil and Stan did not take advantage of inside information regarding this deal.

On August 24, 25, 28, 29 (twice), and 30 (twice), Stan bought shares in Glamis Gold, both in his own trading accounts (17,000 shares) and in those of his sister and brother-in-law (10,000 shares).

On August 31, Goldcorp (Gil's client) announced that it planned to merge with Glamis Gold. In the previous few months, Goldcorp had insatiably taken over Virginia Gold Mines and much of Placer Dome. (Ian Tefler, Goldcorp's CEO, had held information about the Placer Dome takeover so tightly that Gil, Goldcorp's main lawyer, had not heard about it until afterward. John Fraleigh, a Bay Street investor, would later be charged with making $5 million through insider trading on this deal. After that, Stan wrote, "[Gil and I] had a laugh at Fraleigh being such a pig for buying all those options on his inside information and for being lucky enough not to have bought [ourselves].") Soon Goldcorp would swallow Gold Eagle Mines too — and still be hungry for more. This buying spree, part of a consolidation of companies in the precious metals sector, was made possible by sky-high gold prices; gold's price bubble was linked to widespread pessimism about the economic future, for many people bought large amounts of useless gold because they imagined that it would stay valuable forever. (At the time of writing, this gold bubble had yet to pop.)

The Goldcorp president and CEO said, "The combination of Goldcorp and Glamis will create a world class low-cost producer in the Americas with industry-leading growth from an exciting portfolio of development projects."

However, Goldcorp's founder and largest shareholder, Rob McEwen, denounced the deal, claiming that it would harm Goldcorp's shareholders, who were denied a chance to vote on the deal. "This deal is a bad and expensive joke," he said. "It amounts to a very expensive retirement plan for Ian Tefler."

Goldcorp shareholders challenged the deal in the Ontario courts, but the judge sided with Goldcorp, arguing that allowing shareholders to vote on the deal would create "considerable uncertainty."

After the announcement, Stan sold 3,000 shares, for a profit of $25,600. He held on to the remaining shares, which in November would be converted into Goldcorp shares. Then, gradually over the following months, he would sell the converted Goldcorp shares. Altogether on this deal, Stan reaped $158,002 in profits for himself and his sister and brother-in-law.

Having absorbed Glamis, Goldcorp was the third largest gold-mining company in the world (after Barrick Gold and Newmont Mining), reaping about a billion dollars a year in profit. It had mines in Canada, the United States, Mexico, Central America, South America, and Australia. It pumped out 2.5 million ounces of gold a year.

In Honduras, Goldcorp ran the San Martin mine. This was an "open pit mine" where, after rock had been blasted out of the earth and ground into ore by giant machines, sodium- and cyanide-laced water was poured over piles of raw ore to leach out the gold particles. Mercury and lead and arsenic were by-products of this process. The San Martin mine was opposed by local residents, who claimed that mining chemicals were affecting their health. They also raised concerns about environmental harm. An independent human rights report recommended that Goldcorp should stop exploration and expansion at the mine until further consultations were held and that Goldcorp should seek community consent before digging new mines.

When the shareholders of Goldcorp were presented with a resolution that Goldcorp should consult with native groups and seek the consent of local communities before starting new mines, 90% of Goldcorp's shareholders voted no despite the impassioned pleas of a delegation of Honduran community leaders. The actions of Goldcorp should not be blamed solely on its professional managers. Shareholders are morally responsible for the actions of the companies they own.

Shareholders should also be legally responsible for the debts of a corporation. In North America, corporations were largely invented by law in the 1800s to help investors avoid risk, which is not a goal to be blindly encouraged today, at least not in regard to environmental issues. It seems more fair to hold that investors who take profits from a business when the business is going well should also bear some of the costs if the same business is unable to honour its legitimate debts. For example, if a corporation valued at $1 billion carelessly causes $2.5 billion in harm to innocent parties — say by a toxic leak in a populated area, with survivors needing costly medical care for the rest of their lives — who should pay the $1.5 billion in legitimate damages that cannot be covered by selling the corporation's property? It is better for shareholders to return profits than to leave innocent victims unable to pay for care.

Anyway, in early September 2006, Stan filled in a new BMO Nesbitt Burns client account agreement with some updates to his information. Having used kingcityguru@aol.com and kingcityguru@yahoo.com on previous forms, he had by now switched to yet another email address — kingcityguru@hotmail.com.

Stan listed his employer as Punta del Diamante, S.A. He claimed to have worked for this non-existent organization for nine years. It did not matter what Stan filled in on these various forms for various financial institutions — nobody ever seemed to check if his statements were true, nobody seemed to care if he lied or not. As long as he brought in lots of money, which he did, he was free to write whatever he wanted on these forms. As he would later put it, "This 'know your client' shit, nobody gives a fuck."

On September 7, 8, 9, and 13, Stan bought common shares in Cambior — 50,200 in total.

On September 14, Gil's loudly named client IAMGOLD announced plans to merge with Cambior Inc. in a $3 billion (U.S.) transaction. (IAMGOLD was Gil's favourite client, Gil would tell Stan.) The CEO of IAMGOLD, Joe Conway, who worked closely with Gil, would later describe this as one of the key transactions of his career; Joe would call the Cambior takeover "challenging" but "with a great result," creating "one of the leading companies in our sector." It made IAMGOLD the tenth largest gold producer in the world.

IAMGOLD operated, among other mines, the Tarkwa Mine in Ghana, West Africa. Due to tax breaks and other incentives, very little of the income generated by IAMGOLD in Ghana stayed in Ghana; no, it flowed across the ocean to the corporation's shareholders. Like Goldcorp's mines in Central America, this mine also used "cyanide heap leaching technology," poisoning the land and waters around it. IAMGOLD had similar mines in Mali and other places in West Africa.

Stan sold about 10,000 of the Cambior shares before the announcement.

At 9:35 a.m., Gil called Stan from a pay-phone at 25 King Street West to ask about the deal. "Have you seen the press release?"

Stan said, "Yes."

"What's the pre-market?" Gil asked. (The "pre-market" was a sort of stock market that operated when the main stock markets were still closed for the night. Pre-market stock prices usually matched regular market prices.)

Stan told him the pre-market price.

Gil, pleased, said, "Okay, blow it out." (That meant "Sell it all.")

"Okay," Stan said. He sold the remaining 40,000 shares for a profit of $23,100.

Four days later Stan used non-public information provided by Gil on the Toronto Stock Exchange (TSX) and the New York Stock Exchange (NYSE) to reap big-time profits from Denison Mines' merger with International Uranium.

On December 5, inside information from Gil helped Stan to profit from the merger of Direct General (represented by Dorsey & Whitney but not Gil personally) with Fremont Partners and Texas Pacific Group.

The shares were bought and sold on NASDAQ. Gil had learned about the deal by snooping around Dorsey & Whitney's NetDocuments database, trying to see if Jonathan Van Horn was really too busy to help him.

Gil would later say that he got annoyed when he asked other Dorsey & Whitney lawyers for help and they said no. It made him want to get even. He did get even, again and again.

o o o

Stan would later write this:

> The last big deal for which I had inside information concerned Goldcorp, one of the largest gold mining companies in the world, selling off its billion-plus-dollar half-interest in another public company called Silver Wheaton. Two weeks before the transaction was announced I was advised by Goldcorp's legal counsel that Goldcorp was divesting itself of its Silver Wheaton shares in a "bought deal" to a group of underwriters for a near fifteen per cent discount to its then market price. . . . If I had immediately sold short shares in Silver Wheaton after being told of the deal I imagine I would have made [more than] a million. . . .
>
> I did not buy puts on or short the shares of Silver Wheaton because the stock was behaving in a way that screamed to anyone that cared to look that it was being affected by trades motivated by Goldcorp's divestiture.
>
> I was convinced that if I purchased puts or shorted the stock I would immediately be swept up in the dragnet of investigations that regulators would initiate after the deal was announced. . . .

Despite the tens of millions of dollars of trades that "coincidentally" mirrored the status of the private negotiations between Goldcorp and the underwriters, no investigation was ever launched by either Canadian or American regulators.

○ ○ ○

The U.S. housing bubble (caused by Alan Greenspan, former federal reserve chairman and follower of Ayn Rand) did not, to almost all outsiders, seem to be a bubble. Almost everybody behaved as if house prices would go up for eternity.

Angelo R. Mozilo—the boss of the largest mortgage lender in the United States, Countrywide Financial—was a distinguished-looking gentleman with silver hair and several gold-painted Rolls Royces. Mozilo went around telling clients and journalists, "Over the entire history of this country, housing prices have never gone down nationally. . . . [A]ny homeownership over the 10 years has proved to be the best investment that you could ever make. Over any 10-year period, housing prices go up. . . . This is America. People want to own homes." Mozilo made countless statements along these lines in the early and middle years of the decade.

However, at the same time that he was making these statements to gullible clients and gullible journalists, Mozilo was sending a very different message to his co-workers. An email in early 2006 stated, ". . . it is just a matter of time that we will be faced with much higher resets and therefore much higher delinquencies. . . . In all my years in the business, I have never seen a more toxic product. With real estate prices coming down . . . the product will become increasingly worse." Another Mozilo email from the summer of 2006 stated that "borrowers are going to experience a payment shock which is going to be difficult if not impossible for them to manage." In September 2006, he emailed to a co-conspirator that "[t]he bottom line is that we are flying blind on how these loans will perform in a stressed environment of higher unemployment, reduced values and slowing home sales."

The day after he wrote the "flying blind" email, Mozilo started dumping his own shares in Countrywide Financial. Despite the rosy predictions still falling from his lips, he knew how bad the housing market was about to get. On the basis of his inside information about the upcoming mortage crisis, Mozilo started selling his Countrywide

Financial shares. From May 2005 to October 2007, he dumped more than 5 million of them, for a profit of $260 million.

A year later, when the facts about the bad mortgages leaked out, Countrywide Financial would quickly go broke, and its shares would collapse in price. The company would be taken over at a bargain price by Bank of America. Almost all of Countrywide's shareholders would suffer big losses—except, of course, for Angelo R. Mozilo, who had crawled out from the sinking corporation in time.

In June 2009, *Time* magazine would publish the names of the "25 people to blame for the financial crisis." Mozilo's name was at the top of the list.

In late 2010, Mozilo would be charged by the SEC for insider trading regarding his Countrywide stock dumping, eventually being fined $67.5 million—a small fraction of the $260 million reaped by this liar.

o o o

In 2006, former Osgoode Hall Law School dean and respected legal scholar Marilyn Pilkington prepared a report for the Canadian Investment Dealers' Association on how to modernize securities laws, declaring that "It is widely perceived that securities enforcement processes in Canada are inadequate."

In 2007, 33 of 52 large Canadian mergers would show signs of aberrant trading just before the mergers were publicly announced—63%. (In the United States, the rate would be only 41%.) On average, the SEC would prosecute 20 times more insider-trading cases than the OSC, with a higher conviction rate and penalties 17 times bigger—and at a proportionately smaller cost to the taxpayer.

This softness on insider trading was one cause of the "Canadian discount"—the fact that companies would have to sell more securities in Canadian markets to raise the same amount of money as a stock seller would in the United States. The near ubiquity of insider trading in Canada made the country's economy less attractive to foreign investors. If an economy was a bucket of water, and the water in the bucket was the money in the economy, then Gil and Stan were like tiny holes in the bottom of the bucket. The "water" they leaked out made everybody a bit poorer.

Why was Canada so soft on this crime?

One reason was the fact that tipping and insider trading were new crimes; they were added to the Criminal Code only in 2005, and a few decades earlier the acts had been completely legal. Another reason was fragmentation: more than 30 separate agencies, many of them self-regulating, had roles to play in securities regulation in Canada. It was easy to slip through the cracks. Another reason was the cozy relationship between the regulators and the regulated. The stock market police could not change their policies without consulting and negotiating with Bay Street and its powerful lobbyists. Another reason was a void of leadership.

In 2007, the CEO of the OSC, David Wilson, was asked, "Do you think we have a problem with insider trading in this country?"

He said, "I don't have an opinion if we have a problem."

The reporter asked, "What keeps you awake at night?"

Wilson said, "I sleep pretty well."

PART SIX

Spring and Summer 2007

Friendships that are obtained by payments, and not by greatness or nobility of mind, may indeed be earned, but they are not secured, and in time of need cannot be relied upon; and men have less scruple in offending one who is beloved than one who is feared, for love is preserved by the link of obligation which, owing to the baseness of men, is broken at every opportunity for their advantage . . .

from *The Prince*, by Niccolō Machiavelli

21 | AUTHOR'S RANT

Insider trading is not the most action-packed subject to write about. After spending so much time writing about Stan and Gil, I am starting to feel a bit jealous of crime historians who get to write about serial killers, terrorists, crack lords, opium smugglers, assassins, sex fiends, and so on. My last book was about Vikings, rowdy thugs who roved the ocean looting all they could get away with. White-collar crime is too subtle. When writing about insider trading, dramatic scenes are hard to find. After all, what do crooked insiders actually *do*?

Gil is sitting in his office. He stands up. He walks out of his office. He walks to the elevator. He pushes a button and waits. The elevator door opens. Gil steps in. The door closes, then opens again. Gil steps out and walks to a nearby pay-phone. He puts his calling card into the machine, dials some numbers. Gil speaks.

What does a tippee actually *do*?

Stan picks up his cell phone. He listens. He hangs up and starts buying certain shares. Later he sells the shares for profit.

Although the amounts of money involved were often eye-popping — altogether they brought in over $10 million over the two binges — Gil and Stan's criminal acts, in themselves, can be dull when described. I am tired of writing, and you're probably tired of reading, that Gil tipped Stan to buy shares in company X; Stan bought shares in X; after company Y announced that it was planning a takeover of X, Stan sold his shares for profit.

Gil and Stan did this between 100 and 150 times, over 14 years, mostly when Gil was at Sullivan & Cromwell. For huge profits.

But things fell apart in 2007.

22 | TIME'S ARROW

February 7
Gil learns from a tax partner at Dorsey & Whitney, John Hollinrake, that Gateway Casinos is a possible takeover target of New World Gaming Partners Ltd.

February 8
Stan starts buying shares in Gateway Casinos.

February 9
Stan buys more shares in Gateway Casinos.

February 10, 4:07 p.m.
Stan signs "s.j. grmovsek" to an online petition demanding that Conservative Prime Minister Harper fire everybody at the Canadian Human Rights Commission. On another part of the website, Stan reads petition organizer Roger Pearce's comments about "the unfortunately named Mark Steyn" (the Muslim-fearing author of *America Alone*, one of Stan's favourite books). Stan goes to the "Comments" section and writes this: "What is so unfortunate about the name 'Mark'?" Later, Roger explains: "The villain of Thackeray's *Vanity Fair* is the Marquess of Steyn, pronounced 'Stain.'"

February 11, 9:15 a.m.

Stan writes his first-ever post on the Huffingtonpost website. (There would be over 900 to follow on Huffingtonpost, plus hundreds on other sites.) Stan responds to another poster: "You are nuts for being a vegetarian. Don't you know that animals contribute to the CO_2 problem. We must kill and eat them all to save the planet. Ahh, the sky is falling the sky is falling. . . ."

February 12

Stan buys more shares in Gateway Casinos.

February 14

Stan buys more shares in Gateway Casinos.

February 16

Stan buys more shares in Gateway Casinos. Also on this day, Dorsey & Whitney's client Eldorado announces that it plans to merge with Centrera Gold. Gil learned about the deal from another Dorsey & Whitney lawyer, Ken Sam from the Denver office, during a practice group meeting held on a conference call. Stan sells all his Eldorado shares for a profit. (Eldorado ran, among other things, a controversial open-pit mine in Turkey.)

February 21

Stan buys his last block of shares in Gateway Casinos. Now he owns 13,500 common shares.

March 3, 10:41 a.m.

Stan, referring to politician John Edwards, posts this on Huffingtonpost: "He does look a bit faggy to me."

March 4, 11:26 a.m.

Stan on Huffingtonpost, referring to a "Mexican Pop Star": "He looks a bit like Sen. John Edwards. How queer."

March 5, 2:09 p.m.
Stan on Huffingtonpost: ". . . Global warming is a fraud. To be against climate change presumes that the climate is perfect as it is. Judging from this February, as a Canadian I would like it to be warmer. Tomorrow is set to be especially cold—Let me go outside and idle my SUV to help the cause." (Stan does own a SUV, a Lincoln Aviator that is 16 feet long and weighs over 5,000 pounds when empty.)

March 8, 9:57 a.m.
Stan on Huffingtonpost, referring to John Edwards again: "How very gay of him. . . . Dems are a party for losers."

March 9
Stan starts buying shares in Strateco Resources, uranium miners in Quebec, having received a tip from Gil.

March 11, 7:31 p.m.
Stan on Huffingtonpost, referring to the "Apparent Suicide" of comedian Richard Jeni: "Smells like murder to me. . . . I bet it was the girlfriend."

March 12
Stan buys more Strateco Resources shares.

March 13
Stan buys more Strateco Resources shares.

March 14, 9:19 a.m.
Stan on Huffingtonpost, debating overpopulation with "Oldgringo": "Hey Oldgringo, You are a moron. . . . Don't be an idiot all your life. . . . If you are truly worried, get a vasectomy, give all your money and property to charity, and then go jump off a bridge. . . ."

March 31, 8:01 p.m.
Stan on Huffingtonpost, debating environmentalism with "Totalliberal": "Totalliberal, I have two kids and an IQ of 143. It ain't much, but I'm happy."

April 2, 7:44 p.m.
Stan on Huffingtonpost: ". . . Hurray for America!!!"

April 4
Stan sells his Gateway Casino shares for a profit of $176,456. On the same day, Gil asks one of his Dorsey & Whitney colleagues in Vancouver for a precedent. (Precedents, called "model" or "form" documents in the United States, are samples of what certain legal documents are supposed to look like and contain.) Gil's colleague gives him a precedent revealing that Dorsey was representing a company called Liquor Stores Income Fund that was planning to take over a company called Liquor Barn Income Fund, to create, as touted in the press release, "the leading independent liquor retailer in Alberta and BC [with 176 stores full o' booze] and providing opportunities for enhanced growth and the realization of synergies through operational best practices . . . a larger and stronger enterprise." Stan would later say Gil "knew the particulars of it, the price, and the timing."

April 9
Stan starts buying shares in Liquor Barn Income Fund.

April 10
Stan buys his last block of shares in Liquor Barn Income Fund. Now he owns 50,000 of them. The deal is announced. Stan sells all his shares in Liquor Barn Income Fund, for a profit of $152,175.

April 12
Stan sells some of his Strateco Resources shares for a profit of $19,900. Also on this day, Gil turns 37 years old.

April 13
Stan, having been tipped by Gil, starts buying shares in Blue Pearl Mining (Gil's client). Stan is in Las Vegas at the time.

April 14
The *New York Daily News* reports that "A lawyer leaped to his death from a 69th-floor office at the Empire State Building yesterday, severing a leg that crashed to the sidewalk in front of horrified onlookers. . . . 'He was interviewing a client,' said a man who works in the suite. 'He just got up, opened the window, and jumped.'"

April 16
Stan buys more shares in Blue Pearl Mining. Now he owns 40,000 shares. Blue Pearl Mining announces a "resource restatement" regarding how much molybdenum it had, which shows that the company is more valuable than previously thought. The share price shoots up. Stan enjoys a profit of $80,700. (Molybdenum is a metal used in heavy industry and weapons manufacturing.)

April 22, 9:43 a.m.
Stan on Huffingtonpost: ". . . We are not that important and can make no negative impact on the Earth beyond one that affects our own existence. The Earth will spin on long after your favourite celebrity is dead and gone. . . ."

May 3
Stan uses inside information from Gil to profit from the takeover by Coeur d'Alene Mines of Palmarejo Silver (Gil's client). Gil mentioned the takeover to Stan but explicitly told him not to trade on the information because Palmarejo stock wasn't traded very often, so any big purchases would be noticeable, a red flag to regulators. Stan said he would not trade on the Palmarejo Silver information — another lie.

May 4
A broker asks Stan why he purchased shares in Palmarejo Silver. Stan lies, saying that someone at a dinner party recommended it.

May 8
Stan gets a tip from Gil and starts buying shares in Energy Metals. (Gil learned of the upcoming deal from a casual conversation with another Dorsey & Whitney lawyer based in Seattle.) Also on this day, Stan sells some of his shares in Strateco Resources, for a profit of $66,600.

May 10
Stan starts buying shares in Energy Metals.

May 14
Stan buys more shares in Energy Metals. Now he owns 72,400 shares.

May 22
Stan sells 40,200 Energy Metals shares.

May 24
Stan buys 40,000 Energy Metals shares.

June 1
Stan buys 15,000 Energy Metals shares.

June 4
Uranium One (run by Ian Tefler, also the boss of Goldcorp) announces that it has taken over Energy Metals. Stan sells 82,700 shares in Energy Metals for a profit of $270,000.

June 11
Gil gets a "conflict check" firm-wide email. A Dorsey & Whitney lawyer in Vancouver represents the government of China, which is trying to gobble up North American resource companies and is interested in Peru Copper. (Peru Copper is one of the same corporations that "buffetology" and "copperisnot" and others on the Yahoo! chat-board accused Stan of "pumping and dumping" in 2005. Gil represented it then but does not do so anymore.

June 14
The Aluminum Corporation of China announces its takeover of Peru
Copper. Stan sells his shares for a profit. He phones Gil, who is in
Disney World in Florida with his family. Gil talks on his BlackBerry
from Disney World, saying, "That's great, but I'm busy, can't talk."

June 15
Tipped by Gil, Stan starts buying shares in Meridian Gold.

June 20
Stan buys more shares in Meridian Gold.

June 27
Stan buys more shares in Meridian Gold. Now he owns 48,000 shares.
Yamana Gold (Gil's client) announces that, together with Northern
Orion Resources, it will take over Meridian Gold. Stan sells all his
Meridian Gold shares, for a profit of $150,000.

July 9, 8:53 a.m.
Stan on Huffingtonpost: ". . . Don't hate the rich, take a look at what
they do and copy it."

July 17
Six major roads in Honduras are blockaded and demonstrations take
place across the country, protesting against the harmful acts of Canadian
mining companies (such as Goldcorp and Yamana Gold) in Honduras.

July 13, 12:35 p.m.
Stan on Huffingtonpost: ". . . I hate Democrats! . . ." [At 12:39 p.m.,
regarding an article titled "Muslims Are Insulted"] "Oh my, what are
the odds? . . . Ignore comments from these nutjobs and give them a
smack if they threaten existence in the West—they won't stop until the
West is destroyed or they are. . . ." [At 11:17 p.m., regarding an article
titled "Where's the Conrad Black Commutation?"] "Black's books on

Nixon and Roosevelt are quite good. As for the case against him, I believe it was very weak and was only pushed as hard as it was because of the prosecutor involved. Another case of no crime involved for Find-A-Crime Fitz." [At 11:23 p.m.] "Al Gore is the biggest asshole."

July 20, 12:54 p.m.
Stan on Huffingtonpost, referring to "NBA Ref to Be Charged with Betting on Games He Officiated": "The most obvious fix is the one the media are too afraid to cover; namely, how Seattle was robbed by Pittsburgh in the Superbowl [and how in the Superbowl that followed] the refs did everything to rob Pittsburgh against Indy. The rumours of those two games being fixed are everywhere."

August 14
For the first time, Gil uses the Dorsey & Whitney document-sharing database to access "Project Storm." He logs on using his personal password, leaving permanent electronic tracks. He sees checklists, timetables, draft merger agreements, and the list of issues requiring attention. Gil logs off from NetDocuments.

August 17, 1:14 p.m.
Stan on Televisionwithoutpity.com, referring to the show *Californication*: "As a divorced man with children and at a similar level of monetary success and career stagnation as the character in this show, I can say that it was fantastic and spot on. From the conversations with the ex to the promiscuity after the break-up, I thought I was watching my life (which made me quite sad, actually). Any show that can make me laugh out loud is a show that I will go out of my way to watch. By the way, I once was with a woman that had a fetish about being punched in the stomach during sex and punching me . . ."

August 19, 10:01 a.m.
Stan on Televisionwithoutpity, referring to the show *Dexter*: "Woo Hoo, a *Dexter* Forum. Finally! Love, love this show and have pumped it to all my friends. It is not a perfect show, but it does try to stretch itself

and take chances and that should be applauded. There is one scene in season one . . . where I Dexter ["I Dexter" is a Freudian slip—Stan would later admit to identifying with the Dexter character] conveyed a range of emotion and turmoil that I thought only Tom Hanks at his best in something like *Castaway* could. Television has never been better than it has been over the last 5 years with *Sopranos*, *Deadwood*, and now *Dexter*. . . . Dexter conveys the turmoil of doing what is good vs. doing what he is to a degree that I never thought I would see in television."

September 6 , 9:05 a.m.
Stan on Huffingtonpost: ". . . May I suggest that everyone that believes that humans are 'destroying' the planet commit suicide. . . ."

September 8, 6:22 p.m.
Stan on Huffingtonpost: "I think the Democrats agree with everything Osama bin Laden stated except for the cutting of taxes. Osama for Obama in 08."

September 11, 10:01 a.m.
Stan on Televisionwithoutpity, referring to an episode of *Californication* dealing with pedophile priests: ". . . What was with this anti-Catholic shit that, in this episode, added nothing to the story. Sure I am a Catholic and maybe sensitive to the issue. . . ."

September 19
Tipped by Gil, Stan buys 73,500 shares in Northern Orion Resources.

September 20
Yamana Gold (Gil's client) announces a change in its offer to buy shares of Meridian Gold. The shares of Northern Orion Resources (also involved in the complicated deal) go sharply up. Stan sells his shares in Northern Orion Resources for a profit of $41,100.

23 | END AND BEGIN

As the summer of 2007 turned to fall, Gil kept tipping information to Stan, who kept trading with it. No plan to ever stop.

Gil and Susan were active in Toronto society, often donating money to cultural, educational, and religious causes. They were devoted parents.

Stan, an active parent (with the help of his live-in nanny) from Saturdays to Wednesdays, kept trolling on chat-boards during his large amount of free time.

Gil started to prepare for October's Intensive Course in Securities Law and Practice. He was to lecture to a group of top North American corporate lawyers on the topic "Overview of U.S. Securities Regulation Cross-Border Transactions." It would be one of the peaks of his career, marking him as someone who had been accepted by his peers as both a leader of the profession and a role model.

Meanwhile, bitter Gil kept logging on to the Dorsey & Whitney computer network to snoop. Again and again and again.

Compulsively.

Unwisely.

Fatally.

PART SEVEN

2008

If I was ever on [the TV show] *Survivor*, I'd kill
everyone on the first night in their sleep.

Stan Joseph Grmovsek

24 | PROJECT RADICAL

Near the end of 2007, as described in Part 1, Gil tipped Stan about A.S.V.'s upcoming merger with Terex, code-named Project Storm. At the start of 2008, Gil did the same thing regarding an upcoming merger between medical equipment manufacturers Possis and Medrad. Dorsey & Whitney had code-named this deal Project Radical. To steal information about these two transactions, Gil would log on to the Dorsey & Whitney NetDocuments database repeatedly, leaving electronic tracks each time.

Gil tipped Stan about Possis and Medrad during a phone call on Sunday, February 3, 2008. In the following few days, Stan bought 117,602 common shares in Possis. He was trading recklessly, in amounts that he would later call "moronic," because he was obsessed with making up for a recent huge loss on NovaGold. (That was the stock he had lost $600,000 on, a loss that he superstitiously linked to writing "Old crimes have long shadows" on the Facebook page of his ex-fiancée, Jennifer — the woman who, he claimed, liked to steal things and call it art, also liking fisticuffs during sex; the woman who inspired him to get the Latin for "I Am an Honourable Man" tattooed on his right ass cheek; the woman with whom he remained obsessed for many years after their breakup.)

Yahoo! chat-rooms were full of rumours about the upcoming deal.

On the morning of February 11 — the day of the Possis-Medrad announcement — Gil used a pay-phone inside BCE Place, near his office. (Usually, to avoid attention, he avoided that pay-phone.) At 8:22 a.m., he phoned Stan's cell, asking Stan about their profit on the deal.

$612,294.

Both Project Storm and Project Radical were very profitable for Gil and Stan but would destroy them.

o o o

March 16, 1:43 p.m.
Stan on Huffingtonpost, responding to "Pastor's Remark Sparks Debate about Obama Campaign": "Ok, so [Obama's] Pastor of 20 years is an America-hating, race baiting, nut job. . . . [Obama's] wife has expressed the same crazy beliefs as the potato-headed Pastor and you want me to believe that [Obama] does not share those same beliefs, let alone that he has never heard of them before. I call liar. Hmm, lying Clinton and lying Obama — I will go with the true American hero hero: vote McCain."

March 26
Having heard from Gil the day before that "Goldcorp [GG] was talking with Agnico Eagle [AEM], and something might happen the next day," Stan is tempted to trade on the ripe inside information. However, he is also nervous about someone noticing his recent suspicious trades in Possis and A.S.V. (Project Storm and Project Radical). He would later write,

> So I decide that I won't buy Agnico and will not call any non-resident friends about it [i.e.,trade in an offshore account] (though I do tell Gil that I do [and that] there is a 20,000 share position in AEM bought at over $80 using all available funds and some margin). What do I do? I short Goldcorp and go long Yamana on the same day on the theory that if something is announced the next day GG will go down and Yamana may go up. Of course, I am still so shitting in my pants that I first decide not to make this a "big position" and then I am so shitting in my pants that I decide to close out that trade on the same day for fear

that something [will be] announced the next day and my GG short also looks suspicious. Since I did not take enough of a position to justify the "risk," I decide to close it out on a day trade. I lost $1000 or so on the Yamana long and I believe I made just under $10,000 on the GG short. . . . Oh, yes, as almost always, nothing happens and GG does not buy AEM . . . yet!

March 26
Linda Thomsen, the director of enforcement at SEC, makes a speech in which she says, "Last year featured the largest wave of insider trading cases since the days of Dennis Levine and Ivan Boesky in the 1980s. Perhaps even more disturbing, this wave of insider trading featured the active participation of securities industry professionals at the highest levels, including several Wall Street married couples. But almost without exception, the insider traders in this latest wave of cases were under 40, and probably were too young to remember the images of Boesky and Levine being led away in handcuffs. Because they did not learn the lessons of the past, the insider traders of this later generation were destined to repeat them."

April 12
Gil's 38th birthday. At this time, there are only three people working at the Dorsey & Whitney office: managing partner Gil Cornblum, junior lawyer Rachel Smith,* and office manager Basil Parsnip. (The office secretary is on a leave of absence to travel in southeast Asia.)

April 23, 10:42 a.m.
Stan [forgetting that he was a Canadian] on Huffingtonpost: ". . . I guess I am voting for McCain."

o o o

The U.S. Financial Industry Regulatory Authority (FINRA) was a private corporation linked to the U.S. government, with the task of regulating securities trading in the United States. Its advertising boasted that "empowered by the federal government, we're here to protect American investors from fraud and bad practices . . . [and to] keep an eye on the markets. We monitor what's happening in the U.S. stock market — by looking for suspicious trading activity in all stocks, bonds and options traded. . . ."

Stan's suspicious trading activity was discovered in early 2008 when, as explained by Ontario prosecutors, "FINRA's software program twigged the large, well-timed trades with respect to Possis, ASV, and a couple of others, and from that FINRA examined backwards to tie them to additional trades, which led, of course, then to Dorsey & Whitney."

FINRA contacted the U.S. Securities and Enforcement Commission (SEC), which started an investigation into Stan's trades on NASDAQ and the New York Stock Exchange (NYSE). Soon SEC brought in the Federal Bureau of Investigation (FBI) to assist with the investigation. SEC also alerted Canadian authorities — the Ontario Securities Commission (OSC), the Royal Canadian Mounted Police (RCMP), and the Canadian version of FINRA, Market Regulation Services (MRS).

Although Stan and Gil did not know it at first, an alphabet soup of investigators was after them; they were almost out of time.

25 | A VIPER IN THE HOUSE

The senior osc litigation counsel on this case (which was assigned court file number CV-08-00007508-00CL) was Johanna Superina, assisted by Melanie Adams. Ilana Singer—the osc lawyer who had worked closely with Gil on the organizing committee for the International Finance Forum 2005—did not work on this case.

On April 28, 2008, Superina and Adams sent a "direction" (an administrative order, not requiring a judge's signature) to BMO Capital Markets (at 100 King Street West), freezing the trading accounts belonging to Stan, his sister, and his brother-in-law.

On the same day, they sent a direction to E*Trade Securities Corporation (at 60 Yonge Street), freezing all accounts and sub-accounts controlled by "Stan J. Grmovsek, S. Joseph Grmovsek, Stan Grmovsek and Joseph S. Grmovsek."

A third direction was sent to CIBC World Markets (at 199 Bay Street, 2nd Floor), freezing Stan's wealth kept there.

The osc did not know where, other than these three financial institutions, Stan kept his money.

On April 30, an amended direction was sent to CIBC World Markets, correcting several names that had not been properly spelled in the original direction.

o o o

On April 24, 2008, a Thursday, the SEC contacted Dorsey & Whitney's senior partners in Minneapolis. The SEC explained that most of Stan's suspicious trades had involved corporate deals handled by Dorsey & Whitney. The SEC laid out its allegations of insider trading by two lawyers at the firm. Dorsey & Whitney's partners agreed to cooperate in the investigation.

The RCMP started tapping Gil's phones. They gave the investigation the code name Project Logan. (Logan was the "real" name of Gil and Stan's favourite comic-book character, Wolverine.)

Very early on Friday morning, several lawyers from Dorsey & Whitney's head office in Minneapolis flew to Toronto to confront Gil.

At 8:30 a.m., on his way to the office, Gil got a voice-mail message from another Dorsey & Whitney lawyer. Gil called his colleague, who told him that he needed to speak with a partner named Jim Langdon, who would be available for a telephone conference at 9:30 a.m. During the phone conference, Jim told Gil of the firm's suspicions and listed 17 suspicious trades.

The partners asked Gil if he knew someone named Stanko Jose Grmovsek.

Gil said yes.

They asked him if he had ever tipped Stan about deals.

Gil said no.

The Dorsey & Whitney lawyers told him not to touch his computer because, as Gil put it later, technicians were busy "taking a snapshot of my computer and my email, and he was going to ask me to plug in my BlackBerry so he can take a snapshot of my BlackBerry, so I did."

Basil Parsnip, the Dorsey & Whitney office manager, later said,

I knew that something was up, just because of the requests from the Dorsey & Whitney head office for files and the backup requests for computers. I knew something was going on. Originally, I got requests for files from their records department, people I had never talked to before, so that sent up some red flags, and then they had a backup request for their computers: namely, Outlook, so their email. I kind of conferred with Gil as to what was going on. This didn't make any sense to me. I wanted to make sure that Gil was aware of these requests. Gil indicated at that point that there was an investigation. Gil didn't get into any details, but he said there's an investigation and to follow through.

After the teleconference, Gil went for a walk—north to College Street, where he turned around and walked south to the Atrium on Bay and phoned Stan from a pay-phone at 12:38 p.m. Gil said, "We have got to meet. Come down here and meet me right now."

Stan, in the middle of having lunch with Rochelle in a restaurant, said, "I can't." He was hoping to reconcile with his ex-wife over lunch and was getting their kids dropped off at his house later that afternoon. Stan said to Gil, "I'll meet you on the weekend."

"No," Gil said, "we can't meet on the weekend, I'm busy. Come down here Monday morning, first thing."

"Okay."

(After Stan hung up, the reconciliation attempt fizzled.)

Gil could not wait until the agreed time. At 5:00 a.m. on Monday, Gil showed up in a taxi at Stan's rented Woodbridge townhouse. Stan, half-dressed, let Gil in, and they sat down to talk.

"They're on to us," Gil told Stan.

Gil used his BlackBerry to show Stan an email from the U.S. Securities and Exchange Commission detailing 17 suspicious trades (including those connected to Storm and Radical). Gil mentioned that he was confused by some of the trades on the list; they were about deals that he had told Stan about but had also warned him not to invest in to avoid detection. Gil said, "On this list is Palmarejo Silver. We didn't even buy this stock. Why is it on this list?"

Stan lied (yet again) to Gil, denying that he had bought any Palmarejo Silver stock, saying that he had followed Gil's warnings, of course, and had not traded in the companies Gil had said to avoid.

Gil showed Stan a list of names from SEC, around 100 in total. Gil said, "Go through this list and see if you know any of these names."

Stan didn't recognize any of the names on the list and told that to Gil.

(Whose names were on this list? I don't know for sure, but I suspect that the SEC wanted to see if Gil and Stan were part of the alleged Galleon and Raj Rajaratnam insider-trading ring in Manhattan, also being investigated at this time.)

Gil said to Stan, "I've thought about it all weekend. The best solution is for you to, you know, kill yourself. If you do that, I'll take care of your kids."

Stan, secretly shocked, played it cool and said, "I'll think about it."

"Okay," Gil said.

Then they discussed the idea of pretending that they had been gay lovers and that, during their romantic trysts, Stan had secretly stolen information without Gil's knowledge. (They believed that two Toronto men recently in the news for insider trading, stock trader Andrew Rankin and computer guru Daniel Duic, had been gay lovers and that Daniel had used sex to manipulate Andrew into giving him tips. Gil and Stan had often discussed the Rankin and Duic case, a big news story in Toronto for years. Neither went to jail, and Duic ended up keeping most of his illegal gains. The case's ending had reassured Gil and Stan that stock market regulators were too incompetent to worry about.)

Stan was tempted to try to deceive the investigators, he would later claim, but he decided against it because he thought that Gil was acting too irrationally and unstably to pull off a charade. At the time, though, he told Gil, "I'll think about it."

Later Stan would say, "If Gil had stayed rational, we could have worked out a defence."

Stan got dressed and drove Gil to the Yorkdale subway station. Irrational and despondent, Gil took the subway home to his wife and young son.

o o o

That morning Stan "spazzed out" (his words) and hid some trading documents that he didn't want Gil to find out about, then went to meet with

Toronto criminal defence lawyer Edward Greenspan, who was often on TV around that time. (One of the papers that Stan hid was the list of passwords and account numbers for the E*Trade accounts of his family and friends that he controlled. He would forget where he hid that paper and never find it again, probably having thrown it away by accident.)

Later Stan tried to withdraw $450,000 from his BMO Nesbitt Burns and CIBC World Markets accounts. (He was not planning to use the money to flee, he would later claim, but to pay his income taxes for the year.) Stan was told by his bankers that these accounts had been frozen; he could not take any money out of them.

So Stan went to one of his other accounts, CIBC Investor Services, which turned out not to have been frozen yet. He got a $300,000 money order, leaving about $90,000 behind. (Leaving that amount would look less suspicious than emptying the account completely. Later Stan would withdraw another $30,000 from this unseized account.) He used this money to pay his income taxes. He was worried that the cheque would bounce, but it didn't.

From yet another of his accounts, at a financial institution called GMP, Stan obtained a money order for $125,000 and $9,800 in cash. (Any cash withdrawal of more than $10,000 from a bank would trigger a notice to the government. Soon after this withdrawal, Stan's GMP account would be unofficially frozen. Even before the financial institution received an order from the OSC to freeze his assets, GMP refused to let Stan access his own money without the okay of the OSC. It was a legally questionable decision, but what was Stan going to do about it — sue?) The $125,000 was to pay for a lawyer. Stan wanted the best lawyer money could hire. He met with Edward Greenspan, who was regularly in the news due to his unsuccessful defence of Conrad Black in Chicago. Stan handed Greenspan the $125,000 money order as a retainer, warning him that the bank might not honour it if the bank was served with an asset freeze order. Stan dumped $9,800 in paper money on Greenspan's desk, saying, "Look, I want you to get paid if you do something, so here it is."

Stan also tried to hand over 10 ounces in gold wafers toward the retainer, but Greenspan refused them, saying, "I don't want the gold,

I can't account for that. I'll take the cash. You probably need [the gold] more than me. You can sell it if you need it for cash."

Stan took Greenspan's advice, going to Casino Rama and selling the gold there to an "Asian loan shark" for (Stan later claimed) around $6,000—a very low price.

Around this time, one of Stan's child support cheques to Rochelle bounced.

Also on Monday, April 28, Gil met again with the representatives from Dorsey & Whitney's Minneapolis head office. Again Gil was asked if he had tipped Stan, and again Gil denied having done so. The partners showed him some records from the NetDocuments database showing that he had repeatedly snooped into Project Storm and Project Radical. Gil was unable to explain why he had been so interested in files he had never officially worked on or billed for.

He was suspended from work until the investigation was completed.

Gossip about the scandal started flowing around Bay Street.

On Tuesday, Gil phoned Stan, trying to set up another face-to-face meeting. Stan, still remembering Gil's request that he commit suicide, thought that his best friend's behaviour was bizarre. Gil was not speaking in his normal way.

Stan agreed to meet Gil later in the day, but Stan was too scared to follow through. He didn't know what Gil might do. Stan did not show up at the agreed-upon place at the agreed-upon time.

On Wednesday night, Stan had trouble falling asleep. The problems he and Gil were facing seemed inescapable. Stan, under a lot of stress and dread of the future, felt nauseous and dry-heaved. To end the insomnia, he took two sleeping pills. He was back lying in bed, waiting for sleep, when he heard a knock at the front door. It was 2:00 or 3:00 a.m.

Stan carried a steak knife in one hand. He nervously went to the front door. He had leaned a crystal glass against the inside of the door so that, if the door was somehow opened from the outside, the glass would fall and break and make a noise to wake him up. The glass was still balanced on the inside of the door. It was dark outside. Stan couldn't see anybody through the window in the door.

"Who is there?" he called out.

Gil's voice called from outside, "It's me."

Stan was frightened. He said, "Put your hands up onto the window so I can see them. Put your hands on the window!"

Gil's voice said, "They are on the window."

Stan looked more closely and saw that Gil's hands were, in fact, on the window. Stan had not seen them because Gil was wearing a pair of black leather gloves.

"Let me in!" Gil's voice said.

Stan opened the door, and Gil stood there in the doorway.

"Why are you wearing the gloves?" Stan asked.

"It's cold," Gil said.

Stan didn't believe him, thinking he was wearing the gloves so he wouldn't leave fingerprints. Stan guessed that Gil had a knife hidden behind his back and that, once inside, as soon as Stan turned aside or was distracted, Gil would whip out the knife and kill him with it. (Stan remembered that Gil had talked in Manhattan about using a stapler to batter to death any Sullivan & Cromwell lawyer who caught him spelunking.)

Gil saw that Stan was holding the steak knife high, ready to stab down at him.

Stan backed away from the door, going a few steps up the stairway, knife held ready if Gil charged at him. Stan said, "Gil, turn around, because I think you've got something behind you."

"No," Gil said, "I'm not turning around."

Stan said, "Look, I know you have something now. You're trying to get rid of me."

"No, I'm not. I just want to talk."

"Keep your hands up. I know you want me dead," Stan said.

"No," Gil said.

Stan said, "Bullshit. Our interests are adverse!"

(This was legalese for "the situation demands that either you fuck me over or I fuck you over." Wall Street's Ivan Boesky in the 1980s, whose career both Gil and Stan had studied, had expressed a similar sentiment before agreeing to work with the FBI against his long-term buddy, Mike "Junk Bond King" Milken.)

"No, that's not true," Gil said.

"Then turn around and let me see what is behind you."

Gil refused.

Stan said, "I've made a lot of other enemies."

"What are you talking about?"

"All these brokers are all going to be out to get me. They're all going to want to kill me."

(One broker at least, Grover Bismarck, had been making subtle threats to Stan, constantly asking about his children and hinting that something bad could happen to them if Stan cooperated with the authorities. Grover was trying to pressure Stan into telling the authorities that Grover's money laundering was actually the legitimate payment of gambling debts. Around this time, during a meeting in an underground parking lot, Stan asked to borrow money from Grover to help pay his lawyer. Grover said, "Don't worry, I'll take care of you later. When you need help, I'll help you out." But Grover did not give or lend Stan any money.)

Gil said, "Look, you know you're being stupid. Why don't I just give you four, five grand. You know, take a bus. Go to somewhere. Go to like Fort McMurray [in northern Alberta] and be an illegal immigrant, work in the oil sands, and this thing will die down, and I will give you money. You can come back later."

Groggy from the sleeping drug, Stan said, "What am I going to do with $4,000? That won't last me a week. I can't live on the run. No, no, I'm going to serve my time in the U.S. penitentiary, and then I'm going to come out and rebuild my life."

Gil left, then returned very late the next night to resume the conversation. He sat on the living room couch, near the front door. Again he wore the black leather gloves.

Stan sat on the stairs to the second floor, keeping the banister between Gil and himself as a shield. Gripping the handle of the steak knife.

He told Gil that he had destroyed all his files, thrown out all the trading paperwork, broken his computer hard drive with a hammer and thrown it out. He said, "I've hired Greenspan," and he told Gil that Greenspan had phoned the SEC, which had said that Stan would have to serve 15 years in a U.S. prison.

Gil said, "That's just ridiculous."

Stan said, "I'm just going to go in and tell them it's all your fault."

"That's ridiculous!" Gil sputtered.

"Well, that's what I'm going to do," Stan said. "I'm going to say that we were going to split all the money."

Gil, frantic, pleaded, "Why would you do that? Why would you tell them anything? Why would you talk? Why would you do this? You know, you have other options. You can run. You can, you know, you can leave. Why are you destroying everything?"

"There's nothing to talk about," Stan said.

Gil said, "I'm going to kill myself, because this is ridiculous. This leaves me no choice. This is stupid. I'll make it look like an accident."

"Okay," Stan said.

Gil's last words to him were "No matter what happens, I still love you."

Gil left and drove his Jaguar home.

They would never speak again.

Afraid of another nocturnal visit by Gil, Stan had his children move in with their mother full time, and he started sleeping at his sister's house, where he felt safer. Later, his sister would say, "he felt his life was threatened, and he was not in a good place. Mentally, he was in a dark place. He worried us. He worried us very much. He was not rationally thinking at the time. . . . We were afraid for Stan at this point. He was emotional. He was crying. He did not feel comfortable. I did not feel safe with him being alone in the house."

At work, Gil was talking about the SEC letter with the Toronto branch office manager, Basil Parsnip. Gil said, "Basil, you know, I think Stan is being investigated for inside trading, and it's because of things he learned from me."

Basil said, "I can't believe that you would do that."

Gil said, "This is pretty serious stuff." He started to become emotional. He said to Parsnip, "I have had a bad run of things happen to me with regard to my wife's health and my son's health and then this investigation. Why me? Why is this happening to me? Stan really screwed me, and I don't understand. Why is this happening?"

Gil seemed "really angry" with Stan.

A few days after this conversation, on Thursday, May 1, Gil cancelled a meeting with Dorsey & Whitney partner Jim Langdon and went home early and tried to kill himself. He took a large number of Tylenol-brand painkiller pills but not enough to kill him. Susan found him and was very confused by what he had tried to do. Gil did not explain to her.

At 10:00 p.m. or so, Gil went to the hospital emergency room. He was put into a room with three other people the next morning, Friday. He left the hospital on Saturday afternoon. Later he would say, "My life had unravelled. . . . I thought there was no way out."

He took time off work. Susan phoned the office, telling Basil Parsnip, "Gil is sick, he was in the hospital."

On the following Monday, Gil met face to face again with Jim Langdon. They went through the list of 17 suspicious trades. Gil lied and lied and lied. He made up stories for each trade "that sounded logical." He told Jim that Stan must have hacked into his computer and found the NetDocument files himself. The meeting was over by 11:00 a.m. Then Langdon interviewed Basil Parsnip and Rachel Smith. Both Parsnip and Smith described how Gil had seemed under a lot of stress lately, but they had both assumed that it was caused by his son's health issues. Gil had been showing the same signs of stress he had shown during his wife's battle with breast cancer. Langdon was very vague about the nature of the crisis, but Parsnip soon "put the dots together" and figured out that it was related to insider trading. But he was not sure how Gil was involved or if Gil actually was involved.

On Tuesday, Gil spoke on the phone to Greg Gard, a lawyer for the Ontario Securities Commission. He arranged to meet with Gard on Wednesday. He also made arrangements for face-to-face meetings with Dorsey & Whitney partners Jim Langdon and Tom Tinkum on Wednesday.

Wednesday, Gil knew, would be a terrible day.

That Tuesday night, sometime between 11:00 p.m. and 3:00 a.m., Gil tried to kill himself again. He swallowed a large number of his wife's sleeping pills. He made a noise that woke Susan. She found him, called 911. She read the suicide note he had left for her, which said (in part), "Stan and I were involved in bad things and you'll learn all about this afterwards."

Gil was rushed to hospital in an ambulance. Susan had to stay home because Saul was asleep. Gil arrived at the Toronto General Hospital around 4:00 a.m.

Susan phoned Stan at 5:18 a.m. and at 5:21 a.m. Stan saw Gil's number on his cell phone's call display and did not answer the first time she called. The next time he answered. During the 13-minute conversation, Susan asked Stan why her husband had tried twice to kill himself. She suspected that Gil was upset about his son's health. (Saul's slow rate of growth was a concern to his parents.)

Stan broke the news to Susan about the real cause of Gil's anguish. He said, "I think you should get a lawyer. Me and Gil have been in an insider-trading thing." Stan described the Dorsey & Whitney email that listed evidence of Gil's active participation in the conspiracy. After a while, Susan asked Stan to repeat what he had said about the inside trading. He was suspicious that she had just turned on a tape recorder and was going to record his words. Stan said, "Go to the hospital, and get a lawyer," and hung up.

Basil Parsnip arrived at work that morning and listened to a phone message from Susan. Her voice said, among other things, "Gil is in the hospital for testing." Parsnip phoned Susan back, but she did not answer. "I was not sure what was going on," Parsnip later said. He checked Gil's email inbox and his phone messages and learned that Gil was planning to meet with Greg Gard, an official with the osc. Parsnip decided to phone Gard and tell him everything.

Journalists started phoning the Toronto office of Dorsey & Whitney. According to Parsnip, one of the journalists who phoned asked Parsnip if it was true that Parsnip was in the hospital with a stroke. "All kinds of misinformation, things that I could not confirm," Parsnip later described.

During his time recovering in the hospital, Dorsey & Whitney's partners informed Gil that he was fired. The official "cause," Stan would later say, was not insider trading but the second suicide attempt and his inability to work. But Parsnip was under the impression that the "cause" of Gil's firing was insider trading. Gil moved from the Toronto General Hospital to the Western and then back to the TGH. He checked out on May 13.

Around this time, Gil started seeing a psychiatrist. He started collecting disability insurance payments.

It was Parsnip's job to sort through the stuff in Gil's office and pack it.

There was a lot of stuff. I came in on weekends to do that. It took a lot of time to do. He had over 25 boxes of stuff still there. Nothing has been picked up. No arrangements have been made. There's artwork, there's personal items, personal files, books, a wide collection of things. As far as I am aware, Gil has come to pick up nothing. Nothing has been changed. Nothing has been picked up. Nothing has been touched. The room it's all in is locked.

Parsnip talked about the scandal with young Dorsey & Whitney lawyer Rachel Smith. He said, "It does not make sense. No closure." They both did not understand. It did not make sense to either of them. "It still doesn't."

o o o

In April 2008, Stan moved out of his big rented townhouse in Willowdale and started living in a small, low-rent apartment in Toronto.

The last communication from Stan to Gil was anonymous. Stan wrote an unsigned letter (wearing gloves to keep fingerprints and DNA off the paper and envelope and stamp) that told Gil "Don't give up, keep fighting."

o o o

In addition to all the other stress, Stan had to deal with the fact that he and Rochelle had been sued for several hundred thousand dollars by a man named Alfredo Daneluzzi over a mortgage that Stan claimed had been fraudulently placed on his King City house by Donald Berlusconi.

One of Stan's lawyer friends, Reg Mossworth,* represented both Rochelle and Stan. He sent letters to Daneluzzi's lawyer and received letters from Daneluzzi's lawyer. Not much else happened.

This pesky civil case would drag on and on. At the time of writing, it is still going.

o o o

On May 5, lawyers for the OSC appeared before an Ontario Superior Court judge at the 330 University Avenue courthouse. This was a "commercial list" judge, meaning that he or she specialized in corporate matters. The lawyers spoke to the judge (whose signature is illegible) in a "chambers appointment," meaning that it happened in the judge's office, not in open court. It was also *ex parte*, meaning that the opposing side—Stan, his sister, and his brother-in-law—were not told about it beforehand. (In that respect, it was similar to the "emergency" motion Stan had made in family court.)

The asset-freezing directions were only a temporary measure. They would expire after a short time if not endorsed and extended by a judge.

The OSC lawyers presented the judge with a Notice of Application, which requested (in typical litigation lawyer language) "an order pursuant to subsection 126(5) of the Securities Act, R.S.O. 1990, c. S.5 (the Securities Act) continuing the following directions issued by the Applicant. . . ." The application then listed all of Stan's frozen accounts, requesting that the judge turn them into a court order.

Supporting the application was a May 2 affidavit of Stephen Carpenter, an investigator for the enforcement branch of the OSC, describing what the OSC knew so far.

2. Enforcement Staff of the Ontario Securities Commission ("Staff") are conducting an investigation into certain activities carried out by Stan J. Grmovsek ("Grmovsek") and other individuals and entities with respect to trading in Ontario in the securities of several Canadian reporting issuers. . . .

4. The potential insider trading and tipping under investigation includes trading in securities of the following eleven Canadian reporting issuers (the "Reporting Issuers"):

(i) Blue Pearl Mining Ltd. (now known as Thompson Creek Metals Company Inc.);

(ii) Cambior Inc.;

(iii) Desert Sun Mining Corp.;

(iv) Energy Metals Corporation;

(v)   Gateway Casinos Income Fund;

(vi)   Glamis Gold Ltd.;

(vii) Liquor Barn Income Fund;

(viii) Meridian Gold Inc.;

(ix)   Miramar Mining Corporation;

(x)   Northern Orion Resources Inc.; and

(xi)   Strateco Resources Inc.

5. Based on Staff's ongoing investigation to date, there is evidence which demonstrates that the trading activity in the Accounts consists of a pattern of purchases of shares in the Reporting Issuers in the weeks or days before a news announcement of a merger/acquisition or another transaction or matters involving that Reporting Issuer. In most cases, the shares were sold shortly after the news announcement and a profit realized for the account holder. The timely trading by Grmovsek in a number of Reporting Issuers appears to be an indication that Grmovsek may have had access to confidential material information about these publicly traded companies in advance of the news announcements.

6. Staff's review of the potential sources of the confidential material information has revealed that Grmovsek has a connection with a lawyer (the "Lawyer") with a firm (the "Firm") that acted on behalf of several of the Reporting Issuers or other parties involved in transactions or other matters with the Reporting Issuers. Staff are continuing to investigate further connections between Grmovsek and other potential sources of confidential material information concerning the publicly traded companies. . . .

12. Staff have determined that the Lawyer attended Osgoode Hall Law School with Grmovsek. Furthermore, on account opening documents dated April 11, 2006, for an account of Grmovsek with Canaccord Capital, the name of the Lawyer appears as the person who referred Grmovsek to Canaccord Capital.

13. Staff are investigating other potential sources of confiden-

tial material information, including connections between Grmovsek and another lawyer at the Firm. . . .

The affidavit described several of Stan's suspicious trades, ending with this:

48. Staff have been informed that the U.S. Securities and Exchange Commission ("SEC") is also conducting an investigation into the timely trading activities of Stan Grmovsek. I am informed by SEC Staff that on April 24, 2008, the SEC advised a partner of the Firm of its concerns relating to the timely trading activities of Grmovsek, and the Firm's involvement in certain transactions concerning publicly traded companies. I am informed by SEC Staff that SEC Staff also advised the Firm of the names of the Lawyer and one other lawyer at the firm that the SEC Staff believed were involved in certain transactions concerning publicly trading companies. I am further informed by SEC Staff that they were informed that, subsequent to that phone call, a partner at the Firm spoke with the Lawyer on Friday, April 25, 2008, and the Lawyer acknowledged that he knew Grmovsek.

The judge approved the OSC request. The short-term asset-freezing directions were replaced with long-term asset-freezing court orders.

(The "one other lawyer" mentioned was smoked-meat hobbyist Jonathan Van Horn, who would later be cleared of suspicion.)

Over the following months, OSC lawyers would make seven more appearances regarding Stan's assets (always in chambers, never in open court). On August 22, for example, they froze his CIBC Investor Services Account, which they had not known about in May. Other appearances were on May 12, June 12, July 14, August 15, August 29, October 17, and December 17, 2009. These various appearances would be to amend, to extend, and finally to make permanent the freeze on Stan's assets. None of the appearances would take longer than 10 minutes. Only in the later appearances would lawyers for Gil or Stan attend at these secretive "chamber appointments."

The trading accounts of Stan's sister and brother-in-law were frozen too. Their lawyer, from the Bay Street firm McCarthy Tetrault, would not appear at any of these appointments, which were a bit of a rubber stamp. The judge always made the order requested by the OSC.

Most of the important decisions were made between the negotiating lawyers in phone calls and in letters and in face-to-face meetings. Except on TV, that's how litigation usually works. It is usually about as dramatic to watch as insider trading, if not even duller.

o o o

Gil hired top securities lawyer Alistair Crawley to represent him. Crawley "fired" Rochelle, who had hired him first, in order to represent Gil. Crawley delegated much of the work on Gil's case to an experienced and well-respected criminal defence lawyer, Toronto's Ian Smith. Smith had attracted some attention for defending the Conservative ex-attorney general of Ontario, Bob Runciman, during an inquiry into the police shooting of a Native protester at Ipperwash Provincial Park. Smith had also represented a lawyer caught up in the Conrad Black prosecution. He lectured other lawyers at criminal law conferences; one such lecture dealt with lawyers who commit mortgage-related fraud and was titled "A Viper in the House: Real Estate Fraud and You."

Stan wanted a more famous lawyer. He had tried to retain Edward Greenspan, but Greenspan was worried about being paid with "proceeds of crime" and sent Stan away. Greenspan was also annoyed by learning that Stan had, during their initial interview, lied about the scope of the allegations, making the case seem much less serious than it was. Greenspan refunded Stan's money order and cash with a cheque from his trust account for $134,800.

The OSC asset freeze left Stan basically broke. He was trying to start a new career as a professional online poker player but had yet to bring in any profit from that. He had money in his offshore account but didn't dare access it; in his mind, it already belonged to the authorities.

Stan then hired Joseph Groia and gave him the $134,800 cheque from Greenspan's trust account as a retainer. Speaking through his neatly trimmed, greying beard, Groia estimated that the entire case would cost Stan around $200,000.

Groia was not a high-profile celebrity like Edward Greenspan but was more well-known than Ian Smith. From 1987 to 1990 (the year Gil and Stan met), Groia was the OSC's director of enforcement. He then entered private practice on Bay Street, starting his own firm in 2000. He wrote a book, *Securities Litigation and Enforcement*.

Groia taught young lawyers to be guided, as he was, by the five "Cs of defence work: 1, contain the problem if you can; 2, control the flow of information; 3, capitulate only when necessary; 4, counterclaim always; and 5, confound your opponents constantly." (It is unethical to make a counterclaim for purely tactical reasons.)

Groia spoke often at securities law conferences, often arguing that Bay Street needed less regulation, denouncing "the false perception that regulators are not doing enough" and criticizing the OSC for working in the public interest. He opposed adding insider trading and tipping to the Criminal Code.

Groia was involved in the tangled mess of Conrad Black litigation too, representing Hollinger, one of Black's companies. At one point, Groia had also represented Black personally in regard to Black's criminal charges, before Black replaced Groia with Greenspan.

In 2007, the SEC wanted to question Groia, claiming that Groia's friend, inside trader John Fraleigh, had engaged in insider trading while working in Groia's office, reaping over $5 million in illegal profits. The SEC also claimed that Groia had bought some of the same shares that his friend had illegally traded for huge profit. Groia was not accused of wrongdoing.

Groia served on the boards of several mining companies.

He was perhaps most well-known for his successful defence of John Felderhof, who had been accused of reaping hundreds of millions of dollars from insider trading related to failed mining company Bre-X. (This dramatic case, which dominated Canadian newspapers for a long time, involved a fake Indonesian gold mine, a geologist plummeting to his death from a helicopter, and $3 billion lost by investors. Stan owned a single souvenir share in Bre-X.) After a trial that took many years, including an unsuccessful attempt to replace the judge, Groia won the case, and Felderhof, the only person to be charged with anything over Bre-X, would spend the rest of his life in luxury in the Cayman Islands, Bali, and Nova Scotia.

The Bre-X case was not a complete triumph for Groia, however. His client failed to pay his $2-million legal bill. And the tactics that Groia used during the trial — which a later judge called "appallingly unrestrained," "guerrilla theatre," full of "repetitions of his sarcastic attacks" — would come back to haunt him. Groia would be charged by the Law Society for professional misconduct due to his extreme rudeness in court during the Bre-X trial. He had, before a strangely passive judge, repeatedly insulted an OSC lawyer, calling the lawyer unreasonable, unethical, dishonest, untrustworthy, incompetent, and a lazy whiner. (Ian Smith, Gil's lawyer, had been one of the many OSC lawyers opposite Groia in this dragged-out case, but Smith wasn't the one whom Groia rudely attacked.)

The Ontario Court of Appeal would write this: "The problem was not simply with Mr. Groia's conduct. His rhetoric was, in many cases, tied to a view about what constitutes improper prosecutorial conduct that was simply wrong."

At the time of writing this book, the Law Society's misconduct charges are continuing, and it is possible that Groia will be disbarred or otherwise sanctioned.

Obnoxious Joseph Groia was exactly the kind of lawyer Stan wanted.

At an early meeting, Groia asked Stan, "Will Gil cut a deal?"

"No, not if it includes prison," Stan said. He understood Gil's fears very well.

Groia said, "Then let's wait."

When Groia demanded more money, Stan paid him by credit card cheques. Later Stan would borrow $50,000 from his sister and $20,000 from his ex-wife to pay more retainer to Groia. A lawyer and gambling friend of Stan, Marvin Noir* — the inventor of the "guru" nickname — would give Stan $5,000, which also went to Groia.

Assuming that his home phone was tapped, Stan would only communicate with Groia by email or by calling from one of four pay-phones near his home. He mostly used a pay-phone in a supermarket; he could consult his lawyer and buy groceries on the same trip.

o o o

Over the next few weeks, Stan noticed cars following him as he drove around. Was it paranoia or real?

He mentioned it to Groia, also describing how he thought he had seen someone taking pictures of his sister's house before speeding off at his arrival.

Groia said, "Probably private investigators from Dorsey & Whitney."

Groia arranged for Stan to be represented in Washington by Peter Romatowski, a lawyer with Jones Day (the law firm that also employed Michael French, the highly respected corporate lawyer who would later be accused of insider trading with the notorious Wyly brothers). Romatowski oversaw Jones Day's securities litigation and SEC enforcement practice and practised white-collar criminal defence. His website boasted, "As a federal prosecutor in the Southern District of New York [where Gil and Stan would have to appear in court] from 1979 to 1986 and Chief of the Securities and Commodities Fraud Unit, Peter tried cases involving insider trading based on stories that appeared in *The Wall Street Journal*, a successful manipulation that tripled the price of a NYSE-listed stock, and other offences from narcotics to bank fraud."

Gil was represented in the United States by Glenn Colton, whose website boasted,

> Prior to his private practice, Mr. Colton served almost ten years as an assistant United States Attorney in the Southern District of New York. . . . Mr. Colton has handled a broad range of cases and represented a variety of clients in his white collar and government investigation practice, including the representation of the chairman of the board of a public company in an options-backdating investigation, executives of a pharmaceutical company in a kickback and illegal marketing investigation, the

vice president-finance of a public software company in a revenue-recognition fraud investigation, a foreign insurance company in an insurance fraud investigation, a public software company in a consumer-protection investigation, and a critical figure in the KPMG tax shelter prosecution.

Gil paid Glenn Colton and Ian Smith and Alistair Crawley a painfully large sum of money.

o o o

Rochelle did not take the news well. Her first reaction was to gather all of her investment documents and hide them at her father's house, later saying that she was "afraid" to keep them at her home. She was very upset with Stan. She feared government seizure of her investments and the end of Stan's support payments. She had to hire a lawyer to defend her during the OSC investigation. (Her first lawyer was Alistair Crawley, but then Crawley "fired" Rochelle as a client so that his firm of Crawley Meredith Brush could represent Gil instead.)

Stan apologized again and again to Rochelle and told her to tell investigators nothing but the truth, reassuring her that she had done nothing wrong and had nothing to hide.

Rochelle later wrote that Stan "consented to the change of name of the children [to her maiden name] given the embarrassment and shame attached to his name and the fact that all of the children's classmates, the other parents, teachers, and everyone within their circle and the extended neighbourhood knew of the investigations."

On April 30, Stan gave her a handwritten and signed document that said, "I, S.J. Grmovsek, want all to know that I want Rochelle to have custody of my kids and, failing that, her family as she and they see fit."

o o o

On May 8 — the same day that Groia sent Stan his first bill, for $39,772.88 — an article by Jacquie McNish appeared in the *Globe and Mail*, Canada's main national newspaper:

INSIDER TRADING PROBE FOCUSES ON U.S. LAW FIRM

Securities regulators in the United States and Ontario have launched a major insider trading investigation that centres on 11 Canadian takeovers during the past two years and the U.S.-based law firm that advised companies involved in each of the deals.

According to documents filed in the Ontario Superior Court, the Ontario Securities Commission is investigating Toronto business consultant [sic] Stan Grmovsek, his sister Helena Zahir, and his brother-in-law Philip Zahir, alleging they earned a profit of $1.1 million by trading in resource companies shortly before they were engulfed in a frenzied wave of mergers and acquisitions that sent stock prices into orbit. . . .

Joe Groia, a lawyer for Mr. Grmovsek, said his client only learned of the trading probe last week when the OSC applied for a court order to freeze his brokerage accounts. . . .

"I was retained recently and we are working with our client to try and understand the issues," Mr. Groia said. . . .

The article was accompanied by a photo of Stan that Groia had arranged as part of his tip-the-media strategy, hoping to get useful coverage in exchange. Stan stands posing on the front porch of a townhouse that belongs to somebody else, with his SUV and a small tree visible behind him. His hair is short. He seems to be half-smiling at the cameraman, who is standing in the next front yard. Stan is wearing wrinkled bluejeans and a plain sweatshirt. A cell phone is attached to a holster on his belt. He has the thumb of one hand stuck into his pocket, cowboy style, while his other hand twirls a ring of keys.

Gil read this article and saw this photo. Stan's selfish PR move made Gil feel even more upset with him.

During the negotiations with the various authorities, Gil was saddened to learn that his best friend had repeatedly lied to him over the years—Stan had lied to him about changing brokers, about only trading through offshore accounts, about the amount of money received from Grover Bismarck, about so many things. Gil learned that Stan had not only lied to him but also cheated him—the agreement had

been to split profits 50-50, but Stan had secretly taken far more than
his fair share, not to mention all the profit he had surreptitiously reaped
for his family and friends. Learning of Stan's betrayal, and suffering
the shock of detection and the public shame from the growing scandal,
drove Gil deeper and deeper into depression.

The next day another article by Jacquie McNish (with Andy
Hoffman) appeared in the *Globe and Mail*:

INSIDER TRADING PROBE TARGETS CLASSMATES
Stan Grmovsek and Gil Cornblum have been close friends ever
since they met at Osgoode Hall Law School 17 years ago.
Although their careers took different directions, they have
remained in close contact, attended each other's weddings, and
frequently socialized with their families.

Two years ago, the close bond veered into troubling territory
when Mr. Grmovsek, known to friends as Joe, began making
lucky stock bets on companies for himself and two relatives
shortly before takeover bids and other favourable events were
announced. The problem with Mr. Grmovsek's timely trades is
that at least eight companies involved in the deals were clients of
Mr. Cornblum or his law firm Whitney & Dorsey [sic] LLP.

The coincidence has had devastating consequences for both
men. On Monday, Mr. Grmovsek, a 39-year-old self-employed
business consultant in Woodbridge, Ont., consented to an
Ontario Securities Commission demand to freeze most of the
alleged $1.1 million in proceeds from the trades in his brokerage
accounts. He has hired a lawyer and is cooperating with a joint
OSC and U.S. Securities and Exchange Commission investigation, which court documents describe as a "potential illegal
insider trading" case.

For Mr. Cornblum, the scandal has sent his personal and
career life into a horrible downward spiral.

He is currently lying in a Toronto hospital after he was
rushed to emergency earlier this week. Sources close to Whitney
& Dorsey [sic] said his partnership was terminated this week

and he no longer works in its Toronto office. It is understood that the Minneapolis-based firm conducted an internal probe after the SEC alerted it two weeks ago that it was investigating two of its lawyers in relation to the Grmovsek case. It is understood that the firm has taken no action against the other lawyer, whose identity is unknown.

It is a hard fall for a respected corporate lawyer who had won a coveted partnership with a mid-sized U.S. firm, boasted a roster of growing resource company clients and is admired as a devoted husband and father of a young son.

Mr. Cornblum could not be reached for comment. . . . In a written statement yesterday, Mr. Grmovsek said he is "heartbroken" and described Mr. Cornblum as "someone for whom I greatly cared, admired, and respected."

News of the insider trading investigation has stunned Mr. Cornblum's corporate clients and Bay Street lawyers and bankers who worked with him on a variety of transactions involving mostly mid-sized resource companies. They described Mr. Cornblum as an unassuming and pragmatic deal maker.

"He's a guy with a lot of integrity," said Joseph Conway, chief executive officer of IAMGOLD Corp., which hired Mr. Cornblum to advise IAMGOLD on its $1.3-billion takeover of Cambior Inc. in 2006.

"I find it hard to believe that he would actually be willingly involved in something like that," he said.

Peter Marrone, chairman and CEO of Yamana Gold Inc., which hired Mr. Cornblum to advise on two of the merger transactions named by the OSC, said the company had not been contacted by regulators, but it intends to cooperate with any investigation. "I will always hope that the people we deal with will maintain our confidences," he said.

The investigation is believed to mark the first time that a Canadian lawyer has been ensnared in a case involving allegations of insider trading. . . .

IAMGOLD's Mr. Conway said he regarded lawyers as his most "trusted advisors" because they give counsel over a long period of time on a variety of corporate decisions and transactions.

"There's that level of trust and confidence that you have with a lawyer that is much higher than you would have with say an investment adviser or an investment banker. That's the disturbing part about it," he said.

o o o

At around this time, the government of Argentina criminally charged Yamana Gold and Goldcorp (both previously represented by Gil) with "crimes against the environment" as well as tax evasion and corruption.

The criminal charges of environmental contamination were laid because Yamana and Goldcorp, joint operators of the Alumbrera Mine in Argentina, had dumped millions of litres of liquid waste—cyanide, mercury, lead, arsenic, and other deadly mining by-products—into a canal used for farm irrigation and drinking water.

When the Alumbrera Mine closes, the area will never return to its natural state and will need treatment forever. The Canadian mining companies, having made their profits, will abandon the toxic mess to the Argentinean government, which lacks the resources for such a huge problem. The mine will be a permanent toxic crater, clearly visible from the moon, leaking toxins into water that Argentinian kids will have to drink—water much dirtier than that enjoyed by the shareholders of Goldcorp and Yamana.

Compared to that, are the crimes of Stan and Gil such a big deal?

o o o

Four days after the *Globe and Mail* article, Jim Middlemiss wrote for the *National Post*:

DORSEY WHITNEY FALLOUT

The Toronto legal community is still abuzz with the news last week that U.S.-based Dorsey Whitney fired Toronto partner Gil Cornblum after it became public that one of his law school pals,

Stan Grmovsek, is under investigation for alleged insider trading and tipping. According to an OSC affidavit, Mr. Grmovsek "has a connection" with Mr. Cornblum. . . .

As a partner at one of the handful of U.S.-based firms that have offices here, Mr. Cornblum is reasonably well-known in Toronto legal circles and well-respected. One lawyer calls it a "tragic situation."

It's a devastating allegation for a transactional law firm to deal with. Lawyers who take money from clients [are] one thing and many big law firms have survived that type of crisis. However, client confidentiality is sacrosanct in the M&A world and it's unheard of for a law firm in Canada to get embroiled in such allegations and rare to do so in the United States.

While the firm is adamant the Toronto office will continue, some lawyers here aren't so sure. It's a small office, served largely by partners out of the U.S. "They're toast," speculates one top Canadian M&A lawyer, predicting that the firm will quietly close the Toronto office once the dust settles.

A firm spokesman says firmly "we are not going to close the Toronto office." Expect to see more Dorsey lawyers in town more frequently as the firm shifts into damage control mode and tries to calm the corporate waters. It remains to be seen if they can weather the storm.

o o o

May 21
Stan's friend and ex-neighbour Paul Borges is voluntarily interviewed by the Ontario authorities. He appears without a lawyer. He describes his investment knowledge as "poor to none." He says that he has not heard of any of the stocks that Stan illegally traded in his account. He says that he thinks that he met Gil at Stan's son's christening but is not sure.

June 4
Stan takes hope and comfort in reading about the case of Robert J. Downs Jr., a partner in Philadelphia law firm Khler Harrison, who had

been accused by the SEC of earning $308,000 in insider-trading profits. Downs pleaded guilty and paid the SEC $308,000 but did not go to jail.

June 18
Groia sends Stan his second bill for legal services—$43,251.70—which relates to 16.7 hours of work performed by Groia at $700 an hour and 6.6 hours of work performed by Kellie Seaman (Groai's pretty, blonde, and tough associate lawyer) at $320 an hour, plus $2,005.40 for Groia's travel expenses for a meeting with the U.S. attorney in New York, plus smaller disbursements such as $34.20 for photocopying and $32.40 for meals.

June 19
Stan's long-time friend Jimmy DiSantis is involuntarily interviewed by the Ontario authorities. He appears without a lawyer. He describes his investment knowledge as "above average, but not necessarily through experience. . . . I am a lazy investor." He has never heard of some of the stocks that Stan illegally traded in his account. DiSantis has heard of some of them but does not know that Stan bought and sold these stocks in his account. DiSantis says,

> I can probably count on one hand the number of times I have met with Gil Cornblum. . . . He was not a friend of mine but somebody I knew through Stan. . . . Gil's name would come up because I would ask from time to time . . . "When are you coming downtown for lunch?" and sometimes Stan would say, "I'm meeting with Gil." . . . The last time I saw Gil was when I bumped into him in PATH [an underground pedestrian system in downtown Toronto] three or four years ago.

DiSantis says that he is holding off on buying a new car until he learns how much of his profits the authorities want him to disgorge. DiSantis, discussing his own business ethics, says, "I am very sensitive to insider-trading concerns. I have been very careful in the past and left hundreds of thousands of dollars on the table in terms of lost opportunity cost."

Later that day, at 8:27 p.m., Stan emails Groia to thank him for a discount on the latest bill for legal services. Groia emails Stan back: "We should sit down together and see what a realistic budget is going forward and see what can be done to pay it. If we keep giving you this kind of discount (or close to it) we will just break even but I suppose we can live with that. What we can't and don't do anymore is work for free, as we are still trying to work out of our huge Bre-X hole."

June 21, 10:49 p.m.
Stan on Huffingtonpost, responding to a comment on "World Population to Hit 7 Billion by 2012": "You are a nut and a loser. The earth will be fine. You, however, should reconsider your thoughts on suicide as an example to all of us earthlings."

June 23, 2:27 p.m.
Stan on Huffingtonpost: "I think man-made global warming is a fraud. Of course, I also recently installed solar panels from Day4Energy (the most efficient on the market) that completely replace my daytime consumption of electricity (with excess sold back to the grid). Guess I only go to jail on weekends." (Stan does not really have solar panels on his rental apartment. He does, however, own shares in the company he is pumping. The shares, among others, were given to him by his gambling buddy Donald Berlusconi. Later Stan would say that Day4Energy "sucked" and was "a dog.")

June 25
The *Globe and Mail*'s Jacquie McNish reports that Betty Leung, a legal secretary at the Bay Street firm of Bennett Jones, scammed $51,569 using inside information stolen from her boss, Alan Bell. Bell is one of Canada's top corporate lawyers and an adviser to the OSC. McNish writes that OSC officials are "paying more attention to lawyers involved in mergers and acquisitions as part of a broader crackdown on frequent heavy trading ahead of deal announcements."

June 26, 11:54 a.m.
Stan on Huffingtonpost, responding to "Let's Shoot Mugabe and Be Done with It": "That country [Zimbabwe] is just proving that Ayn Rand was correct when she wrote 'Atlas Shrugged.'"

June 29, 8:45 a.m.
Stan on Huffingtonpost: "Obama: The Islamofascists' Manchurian Candidate."

June 30
Stan's younger sister Helena Zahir is involuntarily interviewed by the Ontario authorities. She appears with lawyer David Porter, a partner at the Bay Street firm of McCarthy Tetrault. Helena claims the protection of section 5 of the Canada Evidence Act and section 9 of the Ontario Evidence Act. That means that the testimony she gives cannot be later used against her. She demands an undertaking that her testimony not be shared with the SEC. Helena describes her investment knowledge as "not very good. . . . I am a very inactive trader in the securities. I really still do not understand it. I am trying not to, because it still boggles my mind." She is not familiar with the names of any of the stocks Stan illegally traded in her account. She cannot recall ever meeting Gil, though she knows that he went to school with Stan. She remembers that Stan was living with Gil in New York when her first child was born and that Stan travelled back to Canada to see his new baby niece. In terms of recent events, she said, "I did see newspaper articles that came out just after the OSC action first came out. It had my name on it. No one called me about it, but I did get some looks at my daughter's school. . . . It was interesting to see some looks and some stares. . . . Nobody asked me anything about it. I could just tell that people's body language was different in some way." Asked why she thought Gil and Stan did what they did, Helena said, "I have no sense as to why this arrangement was in place. It's so ridiculous when you think about it. A successful lawyer. I do not understand why. I do not understand it. I cannot wrap my brain around it. It's stupidity."

Later that day, Helena's husband, Philip, is involuntarily interviewed by the Ontario authorities. He also appears with David Porter and claims the self-incrimination protection of the Canada and Ontario Evidence Acts. He also gets an undertaking not to share the testimony with the SEC. He explains that Stan is godfather to Helena and Philip's children. He remembers meeting Gil at Stan's wedding, when Philip was an usher and Gil was Stan's best man. After the interviews, an OSC investigator walks Helena and Philip to the elevator and says, "If you remember *anything* about Gil, call me."

July 1, 8:24 p.m.
Stan on Huffingtonpost, responding to "Bill Gates' Misguided Capitalism": "*The Fountainhead* [by Ayn Rand] got it right."

July 3, 9:21 a.m.
Stan on Huffingtonpost:

> Over 10 years ago I was in a sports book in Vegas chatting up a regular as the NBA played on many of the screens. This guy told me — over 10 years ago — that he did not bet the teams but bet the Refs. I asked what he meant and he said he looked for games with favourites at home coupled with certain refs officiating. He said that the refs could easily throw points to the favourite with foul calls so that the favourite could beat the spread (if they could not beat it on their own). Basketball is the easiest team sport to fix for sports gamblers and it certainly is happening.

July 4, 3:23 p.m.
Stan complains in an email to Groia about his friends and acquaintances, "I am a hard man to hate, but I do get far far fewer calls and emails than I did two months ago (hard to hate, but best to avoid it seems)." Groia's assistant, Seaman, replies (at 8:47 p.m.),

> Thanks for the update. I was in vegas the last few days; lost my shirt (figuratively speaking of course but the real deal would have been cheaper!). It was hot as hell; just the way I like it. I

thought of you as I sat at the fountain outside Paris [in Vegas] but i wasn't sure if that was the fountain you'd mentioned when we talked. Joe [Groia] is meeting the prosecutor in Washington on the 11th. I am away that day but we can schedule a conference call if that's ok. I will give you a number to call in to at a designated time from a pay phone.

July 7, 10:38 p.m.
Stan emails Groia: "Question: From the perspective of my striking the most favourable deal possible with the OSC, would it be better if the OSC had the impression that Gil and I were involved in a close friendship where I was seen by others to be deferential to him; or, we were involved in a casual friendship that was not sufficiently significant to be noted by anyone else in my life?"

July 8, 6:02 a.m.
Groia emails a reply to Stan's question: "The latter as it would make the circumstantial evidence case harder to prove." Three and a half hours later, Stan emails Groia: "OK. My ex only socialized with Gil 2 or 3 times because she did not like him and how he spoke to me in front of his wife. I took a deferential tone with Gil in front of our wives because I knew he was only acting tough and domineering because he was compensating for the fact that I dated his wife long before he did (I introduced them)." That night, Stan emails Groia again, advising him to "use the bureaucratic rivalry between the Americans and the Canadians to control the file to leverage a better deal for me. . . . Even if we decide to give the Americans the cold shoulder there is no need for the OSC to ever know it until a deal is done."

July 10
Jimmy DiSantis' wife, Sonia DiSantis,* is voluntarily interviewed by the Ontario authorities. She appears without a lawyer. She explains that she is a financial services associate at the Canadian Imperial Bank of Commerce. "I work alongside financial advisors and do the administrative work." She met Stan once a year when he came to her house

for a football party. She explained that her investments had suffered a negative 13% rate of return when managed by CIBC, but when Stan took over, "there were more successes than there were losses. . . . I never thought about or checked into whether Grmovsek was licensed or registered to manage money." She works in an office close to that of Sandro Campagna. She says,

> I mentioned specific information concerning the trading that Stan was doing to Sandro Campagna. Campagna was aware that someone else was managing our money. Periodically, Campagna would ask what was in our portfolio and what was being purchased, and I would tell him. Most of the communication between me and Campagna was verbal since we worked so closely together. Campagna would sometimes trade on the information I provided in respect of the actions Grmovsek was taking. . . . [After the story appeared in the newspaper,] I told Campagna that Grmovsek was under investigation and that Jimmy had mentioned that Campagna's name was on "this list." Up until the point that he was interviewed by OSC staff, Jimmy did not know that I had been telling Campagna about what was going on in our trading accounts. . . . I was in Aruba on vacation when the media coverage of Grmovsek began. At no point around the time of the media articles did I discuss it with Campagna. Campagna did not know Grmovsek but knew his name.

Sonia DiSantis says that she was familiar with the names of about half of the stocks that Stan had illegally traded in her account. She had met Gil once, at Stan's wedding, but had never heard Stan or her husband mention his name since then.

Later that day, Sandro Campagna is voluntarily interviewed by the Ontario authorities "regarding allegations that Campagna may have been tipped indirectly by Grmovsek." Campagna (who had studied finance at York at the same time that Gil and Stan were there studying law) described his investment knowledge as "very sophisticated." He admitted that he could not remember any stock recommended by Sonia

DiSantis that he did not buy, but he denied that her tips were the reason he bought these stocks, saying, "The stocks I bought and sold were not because of what Sonia was buying. I invested in what I was investing in because of my trading philosophy and research." He said that he had never heard of Gil. He denied passing on any of the tips to others.

July 11, 8:32 p.m.
Stan on Huffingtonpost: "What a country [Britain] of wimps and losers. America is about striving for bigger, better and more!! . . . USA USA USA USA USA!!!"

July 14, 10:20 a.m.
Stan emails Groia, explaining that Gil was wrong about the total profits of the second phase of insider trading

> because I told him I purchased stock that I did not (I did not because I feared Grover Bismarck was copying my trades so I wanted to buy them in other accounts before using the non-resident vehicle [offshore account].) Unfortunately, the deals were often announced before I had my Bismarck orders filled. I did not tell Gil of non-trades and non-profits because he would have been pissed and demand I dump Grover Bismarck. (I did not want to dump Grover because he was a source of paper cash for me). . . . Bismarck recently advised that it would be "in my interests" to not contact the non-resident vehicle and to not bring it up with anyone until this matter is "all over."

Mid-July
Sonia DiSantis is fired from CIBC "with cause" because she had not informed her employer that she had given Stan trading authority over her investments.

July 16
One of Stan's in-laws, Daniel Zahir, is involuntarily interviewed by the Ontario authorities. He says that he has no investment experience and

cannot read English. He said that he saw Stan once a year at an annual Christmas party at the home of his son, Philip Zahir, but that he never spoke business with Stan on those occasions. He said that, after learning of the scandal, he had not bothered to change the password to his E*Trade account; Stan could still access it. He did not recognize any of the stocks that Stan had illegally traded. He said that he had never heard of Gil.

Achilles Zahir, son of Daniel Zahir and brother of Stan's brother-in-law, is involuntarily interviewed by the Ontario authorities. He describes his investment knowledge as "poor." He initially invested $100,000 with Stan, paying Stan two commissions of $8,000 and $29,500. He says that Stan never communicated with him about his investments. He has not heard of most of the stocks Stan traded for him. He remembers Gil from Stan's wedding and from helping to move Stan's furniture out of Gil's house.

Also on that day, Rochelle (not for the first or last time) yells at Stan for getting her into this mess.

June 18
Groia sends Stan his third bill for legal services — $17,996.22. (Many more will follow.)

July 22
Stan's father, Primoz* Grmovsek, is voluntarily interviewed by the Ontario authorities. He refuses to allow his testimony to be shared with the SEC. He says, "I know nothing of investments. Stan took care of all of that stuff." He describes learning from his son-in-law Philip Zahir that Stan "got in problem and his father in problem with government, probably illegal in that, because he doing some for me investment." He recalls Stan coming to the house in late May and saying, "Don't open the doors to nobody, and don't look through the window. Reporters are going to be watching the house." Stan told his father in late May, "I was doing illegal trading," but otherwise he never talked about it.

July 24

Stan's ex-wife, Rochelle Landry, is involuntarily interviewed by the Ontario authorities. She appears with lawyer Wendy Berman. She demands an undertaking that her testimony not be shared with the SEC. She says that she "does not understand anything about stocks" and would never read any trading confirmations or account statements. She says that she never heard of any of the stocks Stan illegally traded in her account. The interview ends with Rochelle saying, "I don't know anything. . . ."

July 25, 7:37 p.m.

U.S. attorney Raymond Lohier telephones Stan's Washington defence lawyer, Peter Romatowski.

Lohier was Stan's U.S. prosecutor. He was a Democrat; 6′1″, slender, black, a Harvard graduate, and married to an ACLU lawyer, Lohier reminded me of President Barack Obama. Before prosecuting corporate types like Gil and Stan, Lohier had made a name for himself as part of the "War on Drugs," prosecuting New York's drug sellers and consumers. Like Gil, Lohier had lectured to other lawyers about the law. He'd spoken about "Diversity Issues in the Practice of Law," "Federal Criminal Enforcement," and "Conflicts of Laws in Cross-Border Investigations and Prosecutions." Lohier would soon be in the news regarding his leadership of the high-profile insider-trading charges against Galleon Funds and Raj Rajaratnam.

On the night of July 25, Lohier says to Romatowski on the phone,

> I owe you an answer as to the possibility of a non-prosecution agreement in return for cooperation against Cornblum, including both historical and future proactive cooperation. The hangup is the non-prosecution portion. In this context, we're not in the business of providing a non-prosecution agreement to someone who's culpable as a tippee, although arguably not as culpable as the tipper. That said, we are certainly open to a cooperation agreement, but that would involve a felony plea.

Lohier pauses for a long time, with Romatowski thinking that Lohier is about to offer some kind of relief on sentencing, but then the U.S. attorney says, "Now there's really not much more thinking I'm going to do about this unless you have more to add."

Romatowski says, "I don't know where that leaves us or where we go from here."

Lohier says, "I am interested if he wants to cooperate, on either an historical and/or proactive basis. I'm all ears."

Romatowski says, "I will take this back [to Stan], and we will consider what you said, and we may or may not get back to you."

Romatowski chooses not to argue again that Stan's guilty plea in Canada should be enough punishment. The conversation ends. Romatowski records a quarter of an hour of work, and his next bill to Stan will total $15,578.71.

July 26, 5:41 p.m.
Stan emails Seaman (cc'ing Groia):

> You can ask Pete [Romatowski] the obvious: "what is in it for me / why should I cooperate with the Americans unless they at least guarantee no jail time?" As for what I can offer . . . I thought there might be some value in my Chart D listing stocks that were purchased by me on detailed recommendations from Gil, but that did not result in a deal. Such information could be confirmed by the companies involved as the information is not public knowledge and would, therefore, make an even stronger case against Cornblum. . . .

July 30
Stan's brother-in-law, Philip Zahir, is involuntarily interviewed by the Ontario authorities for the second time. He appears with lawyer David Porter. He describes how, after the scandal broke, he questioned Stan and was repeatedly told, "The less you know the better. Just tell [the authorities] the truth." He says that he knew that Stan and Gil were

acquaintances but not that they were friends, saying, "I don't really think that Stan had that many friends. He was just at home with the kids all the time." He describes Stan coming by after Helena's name was in the news: "Stan was crying, and he came over and said, 'I'm really sorry what happened. I feel really guilty for what's happened. I take full responsibility for what has happened. You guys didn't know anything. You had no knowledge of anything.'" Helena hugged Stan, but Philip got angry at him and started yelling at him. Philip then describes a more recent meeting with Stan, two days earlier, when Stan told him about Gil's suicide attempts and said, "Gil's brain is kind of fried" from taking so many pills. Stan also recently talked about a meeting between Groia and Stan's "New York lawyer," complaining that "the Americans aren't giving me a deal" and expressing fear of extradition to the United States. Stan told his brother-in-law that he had told Gil they should stop their illegal activity, but Gil had insisted they continue.

August 12

Basil Parsnip, office manager of Dorsey & Whitney's Toronto branch, is voluntarily interviewed by the authorities. Also participating by conference call are two SEC officials and Jim Langdon, a Minneapolis-based partner in Dorsey & Whitney. Parsnip says that he has worked for Dorsey & Whitney for six years, ever since leaving film school. He says that he never saw Stan or Gil do anything suspicious. Asked why he thought Gil did it, Parsnip says, "I still find that a big question mark. It doesn't make sense to me. Just from what I know of Gil and how important his family is to him, it doesn't add up in terms of the risk involved. . . . I don't think that Gil gained anything himself, so I don't know why he would do that. It doesn't make any sense to me." Parsnip says that Gil often travelled for his work and that he found the Dorsey & Whitney computer system a hassle. He says that many of Gil's lunch expenses involved Cassels Brock lawyer Mark Bennett and that Bennett would often phone Gil at the office. Parsnip describes how Gil would sometimes take time off in the middle of the day to "take Saul, his son, sometimes to a sports hall, kid's activity stuff, and come back" to the office afterward.

September 12, 12:05 p.m.
Stan on Huffingtonpost, regarding criticisms of Sarah Palin: "I find Michelle Obama's voice to be more 'repulsive' because of how it sounds and what she says. . . ." [Two minutes later, again about Palin] "Do you Libs actually think about what you write and say? You are viciously attacking a woman for her voice and appearance simply because you disagree with her politics. . . ."

September 16
Stan buys a computer product called New LobbyEdge Plugin for Internet poker. According to the company, "The New LobbyEdge Plugin is the most advanced Table Selection Tool and Fish Buddy List in existence. It plugs into Poker-Edge's massive player database and instantly tells you exactly where the *easiest and most profitable tables* are. . . . Studies have shown that choosing a weak table over a tough table statistically DOUBLES your expected profits from that session!" With the information from this sneaky software, Stan starts winning lots of money at online poker. He often plays under the username "groiagang."

September 24
Stan pays GoDaddy.com $41.95 to buy the web address www.inside-trader-store.com, plus $152.69 for three years of website hosting.

Late September
Gil is withdrawing from society as a result of the scandal. In one of his few social acts, he and Susan donate between $250 and $499 to the Lorraine Kimsa Theatre for Young People. Donors who give money in that range are honoured with the label "High Jumpers."

October 1
Groia's assistant Seaman does research on the case of Alan Eagleson — a Canadian lawyer, Conservative member of the Ontario legislature, and corrupt sports agent who had stolen large amounts of money from his NHL clients (e.g., hockey legends Bobby Orr and Darryl Sittler). Seaman does this research in the hope that she can find an argument for

Stan receiving a prison sentence as brief as Eagleson's — six months.

October 2
Gil's lawyer Alistair Crawley meets with Seaman to negotiate.

October 3, 4:37 p.m.
In an email to Groia, Stan describes how he believed that Gil had tricked him into not applying for the LLB/MBA program in 1991:

> Long and short of it: He will fuck me if it is to his benefit to do so, whether because he wants to or because his wife wants him to do so. Remember, the last time I saw him he was at my door wearing black leather gloves and hiding something behind his back. In my opinion, nothing good can come of Pete [Romatowski] talking to [Gil's] lawyer. Further, there is a possibility that Gil's U.S. lawyer gets a jump on things and moves up to where we are with the U.S. prosecutor and — intentionally or unintentionally — fucks any deal we are working on with the Americans as they, I believe, do not yet know that Gil is inclined to cooperate.

At 4:52 p.m., Groia replies by email: "Pete agrees with you and will be careful. Let's see what [Gil's lawyer] gives us; he will get nothing in return. There will be no first place award here. And since Gil's lawyers are way behind I will ensure that they do not catch up."

October 6
Fraud on Wall Street leads to a stock-market "crash." George Bush — following his fraudulent election in 2000 and fraudulent invasion of Iraq in 2003 — orders a $700-billion bail-out of Wall Street. Compared to that, are the crimes of Gil and Stan really such a big deal?

October 15
Stan applies to the U.S. Patent and Trademark Office to get a legal trademark for the phrase "inside trader."

October 17, 4:00 p.m.
Stan receives a phone call from Clariden Leu in the Bahamas, telling him that the SEC wants information about his accounts. The bank must respond to the SEC in less than a week. The bank employee asks if Stan wants to take legal action in the Bahamian courts to stop the bank from releasing the information. Stan emails Groia at 4:21 p.m.: "Is there any point in trying to stop that Bank from releasing the info? It did not work too well for Dennis Levine's attempts with Bank Leu nearly 20 years ago." Groia replies, "Let it be."

October 21, 2:51 p.m.
Stan emails Seaman (cc'ing Groia):

> Broker Grover Bismarck called to meet me and told me that the non-resident investigation in Bahamas has been going on since August with Bank Leu agreeing to release the requested info by the deadline tomorrow. Bismarck is nervous because his name is on the account with power of attorney and wires from the account went to a non-resident account of another client of his (in exchange for cash that he gave me here). He wanted to convince me that it was in my interest that, if asked, to go with a story that indemnified him as much as possible and to say that those wires were to cover gambling losses at private poker games. . . . I said I certainly would make statements exculpating him as long as I was alive to do so (hint, hint). I will do my best to avoid an "accident" in the coming weeks.

October 28
Gil signs a Consent and Waiver allowing the OSC to share information with prosecutor John Corelli and the RCMP.

October 29
Stan signs a Consent and Waiver allowing the OSC to share information with prosecutor John Corelli and the RCMP.

November 25, 1:43 p.m.
Stan emails Groia (cc'ing Seaman):

> I was approached yesterday by a person known to the RCMP as being involved in mortgage fraud with a proposal tied to my current "difficult" state and former position as a lawyer in good standing. He suggested that if I gave him and his associates the information needed to get re-instated by the Law Society that they would then do the rest and use my "identity" to facilitate a mortgage fraud scheme that currently involves a network of bank employees on the take, appraisers, and some disbarred lawyers that he says has successfully obtained millions this past year and can get millions more before it blows up and I plead ignorance to the scheme.

Stan told Groia to tell the authorities that he was willing to "lead authorities to a ring of individuals involved in this kind of fraud. I will only do this with the cooperation of the Crown after the promise of some time being knocked off what you negotiate for the inside trading matter. Without that, I won't get involved with either the forces of good or evil."

December 15, 1:50 p.m.
Gil's lawyer, Ian Smith, receives a faxed letter from Ontario prosecutor John Corelli. Gil gets a copy of the letter and reads,

> This is further to my email dated October 24, 2008. I indicated in that email that I would review the materials I received from the Ontario Securities Commission ("OSC") and then contact you to discuss the next steps to be taken in this case. . . . Earlier, we agreed that I will provide you with a range of sentence that, based on my knowledge of facts, the Crown will seek upon pleas of guilty. Next, you are to meet with your clients and, should that range be acceptable, you will provide me with a summary of their anticipated statements, which you have referred to as a

"proffer." I will then re-consider my proposed range of sentence in light of that anticipated incriminating information and advise you as to whether it has changed. Based on my response, you will consult with your clients and advise as to whether or not they will submit to an interview. After the interviews it will again be necessary for me to re-consider the proposed range of sentence having regard to how closely the statements correspond to the "proffers." As well, I must consult with the American authorities to ensure that we have captured all the allegations and to canvass whether the proposed range of sentence is satisfactory to them, i.e. is a fit global sentence. Assuming that the range of sentence that emerges is agreeable, we will then discuss the issue of formally sharing the materials I have with the Americans. We can then begin the process of laying the charges and arranging for pleas and sentencing in both jurisdictions. . . . With this in mind, I can advise you that, based on my knowledge of the facts, I will seek a sentence in the range of 4–7 years following guilty pleas. . . .

The idea of four to seven years in prison terrified Gil.

December 16
Stan, after reading a similar letter, emails his lawyers: "[Four to seven years in prison] is acceptable 'as a global settlement,' but arguably too high in light of Canadian precedent and the applicable limitation period for this jurisdiction. I would also like to see my range differentiated from Cornblum's (maybe 4–5 vs. 6–7 for him)."

December 18
Gil's lawyer Ian Smith talks on the phone with Seaman.

PART EIGHT

....

2009

Why should I be ashamed in the terrible moment when my entire being trembles between being and nothingness, since the past flashes like lightning above the dark abyss of the future and everything around me is swallowed up, and the world perishes with me? . . . I stood above the abyss with outstretched arms and breathed: down! down! and lost myself in the bliss of flinging down my torments, my sufferings! . . . How gladly would I have given my human existence to tear along like clouds with the winds of every storm, to embrace the floods! Ha! And will not one day perhaps this bliss be granted to this imprisoned soul?

from *The Sorrows of Young Werther*, by Goethe

26 | TOM'S THREAT

On January 23, 2009, Tom Atkinson became the OSC's new director of enforcement. He would ultimately be responsible for the prosecution of Gil and Stan in Ontario.

At a pre-lunch speech a few years earlier at Toronto's Four Seasons Hotel — the site of Gil's final lecture — Tom had told an audience of corporate executives the following:

> You need to make sure that employees understand what insider trading is and that it won't be tolerated. But what about those with whom you have "special relationships?" What are you doing to prevent these people from leaking information to the street? These people are also prohibited from trading on undisclosed information. They are what we call "tippees" who pass on tips to others who may benefit by trading on the information. I'm talking about affiliates and associates involved with you in takeover bids, mergers, or acquisitions. I am also talking about people who provide business or professional services to you, like law firms, PR and investor relations agencies, your printer, and so on. . . .

Insider trading is caused by rogue individuals. However, when the finger is pointed at who did the illegal insider trading, the ultimate responsibility may well rest with those who provided inadequate oversight that might have prevented the illegal trading in the first place.

Tom had let the unsubtle threat linger for a while; then he smiled at the executives at their lunch plates and said, "Bon appétit!"

27 | MORE TIME

January 6
To make a list of illegal trades to give to the authorities, Stan spends a morning on Google, searching "1994 takeover," "1995 takeover," "1996 takeover," et cetera. Stan looks at list after list of long-ago corporate transactions, trying to remember which ones Gil had tipped him about.

January 9
Stan's stockbroker and money-laundering partner, Grover Bismarck, is suspended by his employer, BMO Nesbitt Burns. He will soon be fired.

January 11, 5:28 p.m.
Stan emails Seaman: "I still want 'negative' credit for Gil-related purchases that resulted in losses (Nova Gold, for example)."

January 15, 12:04 p.m.
Gil's lawyer, Ian Smith, receives a faxed letter from Ontario prosecutor John Corelli. Gil gets a copy of the letter:

Thank you for meeting with me this morning to discuss the procedure for providing a "proffer" outlining the contents of a possible statement from your clients. . . . With respect to the proffers themselves, we discussed the manner in which they would be presented and recorded. Mr. Smith indicated that his proffer will consist of "nuts and bolts" and will refer to transactions generically, although with sufficient precision to enable us to identify them. It was noted that a number of the transactions involved companies in the same sector [mining] and, therefore, some identifiers will be necessary in order for us to distinguish one from the other. I also noted that we would like to record the proffers to ensure accuracy, both for ourselves and for our discussions with the Americans. Mr. Groia indicated that his client may be prepared to retain a court reporter to produce a transcript of the proffer. We may choose to make an audio recording of Mr. Smith's proffer, which can then be transcribed. . . . Mr. Groia inquired as to whether Mr. Grmovsek or Mr. Cornblum are suspected of any other criminal wrongdoing. I indicated that we are pursuing possible criminal charges in relation to tipping, insider trading, and related offences (e.g. money laundering and possession of the illicit profits) only. I am not aware of any potential allegations for matters such as fraud, theft, etc. . . . [T]he osc will likely seek some public interest orders under s. 127 of the *Securities Act* regarding your clients' future participation in the market. . . .

January 17
Stan emails Reg Mossworthy, his friend and civil lawyer:

> Yah, Groia went to go do the proffer, but they started negotiating the implications and the like so Groia said he wanted an outline of their agreement in writing before they proceeded as he was not on "the same page" as Cornblum's lawyer who wanted just a broad-based guilty plea without any details of the offence. The Crown was not agreeable (surprise). I told Groia that if he could drag it out another 40 years or so I should be ok. . . .

February 6, starting at 10:00 a.m.
Groia makes a proffer statement on behalf of Stan at prosecutor John Corelli's office. He is accompanied by Seaman. Also in the room are Joe Hull and Jim Stuart of the RCMP and Greg Gard from the OSC. Groia says little that the authorities (and the reader) do not already know. An equally cautious Ian Smith makes a proffer statement on behalf of Gil at 1:30 p.m.

February 3
Crawley and Seaman negotiate on the phone.

February 7
Under the username groiagang, Stan comes in first place in PokerStars Tournament #137384917. At 2:36 a.m., Stan sends an email to Groia and Seaman telling them the result and boasting, "I did the name 'groia' proud tonight."

February 9
Gil and Susan send an email to a committee of Toronto City Council expressing their opposition to a neighbour's plan to turn his front yard into a parking lot. Other than this, Gil has almost completely withdrawn from society. He stops taking his family to Holy Blossom Temple and lets his membership lapse.

February 10, 7:42 p.m.
Stan emails Seaman: "Grover Bismarck literally called me over 10 times today. I did not answer and he did not leave a message (I assume it was him as the calls came from a payphone). He is starting to remind me of Gil before he snapped (and we know what happened next)."

February 18, 2:31 p.m.
Gil's lawyer, Ian Smith, receives a faxed letter from Ontario prosecutor John Corelli. Gil gets a copy of the letter and reads that "In my letter dated January 15, 2009 I identified a tentative range of 4–7 years in custody. . . . I am [now] prepared to maintain an offer of 5–7 years. . . ." Gil is not pleased.

February 25

Stan's Washington lawyer, Pete Romatowski, spends 1.5 hours research-ing the "implication of [Stan's 2006] weapons conviction for sentencing." He bills Stan $1,162.50.

February 26

Stan writes a letter (edited by Grover Bismarck) to Doug Cope, man-ager of investigations for the Investment Dealers' Association:

> As you may be aware, I am the subject of an investigation by the Ontario Securities Commission. I have been asked [by Grover Bismarck] to write this letter to clarify my relationship with Grover Bismarck, my former investment advisor at BMO Nesbitt Burns, to assist him in his efforts to obtain employment. All transactions that Mr. Bismarck or his staff executed on my behalf were done at my initiative. There was no discretion used by Mr. Bismarck on any trades executed and all activity was authorized by me.

Stan also sends a copy of the letter to Michael Reynold at Canaccord, where Bismarck was seeking a new job. Canaccord would later hire Bismarck.

March 3, 11:06 a.m.

Stan on Sherdog, a site devoted to mixed martial arts: "I never bet a fight until I see the guy in the locker room just before the fight. . . . I think it is incumbent on the UFC to disclose [injuries to fighters] as soon as possible before a fight to prevent guys with inside knowledge taking advantage of what they know. . . . This kind of non-disclosure can only lead the UFC to a slide to the shenanigans of professional ten-nis (the easiest and most fixed sport by Russian gamblers). . . ."

March 19, 8:57 a.m.

Stan on Sherdog: "We have had Shamrock and Gracie of late as the top names that have used Performing Enhancing Drugs. . . . I am certain that a few more big names will get caught by better testing as they struggle to stick around to earn the bigger paychecks in a growing sport. . . . Most top athletes have used steroids at one time or another. Why should those in the UFC be any different? Since there is no clear test for Human Growth Hormone, I would be shocked if MOST UFC contenders and champs don't use it."

March 23, 11:28 p.m.
Stan on Sherdog: "Google 'Ultimate Bet' and 'scam' and find out that UB insiders and their friends stole millions from players by using a code that let them see everyone's cards. Any poker site that uses an Indian reservation as a home base is off my list."

April 2, 10:40 a.m.
Stan on Sherdog: "Anyone should be free to say anything. Period." [Two minutes later] "To insult someone anonymously is not a very masculine act" [writes "kingcityguru"].

April 12
Gil's 39th birthday.

April 19, 3:59 p.m.
Stan on Sherdog: "I find blood exciting."

April 21, 9:14 a.m.
Stan on Sherdog, referring to water-boarding torture: "This technique was applied over 200 times [on an alleged terrorist] and without any permanent damage done and resulted in valuable information that saved the lives of innocents. Well played."

April 24, 11:35 p.m.
Stan on Sherdog, starting a chat titled "Who Sells 'Proman Dummy' in the Toronto Area?": "Yes, I know I can ship it in from U.S. Internet suppliers; but the shipping costs and duties for this 85 pound bad boy are a bit steep (to say nothing of some customs agent thinking it is used for

S&M rather than training). Anyone know of an outlet that sells it in the Toronto area?" (The Proman Dummy was a rubber punching bag in the shape of a man. Stan wanted to improve his fighting skills before going to jail. But he would later claim that he had bought it for his son, who liked to wrestle with his dad, to wrestle with when Stan was gone.)

May 15, 10:40 a.m.
Seaman emails Stan:

> Gil has basically done the deal and they are now down to the final strokes so there is no chance we are going to get a discount for you being a cooperating witness against Gil (this is something we had spoken with Pete [Romatowski] about during our last call). The issue of Rochelle's house is still on the table and what Corelli is looking for is us to come up with a proposal that has him getting essentially money to avoid going after the house. Joe [Groia] got the feeling that [Corelli] does not really want to do it, but he is also going to use it as a negotiating tactic; Corelli . . . seems to think there is a lot of offshore money that is not accounted for. . . . [I]f we can really demonstrate that we are impecunious and we are putting everything on the table and there is no money hidden, then Corelli might be a little more easy to get along with in terms of the house.

May 16
The U.S. Securities and Enforcement Commission announces that two lawyers employed by the SEC in the enforcement division are under investigation for insider trading regarding a "large health-care company" and a "global oil company."

May 19
Seaman emails Stan:

> I write further to our discussion last Friday (May 15th) with Pete Romatowski and Joseph Groia and specifically to recap our dis-

cussion and to confirm our instructions from you. As we discussed on our call on Friday, now is likely your last opportunity to withdraw from or discontinue settlement discussions with the U.S. and Canadian authorities. . . . Pete advised during the call that in his view the deal that we are contemplating in the U.S. right now is not going to get better. In Pete's view failing a settlement [the U.S. authorities] will almost certainly pursue you. Pete is also concerned that where Gil Cornblum stands now (having almost completed his settlement) they will have a witness.

May or June
Stan works briefly as an expert adviser for a movie about insider trading being filmed in Toronto — Oliver Stone's *Wall Street II: Money Never Sleeps.*

June 4, 4:23 p.m.
Groia emails Stan a single word: "Congratulations." Below Groia's brief correspondence to his client is a forwarded email from John Corelli to Groia, sent at 3:33 p.m. Corelli wrote that, "Further to yesterday's meeting, this will confirm that I am prepared to offer your client a jail sentence of 39 months. . . . I can advise that [U.S. attorney] Ray Lohier is aware of this offer. As I know it is a relevant consideration in making your decision, I can advise that I have agreed to offer Mr. Cornblum a jail sentence of 39 months. I anticipate that he will accept that offer as it is consistent with his expectations."

At 10:28 p.m., Stan emails Groia (cc'ing Seaman) his response to Corelli's offer:

From my perspective and assuming the U.S. angle is not unnecessarily risky and the money laundering charge covers any tax offences connected with using an offshore vehicle, I accept. Can I get some assurances in this settlement regarding the third party accounts I controlled and what authorities intend to do about getting money from them (token payments are best;

or, in the alternative, gains less taxes and fees paid, et cetera)? If necessary, I will trade some more jail time to get those concessions as it is not only the only thing I can do at this point for them, but also the least. You can assure authorities that my memory would be clearer without the stress of worrying about those that I affected.

28 | STAN'S SWORN CONFESSION

RCMP: This is a preamble for the record. The date is July 7, year 2009. Time approximately 9:18 a.m. We are presently in the offices of the Ontario Securities Commission located at 20 Queen Street West, 21st floor, Toronto, Ontario. Present in the room are the following persons: Mr. Stanko J. Grmovsek; Ms. Kellie Seaman, counsel representing Mr. Grmovsek, and Joanna Kourakos, summer law student with Groia & Company; Mr. Greg Gard of the Ontario Securities Commission, Washington D.C., USA; Corporal Jamie Stuart of the Royal Canadian Mounted Police, Toronto Integrated Market Enforcement Team; and myself, Sergeant Joseph Hull of the Royal Canadian Mounted Police, Toronto Integrated Market Enforcement Team. Also in the room is our court reporter, Rachel Rosenberg. . . .

○ ○ ○

After Stan swore to tell the truth, Sergeant Hull started asking questions. The other officials sometimes asked questions too.

○ ○ ○

RCMP: . . . Where were you keeping that cash [from Grover Bismarck]?

STAN: Oh, at home. I have an ottoman that has a secret compartment. I'd stick it in there.

RCMP: What sort of person is [Gil]?

STAN: Gil is very reticent. He comes off as standoffish, a little smarmy at times. Very dry sense of humour, so that's probably why we got along well. Not very talkative, which although I talk a lot right now in front of you and seem very loquacious I'm generally very quiet. And we were both very quiet, so we got along well for that reason.

RCMP: [Asks if Stan has ever traded on information from a law firm where Stan worked.]

STAN: . . . I am never using my own information to buy stocks for myself or telling anyone about it. It sort of was like a line. Like, when I was at Osler Hoskin I had big deals also. I was working on the Shaw Communications takeover back then, the Gemini litigation matter, but I never told Gil about them. He would ask me. I would say, "Oh, I have nothing." It was almost like a psychological line I didn't want to cross. So I'm doing this, which I know is improper, but I don't want to go too far, psychologically at least.

o o o

At one point, Stan went off on a tangent, saying, "No one's totally innocent. Even though you can't convict them of anything, they're not innocent-innocent."

o o o

RCMP: Did [Gil] ever ask to see account statements?

STAN: Never. Zero. Because you got to understand, years ago I had cut him a cheque for $2.75 [million] or something. Because of that, so he trusted me enough—I didn't rip him off then, you know, so why is he going to assume I'm going to rip him off the second time? . . . From Gil's perspective, I've already proved myself to him. I've already given him, like, over $3 million. . . . I could have ripped him off, but I never did [sic]. Say I could have killed him—Gil used this joke: "You could have killed me, you would have had $6 million." And I didn't, so I sort of proved myself to him that he didn't have to worry about me. So he didn't ask questions, he never saw a statement, ever. Ever.

RCMP: . . . Throughout [the second phase of insider trading] what's his mental state like?

STAN: . . . When he was at Dorsey, it seemed like a very good setup to me. Like, he was resentful of the situation, but when I visited him he had the biggest office anyone had, there was no other partner there supervising him after a certain point where he ran the whole show there. He had a lot of clients. He was always taking lunches. Like, he wasn't doing a lot of work, doing deals. He wasn't drafting documents other than a few changes. So it seemed like a good life from my perspective as one that, if I was a lawyer, I would like it. But he was always resentful about it for some reason. So at that period of time he is just resentful about living or being a lawyer, and he did [insider trading] on the side maybe to keep going as a lawyer, he rationalized doing something he didn't like because of [the insider trading]. . . . He just hated [lawyering]. And he didn't work—you know, I worked as a lawyer, articling student, I worked longer hours than he ever did. He'd come in, you know, nine-ish. But the point is no one ever checked up on him. Because it was a U.S. firm, the Dorsey's example, and they're California hours, different hours, and there's no other partner in Toronto, so he's the guy. So he opens the shop, he closes the shop. But he was always complaining about it, always. . . . I think doing this thing with this money over here is almost an "F-you" to the firm that he hates. . . .

RCMP: . . . Is there a mason jar [full of Stan's gold or cash] buried in the backyard?

STAN: I wish there was. . . . No, there's no mysterious place. . . . There's no secret bank account or secret safety deposit box. . . .

OSC: Joseph, this would be a good point to bring up the firm Cassels Brock.

STAN: Sure. Yes.

osc: First off, are you familiar with a lawyer there by the name of Mark Bennett? [Of Cassels Brock & Blackwell, Mark organized the 2007 Intensive Course in Securities Law and Practice. He represented miners and worked closely with Gil on many deals.]

stan: Mark is or was—I knew him as a friend of Gil's. If I met him, I met him at Gil's wedding. I never met him again other than let's say I'm walking down the hallway with Gil, and there's Mark, and we'll say, "Hi." . . .

osc: Do you know any details of the business relationship between Dorsey and Cassels? And if you do, can you tell us about it?

stan: Sure, sure. I understand that Dorsey was sort of the go-to reference for Cassels for U.S. work, so if they needed a U.S. firm they would go to Dorsey as a choice, and vice versa; I think Cassels was Dorsey's Canadian firm. And because Gil has a relationship with Mark he would funnel a lot of work to Gil.

osc: Did Gil ever tell you about the specifics of where he was getting some of this information that he was sharing with you in terms of how it worked?

stan: [Describes several information-gathering methods.] There's a coffee shop in Toronto where poor lawyers and brokers talk, the Starbucks at Bay and Yonge [sic; he means King and Yonge, not far from Bay Street], and he said he heard stuff there all the time, like people talking about deals out loud. . . .

osc: Did he ever tell you specifically that "I got this information from Cassels, this is a deal we're doing with them," or any information like that?

stan: He probably would have said, "I got this from Cassels." Like, "Cassels referred this work to me." Like, that's come up many times.

osc: [Asks if Stan is sure that Goldcorp was Gil's client.]

stan: Gil had told me this many times. I had seen him meet Goldcorp people. You know, he walked down the hall, we'd be walking to lunch or something, and, like, Ian Tefler would say,

"Hey," like a little wave to Gil, walking somewhere down Bay Street. . . .

o o o

At one point, Stan realized just how much detailed evidence the authorities had collected about him. He reacted by joking, "What did I have for breakfast that morning? Do you have that down? . . . Well, you know when I flush the toilets, right? You have my water records, I assume."

o o o

STAN: I'll give you a tidbit you would never know. There's a shirt shop in the BCE Place, called Pace, P-A-C-E. So what Gil would often do was he'd buy shirts and bill that to the firm because it sounded like a restaurant, Pace. So that was his mindset. So every time we had lunch together I would be — he would say, "Who do you want to be today?" And I'd say, "I want to be Ian Tefler today." So if there's a note of a lunch with Ian Tefler, it's not Ian Tefler, it's me. . . .

OSC: . . . Do you ever remember being at lunch with him or maybe even dinner in New York on Canada Day 2006, I believe?

STAN: I don't recall that at all. Could you tell me what happened or what's significant about that?

OSC: Well, the reason I ask is because it's come to our attention that that very thing happened with another lawyer from Toronto where Cornblum claimed to be having dinner with this person and, in fact, the other lawyer in Toronto says he was never in New York on Canada Day that particular year.

STAN: I have not been to New York for many years. . . . It wasn't me.

OSC: But what I heard from you is that it was not uncommon for Cornblum to send expense claims to his firm where you had lunch with him but he claimed it to be somebody else, business-related.

STAN: That's correct, yes. Yes, that's right. That's right. If you want another credibility tidbit issue, he would buy — for example, he would bonus the bills. Like, if you did a deal, you'd bonus the account, you'd charge 120%, as an example. . . . So sometimes he would bill office furniture, like paintings or pictures that he bought for himself which he may have at his home now, he took them from the office. . . . [H]e would hide things into bills that were over-billed and to buy personal stuff. . . .

RCMP: How often would this occur in terms of the lunches where he would mention to you, like you had indicated, "Who do you want to be today?" Was this a fairly regular occurrence?

STAN: When we were having lunch fairly regularly and if we had a lunch that wasn't like a fast food, like a Taco Bell, which we both like to do, it would be that situation. . . . Like, if we went to a fast-food place, it was cash, I would pick it up; you know, $10, $15. But if it was a sit-down lunch, it's because he picked the restaurant, he wants to go there.

○ ○ ○

Stan talked about how Gil built up his client base, explaining that he

represented the AMEX [stock exchange] in Canada, and they would—anyone who wanted to go on the AMEX, usually that was small resource companies—[AMEX] would say, "Well, see our lawyer in Toronto, Gil Cornblum." And that's how he got lots of clients, through the AMEX. So he probably got most of his clients through Cassels on the referrals and AMEX, and they're both probably a good way to get clients because they're not competitive. Cassels doesn't care who he gets because he's a U.S. lawyer, he's not competing; "Here's our U.S. lawyer, Cornblum." And AMEX, Cornblum's their lawyer, he knows how AMEX operates, he knows everybody. "Well, here's our lawyer in Toronto, Cornblum."

Later Stan said,

Okay, I'll give you a flavour, which you would never know otherwise. One time in Vegas, one of our early trips, as you know of my gambling proclivities, I was at the craps table, and I had a $500 chip in my hand, and I threw 500 on the boxcars, which is a 36-to-1 bed, pays 31-to-1. I won $15,500 on this one bet. It was just a feeling I had, first time I ever bet that much on craps. I won! I won some more, so I ended up, left the table with about $17,000 or so. And then I bought him a skull mug as a drink, and for whatever reason he wanted to have a prostitute in Las Vegas, so I paid for one, $500. I remember it was $500. In Vegas, as you might know, they have the magazines of the women. He picked it out, I phoned, I paid, I never saw her, he did whatever it is.

o o o

OSC: . . . So just as it relates to [Stan's long-time stockbroker] Grover, if I told you that in a BMO trading account in his name that there's trading that mirrors almost identically what you did, would that surprise you?
STAN: I would be totally stunned. . . . He specifically said to me, "I never copy my clients' trades." Like, I mean, he looked at my face and said that to me, so I'm totally stunned. . . .
OSC: . . . I know for certain that you bought a fairly healthy share of Liquor Barn April 9th and you sold out your position April 10th. . . . And I can tell you that Bismarck did almost identically the same thing.

o o o

Stan mentioned a stock called Semafo that he had bought based on inside information from Gil. (Semafo was a gold- and uranium-mining company controlled by the king of Morocco that was active in West Africa. Gil had mistakenly told investigators that Semafo was controlled by the king of Monaco.) When the Semafo deal had failed to go through, Stan had been desperate to get rid of the stock at a decent price. He said,

I'm trying to pump that stock to whoever I meet. The police that came to my house during my divorce proceedings, because my wife called the police on me initially as what I call a divorce tactic,

I'm chatting with him, and he's saying, "What stock should I buy?" I say, "Buy Semafo," because I'm trying to get rid of it. It was at 70 cents, so I'm telling the cops, "Buy Semafo." And they should have listened, because it went up shortly afterwards.

o o o

SEC: . . . And all the cash you received from Grover Bismarck has been spent as well?

STAN: It was spent to—whatever I had left at home at that time when my accounts were frozen went to Mr. Greenspan. I might have kept $500. I know I had to let go of my live-in nanny, who was helping with my daughter and my son. I gave her whatever cash I had. I gave her my video recorder and a camera, a digital camera, because I didn't have enough to give her a proper severance. Hang on a sec. I was like—[Stan starts to cry.] Sorry. . . .

SEC: Do you need a minute?

STAN: Yes, because. . . .

RCMP: [To the court reporter] We're just going to pause for a moment.

o o o

When Stan recovered his composure, the questioning continued. At one point, asked if Susan knew of Gil's illegal activities, Stan said, "I'll give you a side point which you wouldn't know which explains why he kept her in the dark. Gil had a hair transplant. She doesn't know he had a hair transplant ever in his life. So that's something I knew from him, and I remember I discussed it with him. He said, 'You know, some things the wife doesn't need to know.' So if he didn't tell her that, he didn't tell her anything."

29 | GIL'S SWORN CONFESSION

RCMP: Good morning, everybody. This is a preamble for the record. The date is July 15, 2009. The time is approximately 9:18 a.m. We are presently in the offices of the Ontario Securities Commission located at 20 Queen Street West, 21st floor, Toronto, Ontario. Present in the room are the following persons: Mr. Gil Cornblum; Mr. Ian Smith, counsel representing Mr. Cornblum; Mr. Greg Gard of the Ontario Securities Commission; Mr. Christopher Nee of the United States Securities and Exchange Commission from Washington, D.C., United States of America. We're also joined by telephone by Ms. Ivonia Slade also of the United States Securities and Exchange Commission in Washington, D.C.; and, of course, myself, Sergeant Joseph Hull of the Royal Canadian Mounted Police, Toronto Integrated Market Enforcement Section. Also in the room is a court reporter, Liz Kichula. . . . Mr. Cornblum, it's my understanding that, during the course of resolution discussions between your counsel, Mr. Smith, and . . . John Corelli, a letter dated July 15th, 2009, outlining the conditions and procedures that apply for this interview had been agreed upon. . . .

DEFENCE LAWYER: Yes. That's correct. We've — I received this letter in its final version this morning, but we've read it and been involved in its drafting, and Mr. Cornblum has been shown this letter and understands it and accepts these terms and conditions. . . .

RCMP: . . . Mr. Cornblum, you may be charged with fraud, insider trading, money laundering, and possession of proceeds of crime in Canada. Do you understand the charges?

GIL: Yes.

RCMP: It's my duty to inform you you have the right to retain . . . and instruct counsel without delay. You have the right to telephone any lawyer you wish. You also have the right to free advice from a Legal Aid lawyer. If you are charged with an offence, you may apply to the Ontario Legal Aid Plan for assistance. 1-800-265-0541 and 1-800-561-2561 are toll-free numbers that will put you in contact with a Legal Aid duty counsel lawyer for free legal advice right now if you wish. I understand you have counsel here. However, it's your choice. Do you understand that, Mr. Cornblum?

GIL: Yes.

RCMP: Do you wish to call a lawyer right now?

GIL: No.

RCMP: Do you wish to say anything in answer to the charges? You are not obliged to say anything unless you wish to do so, but whatever you say may be given in evidence; do you understand?

GIL: Yes.

RCMP: . . . If you have spoken to any police officer or to anyone with authority or if any such person has spoken to you in connection with this case, I want it clearly understood that I do not want it to influence you in making any statement; do you understand?

GIL: Yes.

RCMP: Finally, if you choose to make a statement, it will be recorded in its entirety on audio and videotape media; do you understand?

GIL: Yes.

RCMP: I just ask you, Mr. Cornblum, to sign below where your name is right there, please. [Gil signs, indicating that he understood his rights.] Thank you very much. Now, we'll proceed to the under oath provisions, and I will turn this over to Liz, please. . . .

o o o

Gil swore on a Bible to tell the truth.

o o o

RCMP: Any comments, Greg, from the OSC standpoint before we begin?

OSC: No.

RCMP: Chris Nee of the SEC?

SEC: Mr. Cornblum, my name is Christopher Nee. As was mentioned, Ivonia Slade is joining from Washington with the SEC. I just want to confirm your understanding for the record that this interview is voluntary.

GIL: Confirmed.

SEC: And you've received a copy of the agreement that governs the terms of this agreement between you and the SEC through your U.S. counsel, Mr. Colton?

GIL: Correct.

RCMP: . . . Okay. Please state your name and spell it for the record, Mr. Cornblum.

GIL: Gil Cornblum, G-I-L. Cornblum is C-O-R-N-B-L-U-M.

RCMP: Can you provide us with your current address and telephone number, please?

GIL: The address is 74 Icarus, I-C-A-R-U-S, Avenue, Toronto, Ontario, M4V 1H6. And you said phone number?

RCMP: Yes, please.

GIL: Area code 416, 972-1132.*

RCMP: Okay. And your date of birth as well, please.

GIL: April 12, 1970.

RCMP: Are you married?

GIL: Yes, I am.

RCMP: Any children?

GIL: Yes.

RCMP: How many?

GIL: One.

RCMP: Can you please discuss your education that you've obtained after high school?

GIL: [Describes his education.]

RCMP: Okay. Any other professional designations, Certified Financial Planner, or anything of that like?

GIL: I am a member of the Law Society of Upper Canada. Member of the New York State Bar.

RCMP: Okay. Are you currently employed, Mr. Cornblum?

GIL: No.

RCMP: I would like to discuss your employment history. . . .

GIL: [Describes his employment history.]

RCMP: Very well.

GIL: I have not worked since May of last year, May of 2008.

RCMP: Okay. Going back to your articling period, Mr. Cornblum, how would you characterize your knowledge of investments in the capital markets in general at that point in time?

GIL: I had a degree in economics. So, I would say, depending on — certainly not a professional level. I'd say at the level of an educated reader of the newspaper. You know, someone who follows — follows, you know, news stories, business stories.

RCMP: You know Mr. Stan Grmovsek?

GIL: Yes.

RCMP: When did you meet — when did you first meet Mr. Stan Grmovsek?

GIL: The first week of law school, which would have been September 1990.

RCMP: Okay. How would you characterize your relationship with Mr. Grmovsek at that time?

GIL: In 1990?

RCMP: Yeah.

GIL: I would say we were friends, good friends. I think in that year I had maybe two or three good friends. He was one of my better friends. I found him kind of interesting and amusing and loud and brash. And he — it was his second year, second time taking the first year of law. So, he kind of knew the school and knew what to expect. So, he was, you know, a good guy to have in your corner.

RCMP: How would you characterize his knowledge of the securities industry or capital markets at that point in time? Did you have discussions about stocks or anything of that like?

GIL: Yeah. You appreciate this is close to 20 years ago.

RCMP: Correct.

GIL: I'm sure he was good. I think it was very good. I don't remember if we had very many discussions in 1990 about investments.

RCMP: And your friendship evolved over time. Did you remain to be good friends post–law school?

GIL: Yes, we did.

RCMP: . . . Do you understand when we're talking about material, non-public information as it relates to the securities industry, do you understand what that is?

GIL: Yes.

RCMP: Okay. How would you define that, Mr. Cornblum?

GIL: Information which a reasonable investor would believe would cause a security to rise or fall a material amount.

RCMP: Okay. So, that's materiality. And the non-public component being what?

GIL: Information not generally known to the public, not disseminated to the public.

RCMP: Okay. Have you ever personally traded on material, non-public information yourself?

GIL: No.

RCMP: And going back in time, when was the first time that you had become aware Mr. Grmovsek had traded on material, non-public information?

GIL: I guess it would be 1994.

RCMP: Okay. And can you discuss that in a little more detail?

GIL: While articling [at Fraser & Beatty, now called Fraser Milner Casgrain] I informed him of I think it was a hostile transaction between two forestry companies, Slocan and Canfor. And he traded on those, on that information. I'm not sure what the profits were. I don't believe they were considerable.

RCMP: Okay. So that idea of providing him with that information, Mr. Cornblum, how did that come about? Like, if you can walk me through. You, as I understand, had information relating to this business combination. How did it come about you providing him with that material, non-public information?

GIL: Can you be more specific in your question?

RCMP: Sure. . . . How did you become aware of this material, non-public information in regards to the forestry companies?

GIL: I believe I was asked to do some work on the file, maybe antitrust work, but I can't remember. . . . I think it was a memo on antitrust rules. . . . My recollection is very hazy.

RCMP: . . . Okay. So, now Mr. Grmovsek becomes aware of it. So, how did that happen?

GIL: I told him. Again, I can't tell you if it was in person or by the telephone. It was 20 years ago.

RCMP: Why would you have told him? What was that impetus is what I'm looking for here?

GIL: Well, I mean, that's a longer tale than, you know, you probably want to hear. There were a variety of reasons. I was very down, depressed, gloomy at the time. I think you read the Taerk report that, you know, my psychiatrist prepared several months ago and, I mean, describes my feelings of inadequacy and worthlessness. At the same time Stan had approached me early in my articles. . . . And, you know, had suggested, you know, we could do this, that he would trade. We could split the profits. And, you know, the economy was in the pits. He, I don't believe, was working at the time. You know, I didn't hold much hope that I would be working after my articles were complete. So, it would be a buffer for us and, you know, kept kind of hammering at that for weeks or months. I'm not sure, you know, the evolution of how he came up with it, how he approached me. . . . We would split the profits equally. I guess now maybe is as good a time as any to confirm something that I think Ian has told you. I've never seen records of any trades. So, you know, when you ask me did he trade, you know, again, it's all to the best of my knowledge based on what he told me. I can't confirm if he actually did trade or what the amounts were in.

RCMP: . . . Did you ever advise Mr. Grmovsek to either purchase securities or options? Was there any discussions like that where you may have advised him what particular financial instrument to acquire?

GIL: No. I think my advice, you know, went no further than to be careful.

RCMP: Be careful in what sense?

GIL: Be careful not to get caught, not to do something so egregious, so—not to do something so huge that it would stick out. You know, buy all the options, buy options that expire two days before expiry date, buy 60% of the equity traded in a week, things like that.

RCMP: So, what was the concern there if he went out and bought 60% of the options, what would be the concern?

GIL: Well, as down, as depressed as I was, I was, you know, still aware that trading on insider information is against the law and being caught has negative repercussions.

RCMP: You're talking from a regulations standpoint or a criminal standpoint or both?

GIL: Every standpoint.

RCMP: . . . Do you know why [Stan] quit the law firm [Johnstone & Associates]?

GIL: I think a variety of reasons. I think he probably had made pretty decent money on, you know, a couple of deals before, and I think he was, you know, kind of fired. I think he—later learned he was fired, but I think he either had been fired or had such a terrible personality clash with the . . . guy who ran the firm he had to leave.

RCMP: So, why was he fired again? Was it over a personality clash or some other reason?

GIL: It was personality. I learned this—I mean, he had said he quit. I learned that he was, if not fired, told to go somewhere else in 2006 when—2005, no, 2006. . . . The head of the corporate group at Gardiner Roberts is this guy that Stan worked for. I think his name was Johnson or Johnston, and he'd called me and asked for a reference for this guy who was leaving my firm [to join Gardiner Roberts]. I gave him a good reference and said, you know, would you believe that I actually had lunch with Stan today, and there was a silence on the phone, and then he just kind of went in on how Stan was a terrible person to work with, never paid attention, you know, had destroyed furniture in the office like, I think, you know, kind of ripped up all the lining of the chair and scratched up the desk and could never get a day's work out of him. . . . So, that leaves me to believe that he was fired back in '97.

RCMP: . . . You had indicated earlier you were depressed at one point in time. You were living in fear, in this state of anxiety. Why did you repeatedly honour his request to provide information to him?

GIL: That's a good question, isn't it? . . . It's not greed. Greed is a human constant, but it's not greed. And, you know, I have had the benefit of over a year to think about it and analyze myself and, you know, kind of think of kind of the correct views on the, you know, better views on my life. I think the answer is kind of more subtle, that I was in, you know, what I now know is a very depressed state, very—you know, many times near-suicidal state. I considered suicide on a daily basis in New York, sometimes more, sometimes less seriously, but certainly on a daily basis. I felt like a fraud, that I was worthless. And at Stan's suggestion, and I did go along with it, this did make me feel a little better. It was kind of a window—window out of the helplessness and depression. I mean, it's clear it probably made me more depressed and, you know, more anxious, but at the time it was kind of a result of that—of a depression illness.

RCMP: Did you talk to Stan about it at that time, tell him how you felt about all this?

GIL: I told him it was making me crazy.

RCMP: And what was his reaction to that?

GIL: I don't know if he had one. I think just, you know, "Keep on going." You know, "Won't be long." You know, "Just keep doing it. You're doing great."

RCMP: Did you ever confide in anyone else at that time about how you felt about this? Did you ever have any conversations?

GIL: No. No.

OSC: Did you seek medical help during this period, Gil?

GIL: If only I did, right. No. I did not. . . . I didn't think I was ill. I thought it was normal. And I've had suicidal thoughts from high school, and I thought it was normal. I thought everyone was like that.

RCMP: . . . Why did this all start up again [in 2004]?

GIL: Well, I think the impetus is clear on his end. On my end, I now recognize that my wife's illness, the fact I was passed over for partnership in 2003. You know, one of the reasons they gave for passing me over for partnership was I hadn't been in the office a lot because my wife was ill. I think it led to what now I know is a depressed state, one that made me very vulnerable, one in which, you know, you know, I always know right from wrong, but one in which my—my thinking just became very blurry and fuzzy and very questionable. And, you know, all the while Stan kept saying, you know, "Let's do it, let's do it, let's do it, let's get it started again. . . ."

RCMP: Were you experiencing any financial hardship in and around that time period?

GIL: No. . . . [Money] is not what I stood for. I was a pretty decent lawyer, a family man. I lived within my means.

RCMP: . . . Why don't we take Possis [Project Radical], then. Tell us a little bit more specifically what you did, and then we'll go on to the other transactions more generally.

GIL: I typed in, you know, on a search function Van Horn's last name, and some document related to the Possis transaction showed up. I mean, it's been over a year and a half, so I couldn't tell you —

RCMP: I understand, but try your best.

GIL: . . . A document that made it clear that Possis was in the process of negotiating a takeover.

RCMP: Did you print out the document, or did you just look at it on the screen?

GIL: I looked at it on the screen.

RCMP: Did you see any other documents?

GIL: I'm sure I saw more than one.

RCMP: And why did you look at more than one document?

GIL: Curiosity.

RCMP: Was this over a day, or how long was this process of reviewing Mr. Van Horn's directory to look at the Possis-related documents?

GIL: Oh, I'm sure, you know, I would check every couple of days, I'm sure. Every time I was bored. Every time I was upset that no one was helping me on a file. . . .

U.S. ATTORNEY: . . . Throughout this period of time from 2005, April 2005 on, Mr. Cornblum, did you understand that what you were doing was illegal in the U.S.?

GIL: Yes.

U.S. ATTORNEY: . . . Did you sign, while you were an associate and a partner at Dorsey & Whitney, any policies that you know that it was a violation of Dorsey & Whitney policy to provide material, non-public information to outsiders?

GIL: I don't recall if I saw any, but I knew it was a violation of policy.

RCMP: . . . Do you recall what you did with that money, those two $5,000 payments [through Grover Bismarck]?

GIL: I think in both cases I just used them, you know — I, among other things, go to St. Lawrence Market every weekend, pay in cash. That's the kind of cash-only place and various cash-only, you know, transactions. . . .

RCMP: And [Stan] never discussed with you . . . where the money went?

GIL: No. . . . It is inconceivable to me, absolutely inconceivable, that you have caught even 20% of the cash if, according to the letter that I received from Corelli, you found one-and-a-quarter-million dollars. He has at least 10 in total is my guess. . . . He's not a spender. So, I don't think a single dollar was lost from the first amount [from the first phase]. But he is a big liar. You know, I've said before and I'll say it again for the record, you know, I had no clue that he had engaged in this cottage business for his wife, his wife's in-laws [sic], for his neighbour, you know, probably for Carl Dahomey [sic], for his friend Jimmy. . . . He, you know, lied to me about more than one thing. And my guess is that he lied to me about the size of the investments probably on a deal-by-deal basis. . . .

RCMP: [Asks Gil why he continued to tip Stan from 2004 to 2008.]

GIL: There is another million-dollar question, isn't it? More than that, in my case. I have said before, and you can believe it or not believe it, I believe it, I think I was clinically really depressed. I think my head was in the wrong place. I think I, you know, I think I was very ill. I think my judgment was very clouded. You know, I didn't do it for greed. . . . Well, the answer is that I was insane. My judgment was clouded, and, you know, he had gotten me in various moments of weakness, various moments when, you know, my life was unravelling. You know, my wife was sick, continued to be ill. You know, we haven't discussed it, and I prefer not to, but my son has his own chronic illness. My life has been hard otherwise. Again, it's hard to believe a guy who makes 80 grand a year and then makes a million bucks a year [not including insider trading], but to me my life has been very hard and a lot of struggles and a lot of continual struggles, and work had its own issues, and, you know, for all those reasons, variety of reasons, my judgment was clouded, and he preyed on that.

SEC: . . . You list [on a financial statement] an RRSP account of almost $100,000, and it states that this has since been collapsed.

GIL: Correct.

SEC: What do you mean by collapsed? You took the money out essentially or cashed out the securities?

GIL: It's a Registered Retirement Savings Plan. You're not supposed to, but for limited reasons, take money out of that account until you retire. I took money out of it some time in May, I believe. There is a withholding amount that was left at the broker, and the rest was sent to me by cheque.

SEC: Okay. And what—do you recall what the amount was that you received by cheque?

GIL: I think somewhere in the 60s, high 60s.

SEC: And what did you do with that cash?

GIL: Put it into the bank and used it to pay legal fees, taxes, other living expenses.

SEC: . . . So your disability insurance is the only source of income?

GIL: Correct.

SEC: And your wife is not working; is that accurate?

GIL: Correct. Yes.

RCMP: . . . How long is your disability insurance expected to last?

GIL: Until I go to jail. Two years or until I'm convicted of something.

OSC: . . . Gil, I got some wrap-up questions here, and my questions go back to your employment at Sullivan Cromwell, and I'm going to show you your transcripts that you sent into Sullivan Cromwell. I'm going to show your transcripts for Osgoode Law School, and I want you to have a look at those for me, please.

GIL: Oh, I know that. That I changed marks on the transcript when I applied to S&C. Yeah.

OSC: That's right. Can you tell us why?

GIL: I was desperate for a job. And so I did what I had heard other people had done.

OSC: And you did what other people had done?

GIL: What I heard other people had done.

OSC: Which is what?

GIL: Change marks on transcripts.

OSC: And make them better?

GIL: Yeah.

OSC: . . . It looks like marks were changed in the fall/winter session of '92–'93. And it looks as though a taxation law course that you had a "C" in, the version that was submitted to Sullivan Cromwell reflects an "A."

GIL: Mm-hmm.

OSC: Does that ring a bell?

GIL: It sounds right.

OSC: Okay. And I think — and then a corporate finance and securities regulation course, in the Osgoode version is a "B"; in the Sullivan Cromwell version, it's an "A."

GIL: Yeah. Again, sounds right.

OSC: And I think the same thing for Canada/U.S. business course, Osgoode it's a "B"; Sullivan Cromwell it's an "A."

GIL: Yeah, that sounds right.

OSC: Fall/winter '93–'94, same sort of thing, commercial law course, Osgoode is a "C+"; Sullivan Cromwell is an "A."

GIL: Mm-hmm. Yes.

OSC: Trusts, Osgoode "B"; Sullivan Cromwell "A."

GIL: Right.

OSC: And again it was — it was to get a job?

GIL: Just to get a job.

OSC: . . . There is a version of some of your expense reports from Dorsey Whitney. I want you to have a look there, okay?

GIL: Mm-hmm.

OSC: And in particular I want to ask you about a business called Pace, P-A-C-E.

GIL: Yeah.

OSC: What can you tell me about Pace?

GIL: That was a clothing store downstairs, and I expensed it as a meal . . . I think three or four times.

OSC: . . . Some of the receipts that are attached to the back of some of the expense reports, some of them have handwriting on them?

GIL: Yeah.

OSC: Is that your handwriting?

GIL: Yeah.

OSC: And can you read what some of them say?

GIL: "Lunch for working group." . . . "Meeting with working group" is another one. Here is one "working lunch."

OSC: Is that true?

GIL: No. No. Not true.

OSC: . . . Did you alter the receipts?

GIL: . . . I think I did, yes. . . . I think I was spiralling out of control and falsified an expense report.

30 | THE END OF NEGOTIATIONS

Seeking information, Stan registered with www.prisontalk.com under the username "poorjudgment." He went to the chat-room for Canadians to comment in the following discussions: "Best Discount Collect Call Provider for Ontario," "Who Is the Least Expensive Collect Call Provider in Canada," "Prisoners Can Sue for Harm Done to Them in Prison," "They Don't Make TVs Small Enough!!!," and "Prescription Medication in Prison."

At around the same time, Stan fell down one evening and, as he emailed to Seaman, "exacerbated a degenerative disk problem in my back that may or may not require surgery (honestly, I really can't walk and can only crawl—thank goodness for the Oxycontin)." Much later, Stan would tell me he hurt his back "lifting weights." His email to his lawyer's assistant continued with "If the jail sentence is well off in the future, I will probably get surgery right away if I need it. If it is in October or so I will put it off until after I 'pay my debt to society' as I would hate to enter Millhaven [Maximum Security Penitentiary] as a scrawny dude just recovering from surgery."

o o o

Stan signed a consent order with the SEC on October 9, agreeing to disgorge (which means to "give up") $1,472,000 (U.S.). On October 25, he signed a consent order with the OSC, agreeing to disgorge $1,033,000

(Canadian). He also agreed to never again work in the securities industry. After the signing of these consent orders, almost all of Stan's known illegal profits would be seized by the U.S. and Ontario governments.

Both orders protected Stan from further legal action by the SEC and the OSC — as long as he had told the truth during the negotiations. The SEC had agreed to strip Stan of only $1,472,000, as opposed to the $8,500,000 in total illegal profits they could prove that he had earned on U.S. markets over the 14 years, because he had convinced the SEC that he couldn't afford to pay more than $1,472,000. If it was later proven that Stan had provided false financial information, then the agreement would be nullified and the SEC and the OSC could go after him for further penalties.

Stan's friends and family, who had not known that Stan was managing their accounts illegally, would give up only some of their proceeds — $238,000 in total, or around 15% of their profits derived from his crimes.

Stan had given the SEC a "Statement of Financial Condition." It stated that he had $780 in cash; no real estate; $4,000 worth of furniture in his "1.5 bedroom aprt"; a 2003 SUV worth $12,000; a Registered Retirement Savings Plan worth $1,801.92; a "last month's rent" deposit of $1,137, held by his landlord; a judgment against Donald Berlusconi, in the amount of $214,200, which Stan described as "improperly set aside"; and another outstanding loan to a friend, another gambler, in the amount of $7,850. On the debt side of his personal balance sheet, Stan stated that he owed $33,728.44 on his credit card and $50,000 to his sister. He described the $1,150 he had to pay each year for his term life insurance policy, plus his rent, plus the $4,500 a month he was supposed to pay in support to Rochelle and their children. Stan claimed to have zero income while spending about $10,000 a month on living expenses and family support and about $17,000 a month on lawyer's bills.

Stan had earned many millions in illegal profits from Gil's tips over the years — not paying any income tax on the profits hidden offshore — but, as with Gil, the money would not end up benefiting him that much. On his income tax form for 2008, Stan would claim a net loss of $115,057. He would lose even more in 2009.

As all of their lawyers continued to negotiate and rack up billable hours, Gil and Stan both made preparations in advance of their upcoming guilty pleas.

On October 18, at 9:34 a.m., Stan emailed Kellie Seaman with a request for Groia to "tip" a certain journalist: "I have developed a friendship over the last year or so with Joe Schneider of Bloomberg. He altered his first article to include some corrections I wanted and gives the impression that he would be very agreeable to spinning things in a way that I would likely find agreeable. He also told me that he would include any quotes from me or my counsel that I wanted if we gave him the first heads up."

A few days later, Stan emailed Seaman: "I only ask about the judge because of my choice of attire. I have my 'respectful and contrite' outfit picked out for Tuesday—I even researched it by reading the ideas of professional jury consultants."

On October 22, at almost 9:00 p.m., John Corelli emailed both Ian Smith and Kellie Seaman:

> Here is the latest draft of the agreed facts. . . . I have agreed to refer to just about everyone by their initials. In doing so, I am more than a little perplexed by the notion that this can be done in an agreed statement of facts filed on a plea whereas a publication ban would not likely be granted if this same evidence were called at trial. However, if the press wants to challenge the use of initials we can deal with that later. The unresolved issue is whether even initials should be used. Ian [Smith] would like to use an even less descriptive means of referring to Cornblum's wife.

One of Gil's main concerns during the negotiations was minimizing the embarrassment of his wife.

> But if I do that I will have to refer to everyone else by some equally anonymous moniker—and to what end I'm not sure. Calling someone his wife, as opposed to S.R.* [the initials of Susan's

maiden name], seems to do little to advance the protection of her identity. As well, part of the purpose of this document is to show the friends and family—who do not have access to the statements or Crown Brief—how they were unwittingly implicated in the scheme. . . . In any event, it does not take a sophisticated Google search to find out the names of Cornblum's wife and son, their address, or the synagogue they attend. Accordingly, using some other method of describing her seems cumbersome and futile.

Seaman forwarded Corelli's email to her client at 9:12 the next morning.

Forty-two minutes later, Stan emailed her back with a few suggested changes to the statement of facts, including the removal of his email address. He concluded with "if Ian gives you any lip say that my client has a vivid recollection of dropping off a $600G cheque [for Gil and Susan's matrimonial home] for your client's house at her apartment, her expecting it, and saying thank you for delivering the money (which means she obviously knew of an arrangement between Gil and me)."

Seaman replied to Stan at 11:04 a.m.:

Your email address is removed [from the statement of facts]. However, Corelli may refer to you still as "King City Guru." . . . The cheque. I raised it in the context of para 63 and thought it didn't do much to get things around to our language. It created quite a bit of fuss between Ian [Smith] and Corelli on the identification of Gil's wife. Gil wants her initials removed and her to be just referred to as his wife. His counsel pitched it as she is completely innocent. This prompted Corelli to commence a long diatribe about [Stan's] father. I'm summarizing here but he said in all of this your father is the most innocent person and would be embarrassed to have his name used, yes, but he never even requested that his name not be used. He said Gil put his money in his wife's name and you delivered a cheque to her and these are stages of money laundering. On a final note, there was some discussion about Grover Bismarck and we were asked to let you and Gil know that you will likely be contacted in the next couple of months by IPOC (Integrated Proceeds of Crime) Investigators as they are proceeding against Grover. Corelli added that you do not have to cooperate [i.e., testify against Bismarck] until this is all done. . . .

At 2:24 p.m., Stan emailed Seaman: "On the Grover front, I understand that I do not have to cooperate until this is done, so maybe tell them that I will [cooperate] whenever they want (including [wearing] a wire) if they give a note to the U.S. judge about my cooperating. . . ."

At 7:58 p.m., Stan emailed a copy of the statement of facts to Joe Schneider of Bloomberg News:

Joe, attached is what looks like will be the final version of the Agreed Statement of Facts that should help you get a jump on things. Much of the "flavour" has been taken out, but that can be added after sentencing in a month or so. I am again stating as we agreed that I do NOT want anything released until AFTER the press release by the OSC/SEC is released on what looks like the late afternoon of the 27th. I don't want to give you particulars on the deal right now because I do not know if the OSC/SEC will be including that in their press release (if so, you can obviously punch in what they say; if not and you include it, they will know it came from me). . . . As I have not been formally sentenced and there is still some uncertainty from the U.S. angle, I don't want to piss anyone off by screwing up the deal. In short, use these facts as background for your story, but please wait as we agreed until after the OSC/SEC press release to release your story . . . perhaps a respectable half hour at least. After that, you can call Groia and whomever at the OSC/SEC to get quotes to beef it up on your following updates (but please don't tell them I sent you this statement of facts). I hope that I will be in a position to help you more in upcoming weeks.

31 | THE ABYSS

Very early in the morning of October 26, when it was still very dark, Gil left his house for a walk. He often went for long walks. He was unemployed and withdrawn from society—plenty of time and energy for walking. He locked the door, leaving his sleeping wife and son inside.

Goodbye, he probably thought.

Gil had a lot to think about. He was supposed to meet his lawyer the next morning to finalize the deals that had been negotiated. He was supposed to sign consent orders with the OSC and SEC the next day, just as Stan had done earlier in the month. Gil and Stan were then supposed to appear at a Toronto courthouse to be officially charged with the crimes of insider tipping and trading on the Toronto stock market. Following that, they would travel to Manhattan (in the same airplane) to be officially charged with insider tipping and trading on the New York and NASDAQ Stock Exchanges. Sometime after the charges were laid and the guilty pleas were made, the ex-friends would be both sentenced.

They did not know exactly what the sentence would be—that was up to the judges in Toronto and Manhattan—but they both knew that they were going to prison for a long time. They hoped to avoid being sent to a U.S. prison, much tougher than a Canadian prison. Gil would get a longer sentence because he had breached the trust of his employer and his employer's clients, while Stan had only breached the trust of a co-conspirator — perfectly legal.

Gil was terrified of going to jail. He knew that small, soft men like himself did not have an easy time behind bars. He had heard stories and jokes about people being beaten and raped in prison.

The financial future of his family was also scary. Susan had not worked outside the home in years. After Gil signed the consent orders and was officially charged, the authorities would start seizing his assets just like they had Stan's. He knew that the authorities might consider his and Susan's matrimonial home as "proceeds of crime," for it had been bought with money from the first phase of insider trading. Gil's wife and son loved their beautiful home. Would government seizure force Gil's family out of their home? Where would they live then? With Gil unemployable and having spent a small fortune on lawyer's bills, would asset seizures deny his family an acceptable lifestyle? Gil believed that he had "grown up on the wrong side of the tracks"; was Saul also to have to grow up over there? After Gil had brought home so much wealth and success, would his legal problems send his family into poverty?

As soon as tomorrow came, Gil believed, his family would be on the path to financial ruin. But what if tomorrow were never to come?

If Gil were somehow to disappear before tomorrow — if he had the power of Kwisatz Haderach — then he would not have to sign consent orders, he would not have to plead guilty in court, he would not be sent to jail, and his family's property would be out of the clutches of government seizure.

That was the only loophole — to disappear.

October 26, 2009, was a cool and cloudy morning, a few degrees above freezing. All but a few dry, brown leaves had fallen from the trees. The dead leaves on the sidewalks and streets were mostly still wet from the foggy, rainy morning and afternoon. A few dried-out leaves were rattled and blown around by a wind from the southeast, from New York State. The moon was a thin crescent, barely visible overhead.

Gil walked east, toward the Don Valley. This forested ravine and flood plain around the heavily polluted Don River stretched from the lakeshore in the south to the north end of Toronto. A railway track, a line of electricity towers, and a line of telephone poles ran along the west side of the valley. A tangle of bike paths scribbled through the ravine. The Don Valley Parkway, a busy highway, ran along the east side of the valley. There were several bridges that crossed the Don Valley.

One of them, the Bloor Street Bridge (also known as the Prince Edward Viaduct), had until recently been a "suicide magnet"—a place that attracted people who wanted to jump off. As a result of the many such tragedies on the Bloor Street Bridge, Toronto's city government had recently installed a barrier of metal wires. This "Luminous Veil" effectively blocked would-be jumpers. After it was built, nobody had jumped from the bridge.

But it wasn't the only bridge over the Don Valley. A few kilometres north, Millwood Road crossed the valley on the Leaside Bridge, which—at 45 metres or 13 stories in height—was a bit taller than the Bloor Street Bridge. The Leaside Bridge had become Toronto's new suicide magnet.

Gil walked there.

Passing a Salvation Army building and a transformer station, Gil walked onto the west end of the bridge. The Don Valley Parkway ran under the other end of the bridge.

Six lanes wide and lit by yellowish overhead streetlights, the Leaside Bridge was half a kilometre long. The traffic was sparse so late at night, with only an occasional vehicle crossing the bridge; a heavy bus or a truck would cause the bridge to shake, making the whole structure feel unstable to a pedestrian. From ahead, Gil heard the sounds of the highway traffic flowing under the bridge.

There was a narrow sidewalk on each side of the bridge. There was a low concrete wall, its inner sides moulded into a pattern of eight-sided star shapes, running along the outer edges of both sidewalks, topped by a metal railing. The top of the aluminum railing was about five feet high; Gil was barely tall enough to look over it. The streetlights were held up against the night sky by long metal-sheathed poles; at the base of each pole was a NO STOPPING sign.

Gil stopped walking. He climbed onto the top of the railing.

To the east, on the parkway, a stream of white headlights flowed north, and a similar flow of red tail-lights snaked to the south. Gil could not see inside the darkened cars, but the people in the cars could (if they happened to be looking at the right time) see him on the wrong side of the bridge railing, over the abyss, ready to let go.

To the south, the horizon was filled with the buildings of downtown Toronto, including the Bay Street skyscraper where Gil had worked until the previous year. (Some other Dorsey & Whitney lawyer had taken over his old office there.) Many of the glass-sided skyscrapers were illuminated by fluorescent bulbs inside the offices. The bulging spire of the CN Tower, glowing from top to bottom with red and white lights, stabbed up into the night sky. It was a beautiful sight, a beautiful city at night. Did Gil then remember seeing the city for the first time, in its first wild promise of all the mystery and beauty of the world? He had come to Toronto as a young child; he had been schooled there; he had met Stan there; other than a few years in glamorous Manhattan, he had lived his entire adult life there; he had wooed and married Susan in Toronto, and there he had become a father to Saul. Toronto was Gil's only home.

Beneath Gil, barely visible in the darkness, waited a dark, autumnal forest and flood plain. Dark shadows of clumped sumacs, red oaks, grasses, patches of bare soil, patches of gravel. Several lightning-blasted trees were sprawled on the ground in awkward, unnatural pieces. Gil was high above the tops of the tallest leafless trees.

Numb, senseless, betrayed by his best friend, Gil stood before the abyss; there was no hope or comfort anywhere else to be found, he felt, there was nowhere else to turn.

Driven to desperation by the horrible need in his heart, Gil released the cold metal rail and let himself, finally, fall into the enveloping, embracing darkness; wind shrieked in his ears as he dropped; he felt as if he was floating.

He reached a speed of over 100 kilometres per hour — as fast as the cars on the nearby highway. Dropping 45 metres down, Gil was in the air for almost four seconds.

What was he thinking about on the way down, during those four seconds?

BANG!

His impact shook the earth. His violent embrace of the flood plain echoed from the bottom of the concrete-and-iron bridge and its giant concrete-and-iron legs.

Under the bridge, broken, Gil lay dying.

o o o

At 7:16 a.m. on October 26, half an hour before sunrise, Gil was found sprawled on the soft ground of the flood plain, still barely alive.

During the 40 minutes he lay in the ravine, was Gil ever conscious? Nobody will ever know. Did he realize anything—some insight, some self-understanding, anything—in his extreme final moments? Nobody will ever know.

Paramedics lifted Gil into a vehicle. Police officers took notes. Again, an ambulance with shrieking sirens and flashing red-and-white lights rushed Gil to the hospital. Later that morning, in a hospital bed, Gil escaped.

o o o

The suicide rate among lawyers is six times higher than among non-lawyers. Jumping from a height is unusual (7%)—most escaping lawyers use guns (52%), hanging (22%), or poison (18%).

o o o

Later that day *Globe and Mail* reporter Jacquie McNish asked Gil's wife for a comment. Susan said that her husband's death was "the culmination of a life-long battle with severe depression. He was a wonderful friend to many, and the finest husband and father possible. We are all mourning his absence."

32 | AFTERWARD

On the same day as his death, the criminal charges against Gil were dropped, both in Toronto and in Manhattan. There would be no attempt to seize his widow's home or property.

Asked for his reaction to Gil's death by Bloomberg News reporter Joe Schneider, Stan left a very short message on the reporter's answering machine: "It's a tragedy." Stan would be upset by the story Schneider wrote because Stan thought it quoted him in a way that implied the other information in the piece was also from Stan, which was untrue. (His hurt feelings came partly from the fact that he had considered Schneider a friend.)

The next day, October 27, Stan appeared at Old City Hall at 8:30 a.m. This was his first personal court appearance on the insider-trading charges. He was officially charged by Corporal Jamie Stuart of the RCMP.

Although Stan estimated that he had committed between 100 and 150 illegal trades, the prosecution mentioned only the 46 that they were able to corroborate through supporting evidence. This was the number of trades that would be referred to, incorrectly, in the international media as the total number of Gil and Stan's illegal trades. (The partial list of illegal trades given to the courts and the media did not include, for example, Stan's offshore purchase of Aur Resources shares in 2004.)

Although Stan managed investments for others for profit without a stockbroker's licence, he would not be charged for those illegal acts.

The judge in Courtroom 126 was Robert G. Bigelow. He was a stout, pleasant-looking man with white hair, a pink face, and a bright red sash across his black judge's robe.

The Crown prosecutor was John Corelli. He had a master's degree in law from Osgoode Hall Law School. He was 5′11″, slim, and dark-haired. (I wrote in my notebook "Edgy but nice.") He lectured other lawyers regularly on the topic of asset seizure and forfeiture as well as on the topic (in February 2007) of "Money Laundering and the Legal Profession."

Joseph Groia, assisted by Kellie Seaman, represented the defendant, Stan.

o o o

JUDGE: Good morning.

THE CROWN: Good morning, Your Honour. I'd like to begin by thanking Your Honour and the court staff for accommodating us at this early hour in the morning. I'll share on the record why it is important to start at this time. Before I do that, it's my sad duty to inform you that Mr. Cornblum died yesterday.

JUDGE: Oh, my goodness.

THE CROWN: And therefore will not, of course, be here. But the information was laid without the knowledge that he had died yesterday morning, so I am going to ask that the charges against Mr. Cornblum that are on the information formally be withdrawn by the Crown at this time.

JUDGE: All right.

THE CROWN: And I ask that Mr. Grmovsek, who is present with his counsel, Mr. Joseph Groia and Ms. Kellie Seaman, at the counsel table, I'd ask that Mr. Grmovsek be arraigned on the three counts.

JUDGE: All right. First of all the charges against Mr. Cornblum are noted withdrawn by the Crown. All right. Just before we proceed with the arraignment, Mr. Groia, if I can go through the plea inquiry and make sure that we have matters—I'm sorry, I'm not entirely sure how to pronounce your name, sir.

STAN: Grmovsek.

JUDGE: Grmovsek, sorry. Thank you. I have to confirm a number of things, I am required in the Criminal Code before we proceed to confirm. You are aware that you have a right to have a trial on these matters, and if you do enter a plea of guilty you are giving up your right to have a trial.

STAN: Yes, Your Honour.

JUDGE: All right. You also understand that, in order for me to accept a guilty plea, you have to be prepared to admit the facts sufficient to establish that in fact the offence was committed.

STAN: Yes, Your Honour.

JUDGE: You also have to understand that whatever the Crown says or Mr. Groia says on your behalf I am the final arbiter of what penalty may be imposed.

STAN: Yes, Your Honour.

JUDGE: All right. And no one is forcing you to do this. You are entering this plea voluntarily?

STAN: Yes, Your Honour.

JUDGE: All right. Thank you. That's all three counts, then, I believe?

THE CROWN: Counts one, two, and four.

JUDGE: All right. Thank you.

COURT CLERK [reading to Stan from a piece of paper]: Stanko Grmovsek, charged between September 1st, 1994, and September 14th, 2004, at the City of Toronto and elsewhere in the Province of Ontario and elsewhere, did by deceit, falsehood, or other fraudulent means, with intent to defraud, buy, or sell securities using material not public information that was obtained in circumstances prohibiting them from trading in those securities, contrary to s.381(a) of the Criminal Code. [She went on to describe the other two charges in similarly unnatural, eye-glazing language.] Upon these charges you have the option to elect to be tried by a provincial court judge without a jury and without having had a preliminary inquiry. You can elect to be tried by a judge without a jury. You can elect to be tried by a court composed of judge and jury. If you do not elect now you are deemed to have elected to be tried by a court composed of judge and jury. If you elect to be tried by a judge without a jury, or by a court composed of judge and jury, or if you are deemed to have elected to be tried by a court composed of judge and jury, you will have a preliminary inquiry only if you or the prosecutor request one. How do you elect to be tried on these counts, sir?

DEFENCE LAWYER: Mr. Grmovsek elects to be tried by a provincial court judge.

COURT CLERK: How do you plead to these charges, guilty or not guilty?

STAN: Guilty.

COURT CLERK: You can have a seat. . . .

JUDGE: All right. Thank you. Mr. Corelli?

THE CROWN: Thank you, Your Honour. Before I begin, I have a statement of facts for the guilty plea to file. I actually have a bound copy for Your Honour and perhaps an unbound copy to be marked as an exhibit.

JUDGE: All right. Thank you.

THE CROWN: I also have a copy here for the court reporter to follow along with it while I'm reading it.

JUDGE: The agreed statement of fact will be Exhibit One in these proceedings.

THE CROWN: Your Honour, before I begin, one of the reasons for the early start this morning is that we are on a fairly tight schedule today. Mr. Grmovsek will be leaving the courthouse shortly after these proceedings are finished to go to the airport and then attend in New York to face charges there as well. With that in mind, I do not intend to read the entire statement of facts today, but I would like to read the first six paragraphs into the record so we have a sense of what's going on. The first six paragraphs are just the overview. Before I do that, and I can't tell you how many times this has been proofread, but Mr. Groia opened the first page this morning and noticed a typo. At page two, paragraph five, you'll see on the fourth line down where it says September 15, 2009, it should read September 15, 2004.

JUDGE: All right. I'll ask Madam Clerk if she can make that amendment. Paragraph five, line four, September 15, 2004.

THE CROWN: With that in mind, then, I'll read the overview.

1. The following facts are presented by the Crown upon the plea of guilty by Stanko Joseph Grmovsek to counts of fraud over $5,000, insider trading, and money laundering relating to his trading in securities between 1994 and 2008.

2. All charges emanate from a course of conduct engaged in by Stanko Grmovsek and Gil Cornblum in which they used inside information to buy and sell shares on stock exchanges in Canada and in the United States of America. They then laundered the money through accounts in the Bahamas, in casinos, and elsewhere in order to purchase homes and stock and to pay living expenses.

3. The insider trading took place during two time periods: 1994–1999 and 2004–2008. Cornblum obtained the insider information in the course of his employment as an articling student or lawyer at various large law firms and provided it to Grmovsek, who executed the trades in the accounts controlled by him. Unbeknownst to Cornblum, some of those accounts belonged to Grmovsek's friends and family, none of whom are alleged to have been aware that Grmovsek was engaging in illegal insider trading.

4. It is estimated that Grmovsek and Cornblum made profits of at least $8 million U.S. and $1 million Canadian from insider trading in 46 business transactions. Grmovsek made an additional $925,204 Canadian and $290,113 U.S. trading on behalf of his family and friends.

5. Grmovsek and Cornblum are charged with one count of fraud on the public for the period September 1, 1994, to September 14, 2004. (The count against Mr. Cornblum

having just been withdrawn.) This count covers the tipping and insider trading that occurred prior to the creation of specific insider-trading offences in the Criminal Code of Canada on September 15, 2004. The illegal trading that occurred after that date is charged as insider trading, s.382.1(1), and tipping, s.382.2(2), against Grmovsek and Cornblum, respectively. As well, each is charged with money laundering in relation to the movement of the illicit profits throughout the course of their scheme.

6. The charges against Cornblum are to be withdrawn in light of his death on October 26, 2009, and in fact have now been withdrawn.

Your Honour, that is an overview of the facts. The rest of the document fleshes out those facts in greater detail. I believe we're asking, unless you have any questions, we're asking that you reserve the entering of a conviction or a finding of guilt at this time and adjourn that proceeding to Friday at 9:30 in the morning, that's Friday, October 30th, at 9:30 in the morning, to be spoken to in hopes of then setting a date to then continue these proceedings after we see what occurs in New York this afternoon.

JUDGE: First of all, Mr. Groia, the facts, both as read in by Mr. Corelli and as contained in the statement of fact, are they admitted?

DEFENCE LAWYER: They are admitted. They were the subject of extensive discussions with my friend and also have been carefully reviewed by Mr. Grmovsek, and I can say that they are admitted for the purposes of the proceeding.

JUDGE: All right. Thank you. Unless there is anything further, Mr. Groia, do you have any comments before I adjourn to Friday?

DEFENCE LAWYER: No, I'm content to have the matter put over until Friday morning, Your Honour.

JUDGE: All right. What I will do is I will adjourn this then until Friday morning, that is the 30th, at 9:30 in this courtroom. It is

not anticipated to be a very lengthy proceeding, I gather it is just
to see when we are going to be coming back for the formal sentencing.

THE CROWN: Yes, to complete the reading in of the facts and do
the sentencing.

JUDGE: You don't intend to proceed with the sentencing on
Friday?

THE CROWN: No.

JUDGE: Just to set a date for that?

THE CROWN: Yes.

JUDGE: All right. It is adjourned until Friday at 9:30 in this court.
Thank you.

o o o

Stan and Kellie Seaman left the courthouse and went south through
downtown Toronto to the Island Airport, where they took an 11:15 a.m.
Porter Airlines flight to the Newark Airport, landing at 12:45 p.m. In
Newark, Stan was met by the FBI before he reached customs.

That afternoon, Stan was in Manhattan. He would later write in an
email to Reg Mossworth, after discussing the ongoing lawsuit over the
mortgage on the King City house: "It was quite shocking about what
happened on Monday and difficult to then go to NY and see the places
I saw when I lived with him there a decade earlier. . . . I might die in the
next little while, but it won't be voluntarily."

Stan was taken to the federal courthouse in a tall, pale, granite building at 500 Pearl Street. He was to be dealt with in Courtroom 21A. He
waited there on blue and gold carpets, under eight dangling and breast-
shaped light fixtures. To his right, the Brooklyn Bridge could be seen
downriver. Stan and his paid representatives sat on black leather chairs
with brass studs at dark wooden tables. At the front of the courtroom,
high on the wall, hung a plaque of a bald eagle holding ivy in one claw
and arrows in the other. A slight buzzing sound came from somewhere.

Stan's defence lawyer was Paul Calli, of the Miami firm Carlton
Fields. (One of Paul's colleagues, Mark Danzi, had lectured to Gil about
insider trading at the 2005 International Finance Forum in Toronto.)

He was 5′8″, in his 30s or 40s, with pouffy brown hair. He moved on his feet like a cat and wore flashy clothes. He gave an impression of cheerful tenacity.

The judge was Naomi Reice Buchwald. She had been appointed by President Bill Clinton in 1999 toward the end of his second term. She was 50 or so, with shoulder-length dark hair and a piercing gaze. She spoke with a heavy New York accent.

o o o

U.S. ATTORNEY: Ray Lohier, for the government. With me at counsel table is Robert Napolitano, special agent with the FBI.

DEFENCE LAWYER: Good afternoon, Your Honour. My name is Paul Calli. I need to be admitted *pro hac vice*. [Calli had not been called to the New York Bar and needed special permission to argue cases there.] I'm here on behalf of the defendant Stanko Grmovsek. Also present is his Canadian counsel, not admitted in the United States, Kellie Seaman from the Groia law firm.

JUDGE: Your motion to be admitted pro hac is granted.

DEFENCE LAWYER: Thank you.

JUDGE: Am I correct that this is Mr. Grmovsek's first appearance in court?

U.S. ATTORNEY: That is correct, Your Honour.

JUDGE: Mr. Grmovsek, since this is your first appearance, I want to inform you that the purpose of this proceeding is to inform you of certain rights which you have, to inform you of the charges that have been filed against you, and to consider the question of bail. Now, I want to explain to you that you have the right to remain silent. You are not required to make any statements, and anything that you do say may be used against you, and even if you have made statements to the authorities, you need not make any further statements. Do you understand that?

STAN: Yes, Your Honour.

JUDGE: You also have the right to be represented by an attorney during this court proceeding and at any future court proceeding and at any time that you are questioned by the authorities, and, if you could not afford a lawyer, a lawyer will be appointed for you. Do you understand that?

STAN: Yes, Your Honour.

JUDGE: Mr. Calli, have you received a copy of the information in this case?

DEFENCE LAWYER: We have, as well as the waiver of indictment, both of which I have reviewed prior to this proceeding with my client, and we have both executed the waiver and reviewed the information.

JUDGE: Mr. Grmovsek, you can sit down. Mr. Grmovsek, would you state your full name for me, please.

STAN: Your Honour, Stanko Joseph Grmovsek.

JUDGE: Grmovsek. I'm going to try to get that right.

STAN: Thank you.

JUDGE: Mr. Grmovsek, before you signed the waiver of indictment, did you discuss it with your lawyer?

STAN: I did, Your Honour.

JUDGE: Did he explain to you that you are under no obligation to waive indictment and that, if you did not waive indictment, that if the government wanted to prosecute you, they would have to present your case to a grand jury, which might or might not indict you?

STAN: Yes, Your Honour, he did do that.

JUDGE: Do you realize that by signing this waiver of indictment you have given up your right to have your case presented to a grand jury?

STAN: Yes, Your Honour.

JUDGE: And do you understand what a grand jury is?

STAN: Yes, Your Honour.

JUDGE: Have you seen a copy of the information?

STAN: I have, Your Honour.

JUDGE: Would you like me to read it out loud, or do you waive its public reading?

STAN: I waive its public reading, Your Honour.

JUDGE: How do you plead; guilty or not guilty?

STAN: Guilty, Your Honour.

JUDGE: Mr. Grmovsek, it's really okay if you sit down.

STAN: Thank you, Your Honour. [He finally sits down.]

JUDGE: Could you tell me how old you are, sir?

STAN: I'm 40 years old, Your Honour.

JUDGE: 40?

STAN: 40.

JUDGE: What was the last year in school that you completed?

STAN: Oh.

JUDGE: I don't care what year it was. What level?

STAN: Postgraduate degree [sic], Your Honour, a law degree.

JUDGE: Where did you get your law degree?

STAN: Osgoode Hall Law School, Toronto, Canada.

JUDGE: Are you now, or have you recently been, under the care of a doctor or psychiatrist?

STAN: No, Your Honour.

JUDGE: Have you ever been hospitalized or treated for alcoholism or narcotics addiction?

STAN: No, Your Honour.

JUDGE: Are you under the influence of any drug or alcohol today?

STAN: No, Your Honour.

JUDGE: How are you feeling physically today?

STAN: I feel well, Your Honour.

JUDGE: Mr. Grmovsek, in order to determine whether your plea is voluntary and made with a full understanding of the charges against you and the consequences of your plea, I'm going to make certain statements to you, and I'm going to ask you certain questions. I want you to understand that I need not accept your plea unless I am satisfied that you are in fact guilty and that you fully understand your rights. Now, the charge against you is conspiracy to commit securities fraud in the form of insider trading. The maximum sentence under the statute for this crime is five years' imprisonment. The maximum fine is the greatest of $250,000 or twice the gross pecuniary gain derived from the offense or twice the gross pecuniary loss to a person other than yourself as a result of the offense, a $100 special assessment [called a victim fine surcharge in Ontario, which Stan had been spared after his gun charge conviction], and a three-year term of supervised release. Do you understand that those are the charges against you and the maximum possible penalties under the law?

STAN: Yes, Your Honour.

JUDGE: Do you understand that you have the right to plead not guilty and the right to a trial on the charges against you and, in fact, the right to a jury trial?

STAN: Yes, Your Honour.

JUDGE: At this time, Mr. Lohier, I'd ask you, please, to recite the elements of the crime charged.

U.S. ATTORNEY: Yes, Your Honour. The elements of the conspiracy charged against Mr. Grmovsek are as follows: First, that the conspiracy existed to violate the laws of the United States, in this case, the laws that make it a federal crime to commit securities fraud and, in particular, insider trading; second, that the defendant knowingly and willfully became a member of that conspiracy; and, third, that one of the conspirators knowingly committed at least one overt act in furtherance of the conspiracy during the life of that conspiracy.

JUDGE: Mr. Grmovsek, do you understand that if you pled not guilty and went to trial that the burden would be on the government to prove each and every element of the crime charged beyond a reasonable doubt in order to convict you?

STAN: Yes, I do, Your Honour.

JUDGE: Do you understand that you have the right to plead not guilty and the right to a trial on the charges against you and, in fact, the right to a jury trial?

STAN: Yes, Your Honour.

JUDGE: Do you understand that, at a trial, you would have the right to be represented by an attorney at all stages of the proceeding, and, if necessary, an attorney would be appointed for you?

STAN: Yes, Your Honour.

JUDGE: Do you understand that, at a trial, you would have the right to confront and cross-examine witnesses against you and the right not to be compelled to incriminate yourself?

STAN: Yes, Your Honour.

JUDGE: Do you understand that, at a trial, you would be presumed innocent until such time, if ever, the government established your guilt by competent evidence to the satisfaction of the trier of fact beyond a reasonable doubt?

STAN: Yes, Your Honour.

JUDGE: Do you understand that, at a trial, you would have the right to testify and would also be entitled to compulsory process; in other words, the right to call other witnesses on your behalf?

STAN: Yes, I do, Your Honour.

JUDGE: Do you understand that, if your plea is accepted, there will be no further trial of any kind so that, by pleading guilty, you are waiving your right to a trial?

STAN: Yes, Your Honour.

JUDGE: Do you understand that, if you are sentenced to a period of supervised release and if you violate the terms of your supervised release, that an additional period of jail time may be imposed without credit for the time that you previously spent on supervised release?

STAN: Yes, Your Honour.

JUDGE: Do you understand that, in connection with your plea of guilty, that the Court may ask you certain questions about the offense to which you have pled, and, if you answer those questions under oath and on the record and in the presence of your lawyer, that your answers, if false, may later be used against you in a prosecution for perjury or false statement?

STAN: Yes, Your Honour.

JUDGE: Do you understand that in determining your sentence that the Court is obligated to calculate the applicable Sentencing Guidelines range and to consider that range and possible departures under the Sentencing Guidelines and other factors under the statute which enable the Court to consider the nature and circumstances of the offense and the history and characteristics of the defendant?

STAN: Yes, Your Honour.

JUDGE: Did you sign a plea agreement earlier today?

DEFENCE LAWYER: Yes, Your Honour.

JUDGE: Okay. Mr. Grmovsek, did you sign a plea agreement earlier today?

STAN: Yes, I did, Your Honour.

JUDGE: And before you signed it, did you discuss it with your lawyer?

STAN: I did, Your Honour.

JUDGE: Before you signed it, did you read it?

STAN: I did, Your Honour.

JUDGE: Putting the plea agreement to one side for a minute, have any threats or promises been made to you to make you plead guilty?

STAN: No, Your Honour.

JUDGE: Apart from the plea agreement.

STAN: No, Your Honour.

JUDGE: Again, apart from the plea agreement, have any understandings or promises been made to you concerning the sentence that you will receive?

STAN: No, Your Honour.

JUDGE: Is your plea voluntary?

STAN: It is, Your Honour.

JUDGE: Just to be sure that you understand them, I'd like to review a few portions of the plea agreement with you. Do you understand that as part of the plea agreement there is a stipulated Sentencing Guidelines range of from 37 to 46 months and that it is part of your agreement that neither a downward nor an upward departure from this range is warranted and that you will not seek such a departure and also that you have agreed that a sentence within the stipulated guidelines range would constitute a reasonable sentence?

STAN: Yes, Your Honour.

JUDGE: Do you understand that despite all those agreements that you are free to seek, as is the government, a sentence outside of the stipulated guidelines range?

STAN: Yes, Your Honour.

JUDGE: Do you understand that the sentence to be imposed upon you is determined solely by the Court and that neither the Court nor the probation department is bound by the guidelines stipulation contained in the plea agreement?

STAN: Yes, Your Honour.

JUDGE: Do you understand that, as part of this plea agreement, you have waived the right to file a direct appeal or otherwise challenge any sentence within the stipulated guidelines range?

STAN: Yes, Your Honour.

JUDGE: Are you pleading guilty because you are in fact guilty?

STAN: Yes, Your Honour.

JUDGE: Do you understand that, by pleading guilty, you are waiving any right you might have to require DNA testing of any physical evidence in the case and also waiving any right you might have to have the government retain any physical evidence in the case for future DNA testing?

STAN: Yes, Your Honour.

JUDGE: Do you understand that you are bound by this plea agreement regardless of any immigration consequences of this plea?

STAN: Yes, Your Honour.

JUDGE: Do you understand that this plea agreement does not bind any other federal, state, or local prosecuting office other than the U.S. Attorney's office for the Southern District of New York?

STAN: Yes, Your Honour.

JUDGE: Do you understand that apart from any written proffer agreement that may have been entered into between you and the United States Attorney's office that this plea agreement supersedes any prior understanding or promise between you and the United States Attorney's office and that no additional conditions or understandings have been entered into other than those set forth in the agreement and that none may be entered into except in writing, signed by all parties?

STAN: Yes, Your Honour.

JUDGE: Did you commit the offense that you have been charged with?

STAN: Yes, Your Honour, I did.

JUDGE: In your own words, would you tell me what you did, please.

STAN: I engaged in a process of insider trading with an associate of mine that spanned a number of years and obtained profits from that activity, which I split with my associate.

JUDGE: Were the stocks that you traded traded on stock exchanges in the United States?

STAN: Some of them were, Your Honour.

JUDGE: Did you understand, as you were engaged in this activity, that it was illegal to do so?

STAN: I did after the second transaction going forward, Your Honour, yes.

JUDGE: Mr. Lohier, is there something else you would like me to ask?

U.S. ATTORNEY: Yes. I would like you to ask the defendant if the associate to whom he referred was obtaining material non-public information in breach of a duty that the associate owed to the associate's employer.

STAN: Yes, I knew that.

JUDGE: Thank you. Anything else?

U.S. ATTORNEY: No, Your Honour.

JUDGE: Do you still wish to plead guilty?

STAN: Yes, Your Honour, I do.

JUDGE: Mr. Calli, do you know of any reason why the defendant ought not to plead guilty?

DEFENCE LAWYER: I do not.

JUDGE: The Court is satisfied that you understand the nature of the charge against you and the consequences of your plea and that your plea is made voluntarily and knowingly and that there is a factual basis for it. Therefore, I will accept your plea of guilty. I don't think we've set bail here.

U.S. ATTORNEY: I will proffer one additional fact, Your Honour.

JUDGE: Sure.

U.S. ATTORNEY: That some of the trades occurred on both the New York Stock Exchange and/or the American Stock Exchange in New York, New York, consistent with the information. With respect to bail, Your Honour, Mr. Calli and I have had some number of discussions, and, given the unusual nature of the negotiations leading up to Mr. Grmovsek's plea, I believe that it's appropriate, and propose for your consideration, to enter into a proposed bail package that would involve a personal recognizance bond of $100,000, with regular pretrial supervision only in the form of phone calls by Mr. Grmovsek to pretrial services, and that he be permitted to return to Toronto, Canada. As Your Honour is aware, I think, Mr. Grmovsek pled guilty this morning in Toronto, Canada, to similar, somewhat overlapping insider-trading charges that were lodged against him in the Ontario Court of Justice, and he voluntarily thereafter, in the late morning, flew down to New York to plead guilty before this Court. And as a result of that activity and that conduct, the government believes that the proposed bail package is appropriate.

JUDGE: All right. Bail is set as you've requested. Have you arranged for someone to be downstairs to get a bond signed?

U.S. ATTORNEY: We can probably figure that out, Your Honour.

JUDGE: All right. You just need a body. Do you want us to call down to the magistrate's office and ask them to wait?

U.S. ATTORNEY: That would be helpful, Your Honour. Thank you.

JUDGE: What about setting a sentencing date? What's the plan?

U.S. ATTORNEY: Well, this has also been the subject of the long series of negotiations, Your Honour. I believe, but I will let Mr. Calli speak for himself and for the defendant, that the defendant

wishes to have an accelerated sentencing schedule. I also anticipate, after consulting with our Canadian counterparts, with the
Ontario Ministry of Justice [he means the Ministry of the Attorney
General], that Justice Bigelow, who is the presiding judge in the
Ontario Court of Justice, is likely to provide some sense of the
sentence that is to be imposed in Canada on Mr. Grmovsek within
at least the next month. And with that, I'll leave it to Mr. Calli to
ask for whatever time frame with respect to sentencing he wishes.
DEFENCE LAWYER: Judge, I would concur with Mr. Lohier. I
think within 30 days or perhaps sooner the Canadian court will
have some sort of pronouncement of what its ultimate imposi-
tion of sentence would be. I will tell the Court that, when we
come back up, Mr. Lohier's correct, we will be asking for the
Court to consider an expedited sentencing schedule, which will
include a request from us perhaps even to waive the necessity of
preparation of a presentence report, pursuant to Federal Rule
of Criminal Procedure 2(c)(1)(A).
JUDGE: I don't see why I should be sentencing in the dark.
DEFENCE LAWYER: I appreciate the Court's comment and was
going to elaborate and suggest to the Court that one of the
things that we will have and be able to provide to the Court after
this Canadian hearing is a transcript of the hearing which sets
forth the proceedings in Canada.

∘ ∘ ∘

The judge and the lawyers discussed some complex technical issues,
then agreed on arrangements to bring Stan back to court in Manhattan
after his Ontario sentencing for his U.S. sentencing.

33 | I READ THE NEWS TODAY, OH BOY

I was driving home from Toronto to Hamilton on October 28, 2009, when I stopped to buy a fruit juice at a variety store near the Michael G. DeGroote School of Business (named after a local inside trader who had donated over $100 million of his earnings to Hamilton's university in exchange for an honorary degree and his name prominently installed on two new buildings). When I was inside the variety store, I looked at the front pages of the *Globe and Mail*, the *Toronto Star*, the *Hamilton Spectator*, and, last, the right-wing *National Post*. From one of the *National Post*'s front-page headlines, the word *lawyer* jumped out at me.

(Despite my original intentions, I had ended up working as a lawyer for a long time. After 10 years of practising law solo in downtown Hamilton — representing a wide variety of clients in civil litigation, family court, the landlord and tenant tribunal, criminal court, wherever — I had shut down my practice and surrendered my law licence in 2008 [officially becoming a "former lawyer," as Stan never did] to start a new career writing books. I had just finished a historical saga called *Berserk Revenge* and was waiting for replies from publishers. Occasionally, I had found myself wondering about my next book. What did I want to write about now?)

The *National Post* article was titled "Lawyer Kills Self Day before Charges." Glancing at the story, the familiar names *Cornblum* and *Grmovsek* jumped out at me.

The article, by Kenyon Wallace, told me about Gil's death. It was horrifying to read. I was 40 — still young enough that the death of a peer was a completely unexpected thing. I felt sad to learn Gil was gone. And by suicide!

I read more, learning that Gil had been the best man at Stan's wedding in 2000. That surprised me for some reason. I hadn't seen either of them since law school. I didn't see anybody from law school anymore. I was surprised to learn that Gil and Stan had stayed such close friends for such a long time. For a moment, I wondered if they were gay, then dismissed the idea.

I read that Stan faced "a possible 37 to 46 months in prison." I imagined the TV show *Oz*, where a drunk-driving lawyer named Tobias was sodomized and swastika-tattooed by his cellmate, turning Tobias into a transvestite thrill killer and drooling junkie. Would that happen to Stan?

I bought a copy of the *National Post*.

As I was driving the rest of the way home, I got the idea to write a book about Gil and Stan. I did some research on the Internet, then emailed a pitch of my book idea to some Toronto publishers. ECW Press offered me a contract. I signed it. From that moment on, my main obsession (other than my family) was trying to understand Gil and Stan and their tragedy — so that I could, in this book, sell my inside information to you

34 | SHIVA

At 1:00 p.m. on Wednesday, October 28, 2009, a memorial service for Gil was held at Benjamin Park Memorial Chapel.

Stan did not think that he would be welcome, so he stayed away. He also did not visit Gil's grave. Much later, when I asked him if he would like to see a photo of Gil's grave, Stan refused. Although he had a copy of the transcript of Gil's sworn confession, which he provided to me, Stan claimed not to have read it; he also said it was full of "all those lies." This shows, I believe, that he felt shame over what he did to Gil.

Shiva (the Jewish version of a wake) took place at Susan's home.

Gil would be buried in the Community Section of Pardes Shalom Cemetery, north of Toronto, near King City and Stan's old marital home.

From Gil's obituary in the *Globe and Mail*:

> . . . Until May, 2008, he was a partner at Dorsey Whitney law firm. Gil was an avid art collector and had a keen eye for colour and style. His passions included reading, travelling with his family, and playing with his son. Mostly, Gil lived for his family and was extremely close to his wife and devoted to his only son. Gil leaves his wife and son, his parents and many friends. . . . Donations may be made to the Gil Cornblum fund at either the Toronto East General Hospital or to Canadian Blood Services.

In the "Memorial Book" at the funeral home's website, Grant Vingoe (Gil's one-time supervisor at Dorsey & Whitney) wrote this: "Dear Susan and Saul, I am overwhelmed by your loss and my thoughts and prayers are with you."

Other mourners wrote the following comments.

Susan, Cathy just called me at the office and told me that Gil is gone. I don't know what to say. . . . I am heartbroken. And I am crying for him and for you. . . . No one can know what he went through. May his soul rest in peace. And may you and Saul go on to find a happy life down the road. I am so sorry.

When my parents called to tell me an hour ago I was shocked. We have so many memories together. I still remember going to the cottage together when Gilly and I played Payday [a board game from the 1970s, where players earn money through "deals"] for almost a whole day straight. I feel like I have lost a close family relative that I just haven't seen in a little while. I am very saddened by the news.

Gil was a kind and wonderful man and he will be missed.

We were deeply shocked to read about Gil in the newspaper. We would like to extend our heartfelt condolence to you. If there is anything we can do for you, please call us at any time.

We will remember Gil as the loving son, husband, and father that he was. His devotion to all of you was obvious to anyone who knew him.

I went to high school with Gil. I am very sorry for your loss.

Dear Susan and Saul: Please know Gil loved you very much. May he rest in peace knowing that people forgive him, starting with me.

It took a while for the news to spread to everybody who had known Gil. Over a year later, the news would reach Will Meyerhofer, Gil's friend and fellow fan of classical music from Sullivan & Cromwell. By this time, Will had left law and was working as a psychotherapist and blogger. He wrote this:

> Gil was a nice guy and I miss him.
>
> He shouldn't have stolen the money, but in the grand scheme of things, I think he's more than paid the price for his crimes.
>
> I feel sorry for his family—he must have been a wonderful father—such a sweet soul.

35 | "I AM STAN'S MOTHER"

On October 29, Seaman phoned Smith to discuss the case.

On the same day, at 9:05 p.m., Stan emailed his friend and fellow Ontario lawyer Reg Mossworth:

> I have to tell you, I am a bit pissed with Groia as he told me tonight that he had some photo op for me set up with the *Globe* tomorrow morning (he must have some sort of deal with them to give them stuff in exchange for free press for him). The last time I did that at his urging it made me look like a bit of a knob so I told him politely no; especially so close to Gil's funeral (and the ability for the press to juxtapose photos from that with photos of me still alive).

On October 30, at 12:21 p.m., Stan emailed his friend and fellow Ontario lawyer Marvin Noir about "my conversation with Groia today about Gil's death when he told me that he had heard that things were not as bad as reported. When I asked what he meant he said that apparently [Gil] had 'only' been alive for 40 minutes after jumping. I had thought his death was instantaneous, so [Groia's] good news was actually bad for me."

○ ○ ○

Joseph Groia told Stan to collect reference letters for the sentencing judges. One reference letter came from Marvin Noir:

> Stan has been a long-time friend of mine. I have known him for close to 18 years. . . . I first met Stan while we were both lawyers at a North Toronto law firm. At that time, Stan was an aspiring litigation lawyer and I was a corporate lawyer and we were both starting out. Stan left the law firm after I believe about a year but since that time although we have never again worked together, we have kept in close contact with each other up until today. We have often travelled together on holidays and I thoroughly enjoy his company. Since I have known Stan, he has always been an extremely honest individual and someone as who I would describe as having a great deal of integrity. He is probably the only person I know that if I asked him a question he would always give me an honest answer. I have never known him to be deceitful or evasive. . . . There are very few people in this world who I would take at their word and Stan is one of them. . . . I believe that he is very remorseful for what he did.

Another reference letter came from R. Bartholemew Squib*:

> I am a retired lawyer, having resigned in 2006 after 42 years of practice. . . . I first met Joseph Grmovsek in 2003, when he was introduced to me by a member of my then firm, and we have become good friends over the ensuing years. Joe is a very ebullient, personable young man, and quite intelligent, so it came as quite a shock to hear that he had been involved in insider trading. When we spoke about his problem he seemed to be very embarrassed to have been involved in such a foolish scheme, and it was quite apparent to me that he was very contrite and seemed resigned to face up to the penalties, with his greatest sorrow being the effect his imprisonment would have on his two young children. [He is] very concerned about their well-being while he is in prison and the fact that his support

payments will have to be terminated. . . . He also realizes that he will be disbarred as a lawyer. . . . I hope that any period of incarceration is as short as possible, for I can see little good that this imprisonment can serve other than as a deterrent to others. Joe has lost everything, but I trust that he can withstand the shock of adversity he has suffered and come back into society and make amends.

There was a letter from one of Stan's ex-relatives:

I have known Stan for approximately 10 years, from the time he met and married my cousin. Our friendship has remained intact, even after his divorce from my cousin; due to my high regard of his character. I can confirm that he is a man of integrity, is extremely dedicated to his family, and fair and honourable in his relationship with others. . . . I regard Stan as a dependable, honourable, and honest individual in his relationships with others.

Stan's mom (who knew almost no English) apparently wrote this:

Your Honour, my name is Katya* Grmovsek and I am Stan's mother. . . . His father and I honestly do not know why he did what he did. It certainly had to be for reasons beyond money because he has never been one obsessed with it or to even enjoy spending it. Whether it was because of friendship or loyalty or something else, I do not know. What I do know is that when this matter first came up, Stan visited our home, sat with us at the kitchen table, and said he had done something very wrong regarding stocks, that he knew that he would be punished for it, that his punishment would include jail, and that he was very sorry that we would be affected by what he had been involved in. He told us to just tell the truth so that we would not get in trouble by accident and then promised that he would accept complete responsibility so that there would not be need for a trial that might require us to go through the stress of testifying. He told our daughter the same thing that day and I believe that he has kept that promise to us.

Since this matter started, I can tell you that he has been very quiet, almost always in thought, and focused on preparing his children for his absence from their lives. The loss of his best friend, someone that we also knew well because of the many times we saw them together, has also greatly affected him. . . . I ask you to please please give him a chance to return to help raise his young children as soon as you can and to use any extra time that he could be given to require him to work with the authorities to help prevent crimes so that other people do not end up like him. . . . Thank you very much for reading my letter.

Stan's ex-wife wrote this:

My name is Rochelle Landry and I am the former spouse of Mr. Grmovsek and the mother of his two children, Greg Landry, age 7, and Grace Landry, age 5 (both formerly Grmovsek). While a reference letter from a former spouse may be unusual, I believe that I can provide a useful insight into how my ex husband has behaved since his actions became known to authorities and why an understanding of that can give you an appreciation into who he is and what he is working to become. As soon as he became aware of the investigation into his illegal activities in April of 2008, he voluntarily gave up custody of our children to me (until then, we shared them equally with our children being in his care from Tuesday to Saturday of each and every week) and told me that he had done some very wrong things and that my only concern should be to tell the truth to any authorities that ask. I understand that he gave the same advice to everyone else touched by this matter, while encouraging them to begin their cooperation as soon as possible. From my own knowledge of what kind of a person he is and how he has raised our children, he is someone that always accepts the blame for his mistakes without excuses before doing his best to make things right. In that regard, while we had difficulties in our marriage that led to our divorce, you should be aware that as far as being a father is concerned there are likely few better.

He is incredibly gentle and patient with our children, often to a degree that garners admiring comments from anyone that sees them together. I can assure you that the loss of money, reputation, and freedom connected to what he did and how he will be punished is insignificant to the pain and remorse he feels in knowing the poor example he set (he voluntarily agreed to change their last names so that it would not hinder their future prospects) and how his actions will cause him to be away from his children when they need him the most. I am not certain how to end a letter like this except to say that although my ex husband did bad things he is not a bad person, and I would ask that you give him the chance to show that by allowing him to rebuild his life as soon as possible.

(The prose styles of Stan's ex-wife and his mother are remarkably similar to Stan's.)

Finally, under his own name, Stan wrote to the judges too:

The Honourable Justice Bigelow
The Honourable Justice Buchwald
Your Honours:

I write in regards to the charges that have been made against me in Canada and in United States of America, to which I have pleaded guilty, and my upcoming sentencing hearings in both jurisdictions. In particular I wish to advise Your Honours of my complete acceptance and acknowledgement of the allegations made against me arising from my insider trading activities. I acknowledge that I received material, non-public information, that I used that information to engage in a process of insider trading that spanned a number of years and I obtained profits for that activity. I acknowledge, Your Honours, that I knew the information that was being obtained from the law firms was confidential and that any use of that information to trade in the capital markets was in violation of the law. I accept unconditionally the wrongful acts I have committed. I am truly sorry for my actions and for my violations of the law.

Stanko J. Grmovsek

36 | "THEIR ACTIONS TAINT ALL"

NOVEMBER 6, 2009, AT TORONTO
APPEARANCE REGARDING SENTENCING

THE CROWN: . . . First, the offences are simply deplorable. They are unprecedented in Canadian criminal law. Granted, insider trading has not been with us that long as a criminal offence, but I hazard to guess that we will not soon see an insider-trading scheme of this magnitude again. It is egregious on many levels: in its duration, in the profits it generated, and the number of trades that took place, by the inclusion of innocent family and friends, in its complexity both in terms of the insider trading and in terms of the money laundering, and in its impact on the integrity of the markets. But most of all it is egregious because of its systemic and wanton breach of their duties to their clients and to the profession that they chose, which accepted them, and whose integrity and honour they vowed to uphold. Far from discharging those responsibilities, and far from honouring the trust placed in them by their clients, colleagues, employers, friends, and family, they exploited that trust and those duties for personal gain. The Crown placed in these discussions little difference between Mr. Cornblum, who was the lawyer to the clients, and Mr. Grmovsek, who was also a lawyer, and who encouraged or acquiesced in Mr. Cornblum's repeated and complete breach of his professional obligations. Certainly, we place Mr. Cornblum a little higher on the hierarchy because they were his clients and not Mr. Grmovsek's, but we are mindful throughout that Mr. Grmovsek was trained as a lawyer and fully appreciated the fiduciary duty that Mr. Cornblum had to his clients. He fully knew what it meant for him to breach that duty. Those who read the facts of this case will undoubtedly question how level the playing field is in capital markets and may question how effective the legal profession can be at preventing insider trading by its members. No doubt, Mr. Grmovsek and Mr. Cornblum are the exceptions in their profession, but their actions taint all, and they do so at a time when the markets and the economy are and were already strained. To put this in context, in 2001 the Enron scandal broke, and over the next five years that case, of course, was in the press. In 2006 Mr. Fastow and Mr. Lay, or, sorry, Mr. Fastow, at the beginning, received ten years for his role in it, and later in 2006 Mr. Lay and Mr. Skilling were convicted and received sentences of 24 and 45 years, although I understand, of course, Mr. Lay didn't end up receiving that as he died beforehand. In 2002, the WorldCom scandal broke, and in July of 2005 Bernie Ebbers was sentenced to 25 years. In March of 2004, it was the Martha Stewart scandal, which of course was in the press everywhere you looked. July 2004 was the Adelphia scandal. The principals were looting the cable company, and John Rigas received 15 years. And so it was in that context that in September of 2004 the new insider-trading offences were introduced into Canadian criminal law. But for some reason, and having successfully avoided detection in phase one of their scheme from 1994 to 1999, in which they reaped some $6 million U.S. in profits, for some reason, in the context of all that was going on in that period from 2001 through 2006, they decided to renew their operations at the height of the corporate scandals in the U.S. and to some degree in Canada. Their arrogance in doing so is simply astounding. And they did it with zest and determination for four years. *They were discovered only when* FINRA's *software program twigged the large, well-timed trades with respect to Possis,* ASVI, *and a couple of others, and from that* FINRA *examined backwards to tie them to additional trades* [emphasis added], which led, of course, then to Dorsey & Whitney and eventually to Mr. Cornblum, and then the police became involved. All of this calls for, in my respectful submission, a substantial jail sentence and belies the assertion in many of the reference letters that Mr. Grmovsek is a man of integrity. It belies the suggestion that he is an honest and dependable person. In the Crown's submissions and in our approach to this, he most certainly is not. . . . He is a rapacious thief. He lived off this criminal enterprise for 11 years. Through that time he portrayed to his friends, to his family, and to his community, and to his profession that he was an honest businessman. Everything about his business, his character, his trustworthiness that he was presenting to the community and to his friends was, in the Crown's submission, a lie. . . . Lastly, and to the friends and family of Mr. Cornblum, I would like to say that, as inexcusable as his acts were and although the justice system did have to intervene, it was no one's intention that these proceedings should end as tragically for him as they did. [Corelli wipes away a tear.] I trust that the public, the media, and all those who criticize the adequacy and severity of Canada's penalties for white-collar crime should not forget that there are consequences and repercussions to those who are caught that cannot be measured in days, months, or years of a jail sentence. . . .

JUDGE: Thank you very much, Mr. Corelli. Mr. Groia?

DEFENCE LAWYER: Thank you, Your Honour. . . . I'd like to only really make one fundamental submission, and that is because perhaps unlike Mr. Corelli I have a bit of background in the securities field and the capital markets. And I'd like Your Honour to understand that this is a critically important case in two very significant ways. Firstly, you cannot be a member of the bar and not read repeatedly the criticism that is directed towards

Canadian regulators and the suggestion that they're incapable of investigating and prosecuting insider-trading cases and that as a result our marketplace is sometimes called the wild west of G8 capital markets. What this case, I believe in my submission, amply demonstrates is that is simply not true. *The matters that are before you were uncovered as a result of work done by the compliance office of a Canadian brokerage house, and that information was shared with the Ontario Securities Commission, as well as regulators in the United States* [emphasis added; Groia directly contradicts Corelli on who made the initial detection. Groia also contradicts the Statement of Agreed Facts signed by Groia's client. Later Groia's associate Kellie Seaman would tell me that his statement about the "compliance office of a Canadian brokerage house" was false. It is unclear why Groia made this false statement to Judge Bigelow, Judge Buchwald (by transcript), and *Globe and Mail* reporter Jacquie McNish.] And from the day that the Ontario Commission became aware of the matters, at a stage where they were more than mere allegations but certainly not proven, the Ontario Commission took steps to investigate and to freeze the monies that they found on deposit, and then to move forward with their investigation. . . . Keep in mind that, in prior insider-trading cases, the range of penalty has been in the order of 45 days, 90 days, six months. But for the first prosecution under the new Criminal Code provisions for insider trading, the sentence that is being recommended and urged upon you is 39 months. And that I believe, in my submission, will answer, if it's accepted by you and hopefully accepted by Judge Buchwald in the United States, answer those who say that Canadian regulators cannot police the Canadian marketplace and Canadian courts cannot respond to those concerns. . . . This agreement . . . says to the Americans, "We're able to police our own marketplace and to deal with our own offenders, and we would ask you kindly to respect that in the United States and to accept the agreement that was negotiated and to allow Mr. Grmovsek to be dealt with, essentially, by this Court and our penal system." . . .

What this case will establish, in my respectful submission, is a fundamentally important precedent. Most of the high-profile cases that have come forward in this area, names that are all too familiar to us, have always seemed to end up south of the border, being dealt with by U.S. courts. And that is another criticism that is levied on Canadian regulators. Well, this is not that case. In this case, because of the cooperation of those agencies, if accepted by both yourself and Judge Buchwald, this will be a case that's dealt with by Canadian regulators with the assistance and cooperation of the Americans. . . . The restitution amounts that have been agreed to have been paid. We sent, yesterday, a very large cheque to the United States for their restitution, and I have given Mr. Corelli a copy of that. The monies that are required by Canadian restitution are in the custody of the Securities Commission because they have either been taken or they are still subject to the freeze orders. And all of the other steps that were necessary have been taken. And so Mr. Grmovsek will, at the end of this, be essentially destitute. He will be unable to trade. He will be unable to have any participation in the capital markets of this country or the United States, and he will have to start his life again at the end of his period of incarceration with some very heavy sanctions that he will have to live with long beyond the conclusion of the sentence that is being urged upon you. . . .

JUDGE: All right. Thank you very much, Mr. Groia. I do not intend to repeat either the oral or written submissions that were made by both counsel. I thank them both for their assistance in this. What I will indicate is that I am, first of all, in agreement with both counsel that this is a unique situation. It is, as counsel have indicated to me, the first time that this particular section of the Criminal Code dealing with insider trading has been before a Court on a sentencing, and as Mr. Corelli indicates it is the first time that the fraud provisions of the Code have been used for this type of situation. This is also, frankly, in my experience, the most unique case that I have seen in the 16 years that I have been on the bench of cooperation by accused persons in the process of an investigation. It appears clear to me on all of the facts that, from the time of the first suspicions that were raised, Mr. Grmovsek and Mr. Cornblum, as well, were, cooperative is not nearly enough of a word for what they have done. They have assisted in the investigation enormously. This is a type of matter which, if it had been brought to trial, would have taken enormous resources on behalf of the Securities Commission and the Crown Law Office, as well as authorities in the United States. That is something which has to be given, in my view, great weight in these proceedings. . . . So I am prepared to indicate that it is my intention to impose the 39-month sentence and deal with the forfeiture issues when we return in January.

○ ○ ○

Stan would later say that Groia's speech had been intended less for the ears of the Ontario judge than for the eyes of the U.S. judge, who would read the transcript of the Ontario sentencing and then decide whether to inflict further punishment on Stan — possibly including many years in an *Oz*-like U.S. prison, what Stan feared most.

After the court hearing, Stan said to Groia, "Good speech. I couldn't have done it better myself."

○ ○ ○

A journalist took a photograph of Stan as he walked out of the courthouse. In the picture, his hair is short, and his face is clean-shaven. He is wearing a plain grey sweater. Other than gaining some weight, he looks much as he did in law school. Stan squints at the camera, his face an expressionless mask.

○ ○ ○

Stan was supposed to travel to Manhattan on November 23 for his U.S. sentencing. But when he got to the Toronto airport, U.S. immigration officials would not let him get on the plane. The airport authorities explained that, because he had pled guilty to his U.S. charges the previous month, Stan was now a "convicted felon." It was against U.S. immigration policy to let a convicted felon into the United States, even to attend court.

Kellie Seaman made phone call after phone call to various U.S. authorities, trying to find a way to get Stan to his Manhattan court date, but it was no use. Groia would later bill Stan for "all morning at airport."

Ironically, Stan had often argued that the U.S. government should be tough on criminals and keep undesirables from entering the United States. Those policies now applied to him, throwing his defence plan into chaos.

Stan left the airport and went back home, confused and worried, wondering what would happen tomorrow.

PART NINE

....

2010

Tomorrow, into the valley
Will come the traveller,
Remembering my early glory.
In vain will his eyes
Look for my lost splendour. . . .
Why do you awaken me,
O breath of spring?

from *Werther*, by Édouard Blau,
Paul Millet, and Georges Hartmann

37 | STAN IS BROUGHT TO JUSTICE AGAIN

I had sent Stan an email telling him that I was writing about him and Gil. I had mentioned that I would be at court. I had mentioned that I had spoken with the current editors of the *Obiter Dicta*, who had agreed to publish an excerpt of what I wrote.

Stan had replied with an email from a new address, groia2grmovsek@ gmail.com. Stan's email was titled "Privileged Communication" (even though legal privilege does not apply to things written to a non-lawyer like me):

Hey Mark,

Nice to hear from you and how your contact recalled some good times at the *Obiter.* I am still waiting for my U.S. sentence to be imposed so I have been given an order of silence from my lawyers. . . . To say nothing of how many things have been reported incorrectly—when you are involved in a story you come to realize how much of what gets reported is either wrong or horribly wrong.

My next U.S. hearing is set for December 15. I will contact you after that date.

Best regards,
Stan Grmovsek
—

Contains Solicitor and Client Privileged Material and
Communication [sic]

o o o

On January 7, 2010, I went to Toronto to see Stan's sentencing.

I was sitting on a bench at Old City Hall outside Courtroom 116 waiting. The sentencing was supposed to begin at 10:00 a.m. People scurried past me along the hall. It was easy to tell the confident, well-dressed lawyers from the clients and witnesses, who often looked uncertain or lost and who rarely wore expensive-looking clothes.

Stan walked through the courthouse metal detectors at 9:37 a.m. He was wearing a long black trenchcoat and black pants and shiny black shoes. His hair was short, almost military style.

He walked over to a man standing near me, who was taller than Stan and bald. This was Paul Borges, one of the friends Stan had invested for. They stood in the hallway talking, Stan smiling and looking relaxed. They were so close to me and Stan talked in such a loud voice that, without any effort on my part, I overheard bits of their conversation.

I heard Stan half-shout, "The CO asked me, 'Are you going to kill yourself?'"

Stan and his companion were soon joined by two lawyers who worked for Joseph Groia. The more senior of the pair was Kellie Seaman, now visibly pregnant; I didn't recognize the other lawyer, a young man with glasses. The four of them stood chatting by the stairs to the second floor.

At one point, I heard Stan say loudly to his lawyer "Fifteen years!" with a look of amused surprise on his face. Stan kept both his hands in his trenchcoat pockets the whole time.

He started walking away from the group and toward me. He saw me sitting on the bench and slowed his walk, looking at me as if unsure at first I was whom he thought I might be. Then he said, "Hey, Coakley, how're you doing?"

I stood up, shook his hand, and said, "I'm good. Yourself?"

He grinned. "Come here for the big event, did you?"

"I did. I did. I sent you an email that I talked to the *Obiter* people about doing a story on all this stuff, and actually I'm going to be doing a book."

Stan said, "Really? What's it going—about the whole story?"

"The whole story."

Stan nodded. "That's interesting," he said.

I said, "It's going to be called *In: An Insider-Trading Tragedy*." (My publisher would later convince me to change the title.)

"Yup," Stan said.

"And I'd like to communicate with you after this all is done."

"Sure. Try me in Millhaven, then." Millhaven was a maximum-security prison in Ontario.

I said, "Do you have email there?"

Stan laughed. "No, I have to put you on the list. I'll put you on my visitors list."

"I'll come visit you, then," I said.

"Yeah, come visit me. I'll put Mark Coakley on, then."

"So all I have to do is just write Millhaven and —"

"Millhaven, and it's in Bath, Ontario. I put you on the list, come see me, if they approve you for a visit, come talk to me."

"Okay. I'd like to do that. And I'm actually also going to New York, as well."

"Oh, next week. Is that why?"

"Yes."

Stan quickly said, "Nothing's going to happen there. What is most likely going to happen is that, because they couldn't get me across the border, they're going to sentence me to time served in America, which should be nothing. In theory. But it's not guaranteed yet. The judge could do more. I won't be in New York next week. They can't get me across the border."

"Oh, you won't be there?"

"No."

"So your lawyer will kind of be speaking on your behalf?"

"My U.S. lawyer, Paul Calli."

I repeated, "Paul Calli. Okay. I might show up anyway, because I like Manhattan."

"You can show up there, but I can't get across. And I tried really hard that day. I spent like eight hours in the airport. We phoned everybody, Department of Justice, Washington, but the guy at the border just wouldn't let me go across. Because in America, once you plead guilty, it's considered a conviction."

"Yeah, I heard."

"So they just wouldn't let me get across, because of the conviction. It's crazy."

"Yeah. Wow. Well, ah —"

Stan interrupted me to say, "I gotta go take my last bathroom break as a free man."

I chortled and said, "Okay."

"I'll see you in Millhaven."

I said, "I'll see you in Millhaven."

Stan left.

∘ ∘ ∘

Later I briefly chatted outside Courtroom 116 with a young female OSC lawyer. (There was a whole crowd of OSC types waiting for the door to be unlocked and the show to begin.) I mentioned that I was writing a book about this case, then said, "You guys must be happy how it turned out."

She closed her lips, careful not to say an indiscreet word. But I saw pride and glee in her eyes. This was a day of triumph for Ontario's stock market regulators.

∘ ∘ ∘

In the courtroom, Stan took off his trenchcoat to reveal a green sweater beneath. He sat at the left-hand counsel table with Kellie, chatting with her, while John Corelli stood by the right-hand-side prosecution table. Joseph Groia was not there. At one point, Stan pointed his fingers like a gun at his own head.

The body of the courtroom was filled with 12 or so lawyer-looking people, but I ended up sitting beside *National Post* journalist John

Greenwood. He introduced himself, asked me a few questions, and gave me his card.

Court began with a long discussion of how Stan's friends and family members had paid restitution (also called forfeiture) in the amounts that had been agreed on. Various lawyers (from the Bay Street firms McCarthy Tetrault, Heenan Blaikie, and Borden Ladner) stood up and told the judge about the payments made by their various clients, which Corelli would verify by describing or displaying the cheques.

The restitution from Stan's father came in the form of a Canadian Tire GIC for $20,000 from Scotiabank. This was money Stan's father had counted on for his retirement, after so many years at the sheet-metal factory.

o o o

THE CROWN: Okay. And, Your Honour, there is just one other matter, then, before we get to the formal sentencing. And just with respect to the Clariden Leu money. You'll recall that Clariden Leu—his trading was being done through a Clariden Leu account in the Bahamas. And Clariden Leu, with Mr. Grmovsek's consent and direction, forwarded about $1.5 million to the law office of Mr. Groia for forfeiture, and that money was then used to satisfy the judgment in the United States with the Securities Exchange Commission, and agreements all around. Subsequent to that, on December the 7th of 2009, Clariden Leu sent the law office of Mr. Groia a further cheque in the amount of $6,732.16, which seemed to be the remnants of whatever was in that account. I am not sure how, but there was a little bit of money left over. I am content on behalf of the Crown if that money be used to offset the outstanding legal fees of Mr. Groia.

JUDGE: All right. . . .

THE CROWN: So that I think wraps everything up, and it is time now for the formal sentencing.

JUDGE: All right. [Looking now at Kellie Seaman.] Well, is there anything you wish to say? I mean submissions were made on the last occasion. Anything you wish to say or Mr. Grmovsek wishes to say?

DEFENCE LAWYER: I think Mr. Grmovsek has something he would like to say, Your Honour.

JUDGE: All right. Yes, sir?

STAN: Thank you. I would like to begin by thanking the prosecution as represented by Mr. Corelli for the Crown and Mr. Ray Lohier for the U.S. Department of Justice. They have dealt with me in a very professional and considerate manner, but more importantly they dealt similarly with the innocent third parties, and for that I thank them. I would like to again extend my offer to help regulators on both sides of the border. I engaged in improper trades starting a little over 15 years ago that were probably too numerous for me to recall, despite my best efforts, or for the regulators to list in the materials. And in do doing I found obviously cracks in the system that I slipped through. I would like to help regulators identify future cracks if I can so that there isn't someone else in a similar position standing here before you today. To that end, I would like to apologize for my actions. My decision to engage in this activity 15 years ago and then after a two-year hiatus to agree to re-enter the activity were the two worst decisions of my life, as they cost me everything that I value, and money is not on that list. And, finally, I would like to thank Your Honour for originally agreeing to adjourn the matter to this date to allow for the continued cooperative efforts between regulators and authorities on both sides of the border. On a personal level, it allowed me to spend another Christmas and birthday with my family, and they were both very special days, and for that I thank you. That's all.

JUDGE: A court officer will be here for you soon. Everyone else is free to go.

o o o

Lawyers all around me started getting up, grabbing coats and briefcases, heading back to their offices or wherever. I did not move.

When Stan heard "Everyone else is free to go," he jokingly started to shuffle backward toward the door, as if hoping to sneak out undetected. He chatted with Kellie a bit while putting his trenchcoat back on; then they hugged.

So far, Stan had spent over $350,000 on various lawyers. Although Joseph Groia had estimated $200,000 for the entire case, the final bill was significantly higher than that estimate. So Stan still owed his lawyers money.

The judge left the courtroom by a side door.

A blue-uniformed court officer—burly, bald, and pale—approached Stan, who had a sheet of paper in his hand. It was a sheet of Groia's official letterhead, listing the phone numbers of Stan's friends and family. (His personal information was thus disguised as correspondence from his lawyer, which would be protected by the appearance of solicitor-client privilege and, as such, hopefully not be taken or destroyed by the jail authorities.) Stan put the list of phone numbers into a pocket of his coat.

The court officer said to Stan, "You don't look very unhappy."

Stan said, with a detached shrug, "I'm just accepting what comes."

The officer gestured for Stan to turn around. He turned around. The guard put handcuffs on him. Perhaps annoyed by Stan's comment or attitude, the officer squeezed them on very tightly—the tightest cuffing Stan would ever experience. I heard one ring of steel click around his wrist, then the other. They hurt him. He would have red marks around his wrists for three days afterward.

His arms bound behind his back, metal biting into his wrists, Stan was still smiling and trying to joke around.

The *National Post* journalist approached him.

When Stan noticed John, he said, "I'd shake hands, but . . ."

I chortled at that.

John asked a few questions, and Stan answered them. I realized that I should stand up and go closer to them so that I could hear what Stan said. But I was too shy to walk up to them, so I stayed standing by a bench.

The court officer told Stan it was time to go.

By this time, the courtroom was almost empty.

Guided by the court officer's hand on his arm, followed by his pregnant lawyer, Stan started walking back out of the courtroom. As Stan passed me, our eyes met. He looked pale and tense. So different from law school. Then he was past me and out the courtroom door, starting his 39-month prison sentence.

Stan would later write that "sometime during the first moments after [his] sentence was imposed" he remembered a line from a novel he had last read in high school, *Moby Dick*: "A man can be honest in any sort of skin." He interpreted that ambiguous sentence to mean "You are who you are, no matter where you are."

o o o

In his article for the *National Post* the next day, John Greenwood wrote this:

> . . . While at Osgoode, Grmovsek worked at the school newspaper where he was an outspoken columnist, attracting controversy with his strong conservative views, recalls Mark Coakley, a former classmate who is working on a book about the affair called *In: An International Insider-Trading Tragedy.*
>
> "He was a divisive and controversial figure in some ways," said Mr. Coakley, adding while he had many friends, his critics — often from the left of the political spectrum — occasionally referred to him as cult leader and demagogue.
>
> "I liked him, I thought he was having fun with a stodgy old institution," said Mr. Coakley. . . .

The article was accompanied by a photo I had provided to the *National Post* in a trade for an editor's promise to print my name and the name of my book. The photo was from an old *Obiter Dicta*. It was an outdoor group shot of all the editors and business managers at the end of the 1992–93 school year. Stan (in sunglasses and a white baseball hat) and Gil (in a cozy-looking sweater over a dress shirt with a crisp white collar) stand close together — Stan crouching a bit to make himself shorter, Gil holding up a copy of the newspaper.

Together, side by side in bright sunlight, two best friends smiling.

o o o

In Manhattan the next week, I was the only person in the body of Courtroom 21A (which could hold dozens of spectators) to witness the grand finale of the U.S. charges against Stan, who was still not allowed into the United States for punishment.

To the right of the courtroom were 18 empty juror chairs.

Before Stan's case was called, a heavily guarded Hispanic man was arraigned. It was very quick, lawyers and the judge quoting "section this" and "subsection that" of unfamiliar laws, none of it making sense to me; I wasn't able to figure out what the Hispanic man was charged with before he was led out, ankle chains jingling.

Stan's case was called.

o o o

JUDGE: . . . I should say that I have before me a Rule 43 waiver of the defendant's right to appear personally and/or by video conference and his election to be voluntarily absent during this proceeding, which is signed before a notary public in Toronto and bears a nice red seal. [Smiling, Buchwald held up the Canadian document and its "nice red seal" for the American lawyers to admire.] . . . Under the circumstances, and also considering that Mr. Grmovsek is a Canadian, I sentence him to time served. I guess there is always a special assessment. I don't recall, was it one count?

U.S. ATTORNEY: That is correct, Your Honour.

JUDGE: There is a special assessment of $100. Is there anything else we should be covering? I don't think supervised release makes any sense given that he is not here.

U.S. ATTORNEY: Your Honour, that's entirely up to the Court.

JUDGE: Then we will leave it at time served and a $100 special assessment. Anything else?

DEFENCE LAWYER: No, Your Honour.

U.S. ATTORNEY: Thank you, Your Honour.

o o o

I took the courthouse elevator down with defence lawyer Paul Calli.

I said, "How do you feel about how the case turned out?"

"An extraordinary result," he purred.

38 | ATLAS SHRUGGED

After Stan was sentenced in Toronto, the court officer guided him in painfully tight handcuffs out of Courtroom 116 and down the hall to an elevator, which they took downstairs to the holding cells.

The court officer asked Stan, "So, what stocks are good to buy?"

Stan said, "Ones that are going up."

During the hours Stan spent in the belly of the courthouse, he was locked up with a group of joint-smoking men who became angry with him for having failed to "hoop" in some drugs. ("Hooping" means smuggling something into jail, usually up the asshole or under the tongue.) Stan would later call the courthouse cells "a pit of snakes." Stan saw two lists of names crudely scratched into the paint on the wall—"good lawyers" and "shit lawyers."

At the end of the day, the six men in the courthouse holding cells were shackled together wrist to wrist and led into a fortified van called the "Grey Goose." They were driven through downtown Toronto to the Don Jail—not far from the Don Valley and the Leaside Bridge.

The jail was built in 1862, making it older than Canada itself. A short-term jail, it lacked many basic facilities and was slowly crumbling. Designed to hold 275 people, it now had over 691 people crammed inside. Even so, they were vastly outnumbered by the ubiquitous cockroaches, mice, and other crawling vermin. At least 30% of the people there were mentally ill. People with tuberculosis were often mixed in with healthy inmates. Inmates often had to wear the same clothes, including underwear, for longer than a week. Staff were overworked and sometimes sadistic or incompetent. One Ontario judge said that the Don Jail failed to meet the United Nations' "Minimum Rules for the Treatment of Prisoners"; another said that it fell short of Geneva Convention standards for prisoners of war; many other Ontario judges, lawyers, journalists, and politicians had called the place "cruel" and "medieval." Violence was common; one week before Stan's arrival, a mentally ill man was beaten to death by his two cellmates over a bag of chips. (Ninety-nine percent of the people in the Don Jail had not been convicted of any crime and were just waiting for a court appearance; it was a jail that mostly caged people who were still "presumed innocent.")

At the jail, some guards told Stan to take off his clothes and bend over, facing away from the guards. Using a flashlight, a guard peered inside Stan's asshole. Stan would endure this many times over the next while, often with female guards watching. (Another experience shared by Stan and Conrad Black.)

The ranges at the Don Jail were 5 metres wide and 50 metres long, with 18 cells running along one side. Each cell was about two metres wide and three metres long. Two men would sleep on a bunkbed, while the third man (usually the weakest or most timid of the three) would try to sleep on a thin mattress on the floor; his head would rest beside the toilet, while his feet went under the bottom mattress of the bunkbed. The man on the floor often got wet during the night from urine splashing from a cellmate's use of the toilet or from water leaking through the wall from the showers or from one of the frequent floods from clogged-up toilets.

After half a day spent being processed, Stan was put into the Don Jail's general population. Within minutes of his arrival, another inmate approached him and said, "You're that lawyer who stole that money in that Ponzi scheme."

"I'm not a lawyer," Stan lied, "and I didn't steal anything. Don't believe everything you read."

The guy said, "I didn't read it. I saw it on TV, you asshole."

Stan enjoyed his notoriety and, except when he was in court, showed little remorse. Just before his sentencing, he had boastfully written, "I still have memories of the millions of dollars of profits and the tens of millions of dollars of trades, the respect, the opportunities, and the lifestyle provided to me by near 15 years of turning improperly obtained information into enormous sums of money. . . . I was called the "best" and "most prolific" inside trader in history. . . ."

Stan spent his first few nights sleeping on the floor, sharing a cell with a "whacked-out junkie and an abnormally large Somalian man that had the habit of stepping on me as he went to use the toilet at night." Splashes of hot urine landed around his head each night as he tried to escape into sleep.

Stan felt a lot of stress and uncertainty; he lacked information as to how he was supposed to act in jail, how he could fit into jail society. He would later write that "Every slight or mistake or minor offence is met with an extreme and over-the-top reaction that is always accompanied by insults, threats or actual violence."

During his first week at the Don Jail, Stan was moved into a cell also occupied by a very large crystal meth dealer. The dealer told Stan the cell rules, adding that after Stan washed his hands in the cell's sink he would have to use toilet paper to dry both the outside and the inside of the sink.

"*Inside?*" Stan said, incredulous. "Are you serious?"

The drug dealer charged Stan and slammed him into the wall, pinning him there, putting his face close to Stan's and shouting, "You think this is jokes? Everything is serious! The only reason you ain't knocked out is because you're new here to this!"

Stan apologized.

In the mornings, inmates would crouch or kneel on the cell floor to stick their cups out through a hole at the bottom of the cell door, where the cups would be filled with coffee by a "corridorman." These were inmates who had the job of receiving coffee and food from the guards and distributing it to the other inmates. In some ways, these corridormen ruled the Don Jail. They could deny food to any inmate they pleased. When there were disputes between inmates, the corridormen would resolve them, usually through beatings or by ordering quarrelling inmates to go fight it out in the showers.

Drugs were everywhere at the jail. Men crushed and snorted Wellbutrin pills; others smoked joints made from the wrapping around toilet paper rolls; others got drunk on a jailhouse brew made from fruit, bread scraps, sugar packets, or any other substance that would ferment in a warm place. Stan heard that some prisoners, who were on methadone for heroin addiction, would vomit into a cup soon after drinking a dose mixed with fruit juice; then another inmate would buy the vomit and (re)drink it for a high.

At his first dinner at the Don Jail, Stan was given a plastic picnic spoon. When he was done eating, he threw the spoon away. He learned at breakfast the next morning that he should have saved the spoon and that he would not get another one. So he started eating his breakfast cereal with a folded piece of toast. Eventually, another inmate lent Stan his spoon—on the condition that Stan would wash it and give it back to the inmate during a Bible Study class. This inmate was using his plastic spoon as bait to draw sinning souls to salvation. Stan found it funny to see so many "hard dudes carrying around a white plastic spoon in their pockets like little kids going to play in a sandbox."

Stan met a repeat offender who—after Stan's sister deposited $15 into his account—taught him some of the basics of jail survival.

From 10:00 a.m. to 5:00 p.m., inmates were locked out of cells and forced to mill about the range, which had six tables, four phones, three TVs, and one working toilet shared all day by about 50 men. This lonely toilet was a one-piece stainless steel unit without a seat. To use it for a shit, you had to sit on the urine-covered rim. Stan quickly learned to take off his jail-issued shoes and balance them on the rim of the toilet (with a bias to the outside of the rim so that, if they fell, they would fall outside the bowl); then he would sit on the shoes carefully to prevent them from slipping and thus avoid "butt rash."

The shower area at the Don Jail was surrounded by nothing but a one-metre-high wall, offering little privacy. Stan was amused to learn that, in jail lingo, penises were called "hammers," and inmates who hung around too close to the shower area, presumably to look at the naked men, were derisively called "hammer-hawks," as in "Back the fuck up from the showers, you fuckin' hammer-hawk!"

The toilets at the jail were extremely powerful; Stan was amazed to watch an inmate flush away a rubber-soled slip-on shoe. Inmates did not use garbage bags in their cells, preferring to flush their food scraps and papers down the toilet.

After a week at the Don Jail, Stan was shackled and put into a transport van to Bath, Ontario. He spent his first night in Bath at a "transfer institution." That night he got his first chance to phone his son and daughter. While he was talking to Rochelle, another inmate approached him and whispered into his ear that, unless Stan arranged a "three-way" on the phone, the inmate would stab him in the eye with a comb. Stan was baffled—he imagined that the inmate wanted some kind of sex chat with Rochelle—but soon figured out that the inmate wanted Rochelle to arrange a three-way conference call so that the inmate could connect to an unapproved phone number. Stan looked like "fresh meat" and attracted many bullies, who constantly tested him.

Millhaven Institution had opened in 1971. A famous song about crime and punishment by Canadian rock band the Tragically Hip begins with "Twelve men broke loose in '73 / From Millhaven Maximum Security." The main receiving unit for all new federally sentenced inmates, Millhaven was surrounded by a double three-metre razor fence with observation towers at each corner. Guards drove around in armed patrol vehicles with AR-15 rifles. The inmates were monitored with parabolic microphones, motion sensors, and dozens of video spy cameras. Guards outside the fence had rocket launchers to shoot down approaching helicopters. Built to hold 360 men, it was now overcrowded with 461, along with 381 staff.

Ever since the Canadian government started locking up foreign citizens on security certificates at Millhaven, the place had been known as "Guantanamo North."

Being right beside a dairy farm, Millhaven was oversupplied with milk. There was so much of it that, at night, inmates would play a game of throwing plastic bags of milk out of windows, trying to have one of them land on a coil of razor wire. There were so many scraps of milk bags stuck to the prison wires that they looked like a kind of decoration, fluttering in the wind like decorative ribbons. The razor wire was also decorated with long red windsocks. They were to help the accuracy of snipers shooting into the prison yard.

Stan did not allow any of his family or friends to visit him there.

On arrival at Millhaven, Stan was given a small container of bleach and instructions on how to clean his "works" for injecting drugs. Stan, a non-junkie so far, used his bleach to sanitize toilet seats.

A guard took the Joseph Groia letterhead out of the pocket of Stan's prison uniform.

"What's this?"

"It's a letter from my lawyer."

The guard dropped the sheet with the phone numbers of Stan's loved ones to the floor. He ground the bottom of his boot on the sheet until it was in unreadable smudged shreds.

Welcome to Millhaven.

Stan's first three days were spent in "Orientation" in a classroom setting, done to familiarize inmates with the federal correctional system. Stan's prison number was 4201948.

Stan was put in the assessment unit and made to fill in forms and tests to determine his education and skills. It would be 60 to 90 days before a transfer was possible; Stan was hoping to go to Beaver Creek Minimum Security, also known as "summer camp." He met with his first parole officer. (Later another PO would abuse her position for personal gain by forcing Stan to give her legal advice about the Condominium Act and to write a legal letter for her.)

Stan was quickly learning prison ways. Soon after arriving at Millhaven, he was confronted by the range's inmate cleaner, who started screaming at him and threatening to knock him out, then beat him, then stab him — all because Stan had failed to put his food tray squarely on the one below it. With effort, Stan resisted saying "Are you serious?" and likely avoided harm.

The Millhaven authorities grouped inmates into units A to J. J unit was reserved for "the hardest of the hard" or those who made Millhaven their permanent, or "mother," institution. Each unit was then subdivided into smaller groups or ranges that each held about 40 men. The guards called Stan "Prisoner Gorbachev."

Stan insisted on being put into the "special needs" range. So his first cage was in A unit, a range holding inmates with sex-related convictions, health issues, or fear of other prisoners and those considered "incompatible" with prisoners in other parts of the institution. His first cellmate, Michael, was in prison for manslaughter and was well known for institutional violence. Michael claimed to have been brought to Millhaven with six plastic lighters and "a bale of tobacco" in his rectum. Michael and Stan got along fairly well at first, but Stan's snoring became a problem at night. Michael's complaints quickly switched to threats.

One night, unable to sleep for fear of snoring, wondering if Michael would kill him, Stan fantasized about lifting the TV up high and then crashing it down onto his sleeping cellmate's head. He was tempted to do it, to kill Michael before the guy killed him. But his logic soon returned, and he realized that it was an insane idea.

Stan, alarmed by the threats, gave the inmate boss of the range—a "cleaner" named Cowboy—two chocolate bars, the price for Cowboy telling a guard that Stan needed to be moved out of Michael's cell. Stan was moved into a cell by himself, where he felt safer and happier. The walls, floor, ceiling, and toilet in the cell were "decaying, decrepit steel." He had a TV, which he watched a lot.

Stan's cell was no larger than a king-size bed, with a small window in the steel door and another small window (that could open and close) overlooking the prison yard.

Stan thought that Millhaven's food was terrible. He also complained that he was only given three meals a day, with no treats or snacks. Everything was eaten with "sporks" (spoon and fork combinations). The main way of cooking food was boiling—for example, boiled potatoes and boiled frozen vegetables. For one of his first breakfasts, he was served boiled oatmeal mixed with pineapple pieces. Stan, a bit paranoid by this point, mistakenly imagined that it was actually the vomit of an inmate cook and refused to eat it; another inmate happily wolfed it down. A typical dinner would be one boiled potato with skin left on, a pile of still-cold frozen beans, and two nasty-looking "fish sticks."

Stan felt many annoyances, some minor, some not. He was not allowed to have a pencil longer than four inches. He could not use a computer or make outgoing phone calls before 8:00 p.m.

Stan had never been a good sleeper, and his restless nights had become worse as he grew older and developed an inflammation of his prostate gland, which made him have to get up often to pee. His sleeping problems were aggravated by the stress and anxiety and fear he felt every day as well as by all the noise at night and the red lightbulb in his cell that burned all night long. Stan would cover his head at night and use "ear plugs" made with balled-up Saran Wrap. He would usually notice when the guard, every hour on the hour, opened the window in his cell door to peer inside. The guards would move about loudly at night and sometimes tap on his door to see movement.

Sometimes an inmate in one cell would shout through the crack at the edge of the cell door, starting a conversation with an inmate farther down the range. Once Stan lay sleepless as several inmates discussed how replacing the pellets in a shotgun shell with dimes would make it more effective against police officers in bullet-proof vests.

Stan would wake up in the morning to the sound of the gates at the end of the range clanging shut. He would open his eyes to see, to the right of his bed, a calendar he had hung up. Every morning, just like the prison cliché, he would put a slash through the day that had just passed. There was a circle drawn around the day that he expected to be transferred to an easier prison in Ontario, hopefully the "camp" at Beaver Creek.

Cigarettes were banned at Millhaven and all federal institutions. To have a smoke, inmates would place nicotine patches into a pot to burn off most of the plastic adhesive, then they would crumble up the nicotine residue and blend it with some dried potato skin, then they would roll the mixture into a scrap of paper ripped from a Bible, light it, and smoke it under the exhaust fan of a kitchen stove.

Stan made good use of his business skills at Millhaven. He kept a journal of meals, soon realizing that the amount of protein from eggs served each month exceeded that of chicken. With that information, he found a prisoner who agreed to a deal in which Stan gave all his chicken to the other prisoner, who gave all his eggs to Stan. It was a clever, win-win deal; Stan got extra protein, while the other prisoner got more chicken (which he liked more than eggs). Despite such attention to nutrition, Stan's weight went down.

In early February 2010, the TV news was filled with reports about an orca whale at Seaworld that had killed its trainer after being involved in two previous human deaths. On the way to breakfast one day, Stan kept talking to two other inmates about this whale with "blood on its fins" and how it should never again be allowed to interact with humans. On the way back to his cell later, Stan started babbling in amusement about the news story again, until one of the other inmates said, "Enough about the fucking whale!" Stan realized only then that both of his companions were man killers too. Stan found *Moby Dick* at the Millhaven library and read it for the first time since high school.

I wrote a letter to Stan at Millhaven that was delivered to him weeks late and torn into four pieces. As the canteen for buying stamps had been shut down for months, the only way he could get a stamp to write me back was through a trade with another inmate, who was in prison for killing two men (his girlfriend's brothers) and cutting off their heads, hands, and feet. In return for the stamp, Stan had to give the double slayer a syrup packet, 10 sugar packets, two jam packets, and two juice bags.

Stan often wondered what he would do for a career when he was released. He was barred from stock trading for the rest of his life; the Law Society was going to disbar him; professional poker playing seemed a bit unreliable and disreputable; but what else could Stan do? He had the idea of starting a side project after release called "First-Time Prisoner Consulting," in which he would counsel and advise first-time white-collar prisoners on how to survive in "the system." He wrote that the biggest worry for such criminals was

> fear of [the] unknown—something that I believe contributed
> to my friend and co-accused deciding to take his life. (I know
> that I have never written about him before; but, I do think about

him every day.) While he would have had his difficulties, I know that what I have learned could have helped him get through it. If an hour of my time can convince another white-collar criminal facing a prison sentence that things will not be as bad as his fears lead him to believe, then I think I need to make that available. Throw in a job with the OSC helping to identify inside traders . . . and I think I will be well on my way to making my amends to society.

My letter (which included a stamped, self-addressed envelope for his reply) helped get Stan into trouble. Several of his other correspondents had also mailed him stamps, some of them sending a lot. At the end of February, the mail-screening guard called Stan to his office. The guard greeted Stan by yelling "You are becoming a real pain in the ass!" and then accused him of encouraging outsiders to smuggle in "a shitload of stamps" so that he could become a "big man" on the prison range. Stan claimed that he had not encouraged anyone to mail him stamps (a lie). The guard threatened that Stan could get "max time" for this and that "this shit has got to stop!"

Also due to the shutdown of the canteen (caused by the underfunded administrators of Millhaven Institution running out of money until the start of its next fiscal year in April), prisoners could not buy new toothbrushes, laundry soap, razors, nail clippers, Mr. Noodles, lined paper, long-distance phone cards, apple juice, or any of the other semi-necessities inmates were usually able to buy with their one-dollar daily allowance.

Now and then Stan had to piss on demand for a random drug test. The first time this happened, he had just emptied his bladder a minute before, so it took him over two hours to be able to provide the sample.

Time moved slowly in prison. Stan watched a lot of TV. During the Vancouver Winter Olympics, he cheered on North Korea—reasoning that, since that whole country was run as a prison, it was now his "home team."

The most difficult part of prison life, Stan would later write, was hearing his children on the phone during his rare calls, hearing them say how they missed him and wanted him back; Stan would suffer from the frustration of not being able to comfort them.

There had once been microwaves at Millhaven, but no longer. Stan met an inmate there with horrible scars all over his face and his left arm. This inmate's cellmate had, for reasons that remain unclear, used the microwave to heat some margarine to a boil and then threw the sizzling yellow grease onto the now-scarred inmate. Stan heard a similar story about liquid hand sanitizers like Purell, which had been allowed at Millhaven until, during the worst of the H1N1 flu epidemic, an inmate had covered his body with hand sanitizer and then drank a whole bottle, killing him. After that, hand sanitizer was removed from all Canadian prisons.

Stan learned that "goof" is the harshest insult you can call someone in prison. He witnessed the word said in anger three times at Millhaven; each time the person so described responded with immediate violence. Assaults that did not kill or cause serious permanent injury would only add 90 days to an inmate's sentence, not much of a deterrent for long-timers (or the mentally ill).

Stan had difficulties with two other men on the range, both of whom were considered "incompatible" with the general prison population.

One, Steven, was serving a life sentence for cutting up his girl-friends' brothers. (He had been represented by Edward Greenspan.) Steven was nice to Stan at first, as shown by his willingness to trade stamps for condiments, but that gradually started to change. At first, he just slapped Stan on the back as they went to breakfast in the morning. Later he touched Stan's chest in an inappropriate way; another time he kneed Stan in the back of the legs as Stan talked on the phone. Steven always did these things with a friendly smile, as if he was only joking.

One day Stan was returning to his cell from the shower when he heard a voice call out to him from one of the cells. It was Steven. When Stan moved closer to the crack at the edge of the door to hear what he wanted, Steven blew a stream of smoke directly into his face. Stan kept his gaze on Steven as he stepped back and said, loudly enough for others to hear, "It stops now! This door isn't thick enough!" Stan waited two heartbeats, then walked away. Steven stopped bothering Stan after that and became friendly again. Steven boasted to Stan that, even though he had been in prison for 20 years, he had apparently fathered eight children with his girlfriend (the same girlfriend who had helped to hide her brothers' severed body parts) during conjugal visits.

Another scary inmate, also an "incompatible," was named Jay. He was a Native with bipolar disorder serving a life sentence for two separate murders. When Jay learned that Stan was hoping for a transfer to an easier prison, Jay started trying to provoke him into a fight, which would make Stan ineligible for the transfer. Sometimes Jay would bump Stan when they were in line for food. Once, when Stan was shooting hoops in the yard, Jay threw a basketball at his head. The next day Stan did not go to the yard for exercise. During shower time that night, Jay went to the door of Stan's cell and started yelling through the door that Stan was a "fucking goof!" and that Jay was going to give him "two black eyes."

Through the door, Stan explained that, if they were to fight, all that Stan would get out of it was time in the hole and cancellation of his transfer. "So there's no upside for me."

Jay replied, "Yes, there is. Two black eyes!"

Stan was not persuaded by the logic of that argument; he tried to avoid Jay, staying in his cell as much as he could stand. When they did meet, Jay would sometimes be a bully; other times he would be nice to Stan; and sometimes he would be completely indifferent to him—all depending on where in the bipolar cycle Jay happened to be.

During a conversation with his ex-wife about Greg and Grace, Rochelle changed the subject to ask, "So, ahh, were you raped at Millhaven?"

Stan said, "I'm offended by that question. Is it not possible that, instead of being raped, that I was the one doing the raping?"

She laughed.

While at Millhaven, Stan was served with legal papers from Rochelle. One document was a Notice of Motion for permanent sole custody of Greg and Grace. The other documents included her affidavit. Stan's crime, she swore under oath, is currently the cover story in *Canadian Lawyer* under the title "When Temptation Bites." . . . [Rochelle, the Applicant mother] voluntarily paid to the OSC $78,265.00 Cdn and incurred great expense for a lawyer [first Alistair Crawley, then Wendy Berman of Heenan Blaikie] to deal with the investigation. . . . [Before Stan went to prison, his] daily visits had resulted in his belittling of the Applicant mother in front of the children and his extremely narcissistic behaviour in front of the children and in his total control of the family, albeit the fact that he and the Applicant mother were already separated and divorced. . . . [She described how Stan had signed up Greg for a three-year contract of almost daily karate training despite the unwillingness of both Rochelle and Greg.] . . . The relationship between the Applicant and the Respondent as co-parents was increasingly strained during the last months of the Respondent's freedom. . . . [P]rior to his incarceration, the father was attending in the mother's home to spend time with the children from 4 hours a night and was frequently extremely verbally abusive to the Applicant mother. . . . The Applicant mother can no longer afford her home in Woodbridge. She will need to utilize her RRSPs to finance her studies [to become a legal administrative assistant] and the expenses of the home. . . . Her current home will have to be sold as a home of this luxury is no longer affordable. . . . [T]he Respondent's position that there are no rules that apply to him has been extremely difficult for the children. . . . [T]he training given to the son that he has to be strong and tough and that kindness and sensitivity are qualities to be derided must be reversed. The Applicant is also extremely concerned that on-going phone calls from the Respondent father are a negative influence on the children as he sets out to control the family from behind bars and to check up on the Applicant mother. . . . She is content that access, once the Respondent is released, be worked out on a gradual basis and that it should be supervised and restricted unless he works on his parenting and control issues. . . . [A]ll child and spousal support in the amount of $4,500.00 per month has ceased. . . . I want my ex-husband in counselling and parenting education programs when he is out of jail. . . . At no time may he enter my home. He must be respectful of boundaries. . . . Telephone calls restricted. . . . The Respondent showed no remorse about his friend's suicide, calling him weak and a coward and selfish. . . .

On April 1, April Fool's Day, Stan was told that his transfer had gone through — he was being sent to Beaver Creek minimum security prison. That was where he had hoped to be sent; deep in the cottage country north of Toronto, it was the softest, nicest prison in Ontario.

Stan told some other inmates on the range that he was leaving. They were jealous.

That evening Stan was put into a transport van to take him to Beaver Creek. In shackles, he sat there in excitement to be leaving Millhaven. A few minutes later, he was taken out of the van. The guards told Stan that his transfer had been cancelled.

"Why?"

Because the Law Society of Upper Canada, the regulatory body for Ontario lawyers, had sent a letter to the warden at Millhaven stating that a representative of the Law Society wanted to visit Stan there on April 6. The meeting would have something to do with Stan being disbarred. He hadn't practised law for 15 years and did not care if he was disbarred or not. He had no interest in talking to the Law Society — but the letter still screwed up his transfer.

Fifteen minutes after Stan was taken out of the van, a guard went on the internal loudspeaker system to announce a lockdown order. All the inmates in Stan's range were sent to their cells, and the doors were sealed shut.

During a lockdown at Millhaven, prisoners were kept in their cells 24 hours a day, except for 15 minutes for a shower or a phone call every three days. Food would be shoved in through a slot in the cell door. Lockdowns happened a lot, sometimes for several days at a time; there had just been a four-day-long lockdown the previous week.

From his cell, Stan looked out of his window to see a cloud of thick white smoke floating over the prison grounds: a mix of tear gas and pepper spray. A yelling, chaotic mob of inmates from other ranges was rioting in the prison yard. Stan saw oval metal gas canisters bouncing around the concrete surface, spewing out clouds of rising chemical steam. He saw what looked like fresh blood smeared on a table in the yard. Someone had just been stabbed.

Stan, coughing, closed his window to the incoming fumes. The noxious gases still made it into his confined metal cell. He covered his face with a wet towel. His eyes, nose, and throat burned from the harsh chemicals. The painful irritation soon spread to the inside of his ears and under his arms. Stan writhed, alone, on the bed in his small metal cage, scratching at his itching and burning skin, with snot dripping out of his nose and tears flooding out of his bloodshot eyes.

He heard snipers in the guard towers shooting live bullets at the shouting rioters, who charged in a mass at the fences, trying to break out.

The lockdown would last eight days.

Like Rigoletto in the opera review Stan had once written for the Osgoode Hall newspaper, he was "alone within his own personal torment . . . isolated, pitied, mocked and damned. . . ."

39 | GOODBYE, GIL;

OR, THE SECRET GARDEN

April 12, 2010, was a warm, clear spring day. It would have been Gil's 40th birthday.

I travelled north from lovely Hamilton, first visiting the Leaside Bridge and Don Valley, then travelling north past Toronto on Highway 400, past Osgoode Hall Law School, to Vaughan, where I found Pardes Shalom cemetery.

The cemetery was surrounded by newly built suburban houses, more houses that were under construction or coming soon, a golf course, and a gravel mine. The cemetery gates were made of heavy iron, with a sign in both English and Hebrew. Also by the front gates were a well and a hand-washing pump.

Hundreds of tall pine trees dominated the pretty cemetery, with a few big broad-leafed trees visible here and there. The sky was blue and warm. The twisting road into the cemetery went through fields of closely packed gravestones. Cemetery staff were working among the graves, clearing away leaves and fallen branches from the fall and winter. Many of the gravestones had smaller stones piled on top. This custom showed that the dead had not been forgotten and was often accompanied by someone saying in Hebrew, "He remembers that we are dust."

Speaking to the cemetery manager, I learned that Gil was buried in a "Community Section," for folks who did not belong to a particular synagogue. He had once belonged to the Holy Blossom temple, but after the scandal that had been one of the social ties that Gil had cut. The manager also told me that Susan had visited Gil's grave earlier in the morning.

In the middle of the warm afternoon, I found Gil's grave near the back of the cemetery, on "Elm Street," in a newly expanded section. It was across the road from a wooded ravine. There were a few light construction machines nearby and a few cemetery workers, who held rakes and stood around a little tractor, which made an annoying noise.

Gil's grave was at the bottom of a gentle little hill, near the edge of the road. There were no other graves nearby. The cemetery manager had told me that Gil's family owned three more plots beside his. His grave was surrounded by newly sprouted green grass, on which I could see the tracks of the heavy backhoe that had dug the hole in October.

The surface of the grave was a rectangle of broken-up brown dirt. There was no permanent marker yet, just a sort of plaque. Over the name of the funeral home, it read,

CORNBLUM
In Memory of
Gil Cornblum
October 26, 2009 — 8 Cheshvan 5770
Forever In Our Hearts

To the left-hand side of this plaque was a round grey stone that looked like it had been left by a visitor some time ago. At the front of the plaque, Susan had earlier left Gil's favourite food — a chocolate cupcake, topped with a yummy-looking smear of vanilla icing. The sweet treat still looked fresh. Near the cupcake Susan had lain three bunches of pretty yellow and orange flowers. Under the flowers, toward the middle of the grave, she had lain a round white stone.

I walked back to the road and crossed it, to a wooded area where a pile of dirt and garden cuttings had been dumped. The first suitable stone I found was a smooth, round, dark one. Feeling a bit self-conscious, I took the stone back to Gil's grave. The smooth stone became warm in my palm.

I thought, *I can't believe that Gil is inside there.*

The grave looked so small. There were clumps of last fall's oak leaves along the edges of the rectangle of brown earth.

He is inside there.

After looking around to make sure that the cemetery workers were too far away to hear me, I said, "You didn't have to do this, Gil. Was it the shame, the scandal, Stan's betrayal, fear of jail? Did life suck so bad that you would have done this anyway, even without the scandal? Why? You were so smart. What didn't you figure out? Or what have the rest of us not figured out? What you did wasn't so bad. People don't hate you for it. You weren't a child molester or killer. What you did was legal a few decades ago. Anyway, here's a stone, I guess that's the tradition."

I put my stone on Gil's grave.

Staring down at the sun-warmed soil, imagining the changes happening to Gil beneath the surface, remembering the friendly and impressive guy I had known in my youth, I cried. Sobbing, I felt the tears flowing down my cheeks.

Afterward, I read out loud a part of Gil's favourite childhood book, *The Secret Garden.* I started reading at the place where I had left off: the first paragraph of Chapter 24, titled "Let Them Laugh." After reading the paragraph, I said, "I'm sure you know the rest of the book very well, Gil."

The nearby cemetery workers were hanging around, not doing much. I got the feeling that they were waiting for me to leave so that they could do their work. I felt self-conscious and wondered if I belonged there.

I said, "Goodbye, Gil," and walked away in bright sunlight.

MAIN WORKS CITED BY CHAPTER

CHAPTER ONE
Goodwin v. Agassiz, 283 Mass. 358, 186 N.E. 659 (Mass. 1933).

CHAPTER FIVE
Obiter Dicta, various issues.
Ayn Rand, *We the Living* (New York: Macmillan Publishing, 1936).

CHAPTER SIX
Obiter Dicta, various issues.

CHAPTER SEVEN
Obiter Dicta, various issues.
Wilfred Funk and Norman Lewis, *30 Days to a Better Vocabulary* (New York:
    Pocket Books, 1970).

CHAPTER EIGHT
Jules Massenet, *Werther*, quoted from www.abmusica.com/werther.htm.
Obiter Dicta, various issues.
Johann Wolfgang von Goethe, *The Sorrows of Young Werther*, trans. Burton Pike
    (New York: Modern Library, 2005).

CHAPTER NINE
Obiter Dicta, various issues.

CHAPTER TEN

Joan Bryden, "Election-Finance Poison Pill Threatens Three Cabinet Ministers," *Globe and Mail* (online), May 20, 2010, http://www.theglobeandmail.com/news/politics/election-finance-poison-pill-threatens-three-cabinet-ministers/article1576229/.

"Directory—Firms, Fraser's," www.lexpert.ca.

"Firm Profile," http://www.bratty.com/firm_profile.php.

Fraser Milner Casgrain, "About FMC," www.fmc-law.com.

"The Man Who Built Toronto," *Globe and Mail* (online), December 16, 2008, http://www.theglobeandmail.com/report-on-business/article728526.ece.

Don Martin, "Harper Keeps Everyone with Supersized Cabinet," *National Post* (online), October 30, 2008, http://network.nationalpost. com/np/blogs/fullcomment/archive/2008/10/31/204221.aspx.

Osler, Hoskin & Harcourt, "Firm Profile" and "Our History," www.osler.com.

R. v. Grmovsek, Ontario Court of Justice, Statement of Facts.

"Tories Overspent on Election by $1M: Warrant," CBC News, April 22, 2008, http://www.cbc.ca/canada/story/2008/04/20/rcmp-torieswarrant.html.

CHAPTER ELEVEN

F. Scott Fitzgerald, *The Great Gatsby*, ed. Matthew J. Bruccoli (Cambridge: Cambridge University Press, 1991).

Milo Geyelin, "Leaky Credibility: Big Law Firm's Gaffe over Sealed Records Raises Troubling Issues," *Wall Street Journal*, October 4, 1994.

Sullivan & Cromwell, "About Us," http://www.sullcrom.com/about/overview/.

CHAPTER TWELVE

Book Larmer, "The Real Price of Gold," *National Geographic*, January 2009.

No Dirty Gold, http://www.nodirtygold.org/home.cfm.

Sworn Confession of Stan Grmovsek, July 7, 2009, Toronto.

CHAPTER THIRTEEN

William Keates, *Proceed with Caution* (Minneapolis: Harcourt Brace Legal, 1997).

Cameron Stracher, *Double Billing* (New York: Quill William Morrow, 1998).

Sworn Confession of Gil Cornblum, July 15, 2009, Toronto.

Benjamin Weser, "Lawyer's Suicide Touches a Nerve within Profession," *Wall Street Journal*, November 14, 1994.

CHAPTER FOURTEEN

Schulte, Roth & Zabel, "Firm Overview," ww.scr.com.

Cameron Stracher, *Double Billing* (New York: Quill William Morrow, 1998).

Sworn Confession of Gil Cornblum, July 15, 2009, Toronto.

Sworn Confession of Stan Grmovsek, July 7, 2009, Toronto.

CHAPTER FIFTEEN

Sworn Confession of Gil Cornblum, July 15, 2009, Toronto.

Sworn Confession of Stan Grmovsek, July 7, 2009, Toronto.

CHAPTER SIXTEEN

Grmovsek v. Grmovsek, Respondent's Affidavit, November 16, 2004, Newmarket
    Family Court.

Sworn Confession of Gil Cornblum, July 15, 2009, Toronto.

CHAPTER SEVENTEEN

Sworn Confession of Gil Cornblum, July 15, 2009, Toronto.

Sworn Confession of Stan Grmovsek, July 7, 2009, Toronto.

"White Collar Crime and Civil Fraud Update," www.dorsey.com.

CHAPTER EIGHTEEN

Grmovsek v. Grmovsek, Applicant's Affidavit, October 30, 2004, Newmarket Family
    Court.

Grmovsek v. Grmovsek, Respondent's Affidavit and Exhibits, November 16, 2004,
    Newmarket Family Court.

Grmovsek v. Grmovsek, Respondent's Affidavit, November 18, 2004, Newmarket
    Family Court.

R. v. Stanko Grmovsek, "Statement of Facts," Ontario Court of Justice.

CHAPTER TWENTY

John Gray, "Gold Handshake: Goldcorp's Glamis Takeover," *Canadian Business
    Online*, September 11, 2006.

Tyler Hamilton, "Why the osc So Rarely Gets Its Man," *Toronto Star*, December 1, 2007.

Dristine Owram, "Goldcorp Shareholders Reject Proposal to Consult Local
    Groups," *Globe and Mail*, May 20, 2010.

R. v. Stanko Grmovsek, Guilty Plea, Ontario Superior Court of Justice, March 9, 2006.

"Report on Business," *Globe and Mail*, August 14, 2006.

"U.S. Prosecutions Cast a Long Shadow," lawtimesnews.com, February 25, 2008.

Jennifer Wells, "osc Chief Takes It All in Stride," *Toronto Star*, December 3, 2007.

http://www.whoswholegal.com/profiles/29467/0/Turner/john-sm-turner/.

CHAPTER TWENTY-TWO

Kerry Burke, Xana O'Neill, and Robert F. Moore, "Lawyer Dies in Empire Suicide
    Horror," *New York Daily News*, April 14, 2007.

Sworn Confession of Stan Grmovsek, July 7, 2009, Toronto.

CHAPTER TWENTY-FOUR

"Get to Know Us," http://www.finra.org/AboutFINRA/.

R. v. Stanko Grmovsek, Crown's Submissions on Sentencing, Ontario Court of
    Justice, November 6, 2009.

CHAPTER TWENTY-FIVE

"Environment — Argentina Lays Criminal Charges against Alumbrera," *Canadian*
    Mining Journal, June 29, 2008, http://www.canadianminingjournal.com/issues/
    story.aspx?aid=1000080117.
Joseph Groia, Donald Park, and Matthew Scott, "Surviving 'Rogue' Brokers . . . ,"
    presentation at the Ontario Bar Association, May 29, 2002.
Joseph Groia and Kellie Seaman, "Commercial Crime," www.groiaco.com/pdf/
    commercial_crime.pdf.
———, "Enron, Fear, and Loathing on Bay Street," presentation at the
    Ninth Queen's Annual Business Law Symposium, November 8–9, 2002,
    http://www.groiaco.com/pdf/enron.pdf.
Bruce Livesey, "The Buck Stops Where?" *Canadian Lawyer*, January 2008.
Janet McFarland, "SEC Puts Fraleigh Witnesses in Spotlight," *Globe and Mail*,
    September 3, 2007.
Jacquie McNish, "Insider Trading Probe Focuses on U.S. Law Firm," *Globe and Mail*,
    May 8, 2008.
Jacquie McNish and Andy Hoffman, "Insider Trading Probe Targets Classmates,"
    Globe and Mail, May 9, 2008. Reprinted with permission (license 3.8425-54672).
Jim Middlemiss, "Dorsey Whitney Fallout," *Financial Post*, May 13, 2008. Material
    reprinted with the express permission of National Post Inc.
R. v. Felderhof, [2003] O.J. No. 4819 (Ont. C.A.)., per Rosenberg J.A.
John Saunders, "Groia's Court Manners Defended," *Globe and Mail*, June 20, 2003.
Sworn Confession of Gil Cornblum, July 15, 2009, Toronto.
Sworn Confession of Stan Grmovsek, July 7, 2009, Toronto.

CHAPTER TWENTY-SIX

David Scheer and Jesse Westbrook, "Two SEC Lawyers Examined over Insider-
    Trading Concern," *Bloomberg News*, May 15, 2009.

CHAPTER TWENTY-EIGHT

Sworn Confession of Stan Grmovsek, July 7, 2009, Toronto.

CHAPTER TWENTY-NINE

Sworn Confession of Gil Cornblum, July 15, 2009, Toronto.

CHAPTER THIRTY-ONE

Canadian Bar Association, 1997 LPAC Lawyer Suicide Study, referred to by Debra
    Weiss, "Lawyer Personalities May Contribute to Increased Suicide Risk,"

April 30, 2009, http://www.abajournal.com/news/article/lawyer_personalities_
   may_contribute_to_increased_suicide_risk/.
Emily Friedman, "Inside the Mind of a Suicide Jumper," ABC News, July 2, 2008.
Jacquie McNish, "Lawyer's Death Came on Eve of Deal," Globe and Mail,
   October 27, 2009.

CHAPTER THIRTY-TWO
R. v. Stanko Grmovsek, Guilty Plea, Ontario Court of Justice, October 26, 2009.
Joe Schneider and David Glovin, "Ex-Trader Grmovsek Pleads Guilty in Canada,
   U.S. in Fraud Cases," Bloomberg News, October 28, 2009.

CHAPTER THIRTY-THREE
Kenyon Wallace, "Lawyer Kills Self Day before Charges," National Post,
   28 October 2009.

CHAPTER THIRTY-FOUR
Obituary for Gil Cornblum, Globe and Mail, October 28, 2009.

CHAPTER THIRTY-FIVE
R. v. Stanko Grmovsek, Exhibits to Guilty Plea, Ontario Court of Justice,
   October 26, 2009.

CHAPTER THIRTY-SEVEN
John Greenwood, "Prison for Inside Trader," National Post, January 8, 2010.
U.S. v. Stanko Grmovsek, Sentencing, United States District Court, Southern District
   of New York, January 13, 2010.